TOP LGBTQ+
FRIENDLY PLACES
IN EUROPE

THE ROUGH GUIDE

First edition

ROUGH
GUIDES

Publishing information

This first edition was published in 2023 by Apa Publications Ltd.
7 Bell Yard, London, WC2A 2JR

Distribution

UK, Ireland and Europe
Apa Publications (UK) Ltd; sales@roughguides.com

United States and Canada
Ingram Publisher Services; ips@ingramcontent.com

Australia and New Zealand
Booktopia; retailer@booktopia.com.au

Worldwide
Apa Publications (UK) Ltd; sales@roughguides.com

Special Sales, Content Licensing and CoPublishing
Rough Guides can be purchased in bulk quantities at discounted prices. We can create special editions, personalised jackets and corporate imprints tailored to your needs. sales@roughguides.com.

roughguides.com

Printed in Czech Republic

Credits and acknowledgements

Concept: Annie Warren
Commissioning editor: Annie Warren
Head of Publishing: Sarah Clark
Picture editors: Tom Smyth and Piotr Kala
Layout: Pradeep Thapliyal
Cartography: Katie Bennett
Proofreaders: Beth Williams and Sarah Clark
Indexer: Penny Phenix
Head of DTP and Pre-Press: Rebeka Davies
Thanks to all our writers and photographers, credited at the back of
the book, for their great ideas, fine writing and beautiful pictures.

CONTENTS

INTRODUCTION

This is a book for everyone.

Many will agree that travel is one of the most enriching experiences a person can have, and one of life's great pleasures – yet it is also one that has historically been more dangerous and therefore inaccessible to queer people than for others. Even now, most queer people will be familiar with the experience of Googling 'Is [city] safe for LGBTQ+ people?' before booking a flight. Will there be a place for me there, we wonder? Will I feel comfortable holding my partner's hand? Am I putting myself at risk? Yet queer people have always existed, as the powerful collection of LGBTQ+ icons included within these pages goes to show.

While things are improving in some places, with individuals and communities across the globe becoming more informed and open-minded and new spaces continuing to crop up that are welcoming and accessible to all, the unfortunate reality is that this is not always the case. This book celebrates the inclusive spaces that do exist in the hope that they multiply exponentially in the years to come; this would be a wonderful development not only for queer communities, but for everyone. The safer we all feel, the freer we all become.

This guide brings together fantastic writing from new and seasoned travel writers to highlight some of Europe's most majestic, queer-friendly places. From the cosy *hygge* vibes, Christmas markets and Winter Pride festival of Stockholm to the elderly-run kitschy Vollpension cafés of Vienna to an interdisciplinary-art-show-cum-electronic-music-festival in an eighteenth-century farmhouse in Puglia, the *Rough Guide to the Top LGBTQ+ Friendly Places in Europe* is a compendium of queer culture. Most destinations found in this guide are perfect for year-round visits, but we have split them seasonally to give you a flavour of some of the most exciting times to plan your trip.

This is a book that brings together some of the best places in Europe to be joyfully, unapologetically yourself.

This is a book for you.

Annie Warren, Commissioning Editor

#RGQueerEurope

ICELAND

REYKJAVÍK

GLASGO

IRELAND

DUBLIN

ATLANTIC
OCEAN

Bay of
Biscay

PORTUGAL

SPAIN

MADRID

LISBON

MOROCCO

AMSTERDAM
Spring

The trill of bells as bicycles whizz by, the gentle lapping of waves as a tour boat putters through the Grachtengordel, the faint whiff of a gaggle of tourists smoking marijuana; there's nowhere quite like Amsterdam. Although the picturesque canals are certainly a showstopper, Amsterdam has much more going on than just its pretty scenery. Few cities can effortlessly pull off the combination of a bustling, cosmopolitan atmosphere and quaint, homely feel the way Amsterdam does. From live storytelling next to the IJ (pronounced "eye") river to all-night raves on the outskirts in Ruigoord, anything is possible in the queer heart of Europe!

Bicycles and bridges

HISTORY

Amsterdam is truly remarkable. You could be sitting nursing a drink outside one of its cafés, chugging along its canals by boat, or riding its cheerful trams, and you'll know immediately that you couldn't be anywhere else in the world. What is it that makes the place so exceptional? Well, its watery cityscape means that much of the centre is off-limits to traffic; its architecture is, for the most part, on a human rather than a grandiose scale; and its people are a welcoming bunch on the whole, proud of their city but not stuck in the past. Amsterdam is always changing but has an uncanny – and reassuring – ability to stay much the same as it has always been.

The city we know today began as a fishing village in the twelfth century, located on the dykes holding back the Amstel River by the IJ. Several buildings from Amsterdam's earlier days still exist today, such as the thirteenth century's Oude Kerk, the fifteenth century's

Nieuwe Kerk, and the seventeenth century's Royal Palace.

Amsterdam's Golden Age began in the seventeenth century, as ships set out on trading voyages to the Indies. The industry was soon dominated by the famous Dutch East India Company (*VOC* in Dutch), established in 1602. The city quickly catapulted to unprecedented levels of economic success: the stunning canal houses represented the immense wealth merchants had gained, with the attics often being used to store imported goods such as tea, sugar, and spices. The cultural scene flourished as well; Rembrandt, P.C. Hooft, and Descartes are some of the great names who either came from or lived in Amsterdam during this time.

Although Amsterdam had become a force to be reckoned with, this eminence came at a sobering cost. Half a million enslaved people were transported

between Africa and the Americas by Dutch trading companies, usually in horrifying conditions; they were bought and sold and forced to undertake hard labour. The Dutch colonised islands such as Bonaire and Sint Eustatius in the Caribbean, eventually moving the slaves to Spanish colonies. The slave trade was banned in 1814, although effects are still felt today across the Black Dutch (Caribbean) community.

The city underwent dramatic change as its population exploded in the nineteenth and twentieth centuries, with cheap new neighbourhoods such as De Pijp built to accommodate the new inhabitants. World War II barely scathed Amsterdam, but as the population continued to expand, more neighbourhoods such as Slotermeer in the west or Bijlmermeer in the southeast had to be built, the latter a failed attempt at an urban utopia.

Amsterdam was famous for being socially progressive in the 1960s and 1970s: its tolerance of some drugs (such as marijuana and magic mushrooms) made it a popular hippie destination, and squatters frequently protested and fought with the police against real estate investors who bought out already-scarce housing options. In 2001, the Netherlands became the first country to legalise same-sex marriage, with four gay couples married by Amsterdam's mayor on the day the law came into effect, the 1st April.

Today, Amsterdam is a true tourist capital. The tourist campaigns from organisations like I Amsterdam have been too successful, if anything; the tiny city of around 820,000 saw over 21 million overnight stays in 2019, leading to efforts to transform mass tourism into a something more sustainable, which has included Airbnb restrictions and increased tourist taxes.

In part it's the liberal traditions of the city that have given Amsterdam its distinctive character, but there are also more subtle qualities that are encapsulated by Amsterdammers themselves in the word *gezellig*, a very Dutch concept which roughly corresponds to "warmly convivial".

ICON

Glenn Helberg was born on Curacao, a Caribbean Island off the coast of Venezuela that the Dutch colonised; today, it's officially a constituent country within the Kingdom of the Netherlands, and part of the ABC islands, which include Aruba and Bonaire. He's a prominent LGBTQ+ psychiatrist and activist with a particular focus on the queer Dutch Caribbean community. In fact, he was called "the mental health father of the queer community" after receiving the Jos Brink Ouevre Prize in 2021, awarded to people who've made a meaningful contribution to improving the societal standing of the LGBTQ+ community within the Netherlands.

Helberg moved to the Netherlands from Curacao to study medicine at Utrecht University, and after working as a doctor in Curacao, he eventually specialised in psychiatry back in the Netherlands, focusing on child and adolescent psychiatry. In addition to studying Western models of psychiatry, he also studied and utilised non-Western psychiatric practices, as he believed that colonial mindsets had played a detrimental role in psychiatry and that those models were not appropriate to treat an increasingly bicultural society. He co-founded the Expertise Centre for Transcultural Therapy in Amsterdam, aimed at providing a holistic, broader approach for viewing and tackling mental health problems through methods that go across and beyond cultures. In his own words, "traumas cannot be solved with one theory".

In addition to his psychiatric work, he's a vocal activist, both in the Netherlands and back on the islands. For example, he was a member of the Advisory Council of the Netherlands Institute for Human Rights and was also chairman of the Consultative Body for the Caribbean Netherland for nearly a decade. He also played a key role in giving the queer Dutch Caribbean community a visible presence by organising the first Dutch Caribbean boat for the annual Amsterdam Canal Parade. He was awarded the Black Achievement Award in 2019 for his work, and was royally decorated into the Knight of the Orange-Nassau Order for his dedication to improving the social standing of the Dutch Caribbean community – and he shows no signs of slowing down any time soon.

HIGHLIGHT

One of the most celebrated days of the year is *Koningsdag*, or King's Day: a national holiday to honour the current King Willem-Alexander's birthday on 27th April – although it's really just a chance to throw one of the biggest street parties across the country. If you're visiting Amsterdam over King's Day, it's essential to book your accommodation as far ahead as possible, as this is one of the most expensive dates to visit the city.

Whether you're on the canals, in the park, or roaming the streets, the entire city and country will have exploded in *oranjegekte*, or orange madness, in honour of the Dutch royal family. Boats, balconies, and buildings will be festooned in bright orange decorations, and most people will wear orange clothes or accessories, so make sure to bring or buy something of the right colour if you're visiting Amsterdam in April – you'll stand out like a sore thumb without wearing the compulsory uniform!

King's Day begins with King's Night celebrations the night before, which is the perfect time to see a live DJ or go clubbing into the wee hours. Almost all clubs or bars will host a special King's Night party, but it's best to grab tickets in advance for bigger venues (such as those in Westerpark) to ensure you'll get in – these events are very popular and do tend to sell out early. To have enough energy on King's Day proper, it's best to not go all out on King's Night at all, and instead opt for a sensible early night!

A big part of King's Day is the *vrijmarkt* (essentially a nation-wide garage sale) since it's the one day of the year that no permits are needed to sell goods. One of the most popular areas for this tradition is in Jordaan, a

De Wallen, Amsterdam's red-light district

part of town primarily populated by Mokummers, the old Amsterdammers. If you've forgotten to buy something orange, you'll be sure to find something here! The *vrijmarkt* starts early, so it's best to peruse the offerings in the morning before all the good stuff gets snapped up.

The best ways to see the King's Day festivities are on a boat (although, as you may have guessed, getting a boat party ticket can be pricey) or from a canal bridge. While there are lots of King's Day festivals, it's not the most ideal way to soak up the true spirit of the day as they can be too overcrowded to move around easily and can get very pricey. Instead, a better idea is to grab some drinks from a supermarket (ideally purchased the day before if you're organised enough, as Amsterdam has strict alcohol purchasing rules for the holiday that surprise many visitors), and weave through the crowds to catch a view of the revellers on land and water. Visitors will hear music coming from public squares, cafés, bars, and even canal house balconies, so if the current jam isn't quite to your liking, it's super easy to just move a few metres away to the next party!

If you want to partake in King's Day but aren't too keen on partying hard, a good tip is to move out of the Canal Ring, where you'll usually find a much quieter, calmer and more family-focused affair. Stroll through Vondelpark while eating a delicious orange *tompouce* (a cream-filled pastry) and watch children selling their handmade crafts, lemonade, or toys – with locals perhaps offering them more than the asking price in a show of kind-heartedness.

If King's Day sounds up your alley, but you're not in Amsterdam in the spring, the only other event that can top it is Amsterdam Pride's Canal Parade, held during the first weekend of August. It's a real must-see event, with rainbow-laden boats making their stately way down the canals. Again, you should absolutely arrive early to claim a good spot along the canals or the bridges to watch the spectacle, and then join the partygoers at one of the many open-air parties afterwards. Much like King's Day, be prepared for a long day of walking, dancing, singing, crowds, music and pricey alcoholic drinks.

LISTINGS

STAY

Amsterdam is a notoriously expensive city to stay in, due to its small size and government regulations that make housing more accessible for citizens. It's best to book your stay as early as possible and expect to pay a handsome amount for smaller rooms during peak times. Don't be afraid to find a place to stay that it outside of the centre, as the robust public transport network and biking options will get you into the heart of Amsterdam in under 30 minutes.

Conscious Hotel Westerpark Haarlemmerweg 10; conscioushotels.com/hotels/westerpark-amsterdam. You'll find this former office in the centre of the sprawling Westerpark. It's 100% electric and organic—the perfect layaway for the environmentally conscious to bunk down in.

Generator Amsterdam Mauritskade 57; staygenerator. com/hostels/Amsterdam. A rather stylish zoological university building-turned-hostel, it is located next to the lively Oosterpark and is a stone's throw away from the hip De Pijp neighbourhood. With a library, café, terrace, bar and bike hire, all bases are covered here.

Volkshotel Wibautstraat 150; volkshotel.nl/en. More than just a hotel, this former newspaper headquarters holds an underground soundbar, rooftop bar and restaurant, hot tub and weekly haircuts and massages, as well as eight designer rooms.

The Winston's Hostel Warmoesstraat 129; st-christophers.co.uk/amsterdam/winston-hostel. This rowdy backpacker's hostel is as central as it gets: the Red Light District, Dam Square and Centraal Station are all just 10 minutes away on foot. The hostel offers free walking tours and generous happy hours.

Zoku Weesperstraat 105; livezoku.com/amsterdam. This sustainable apartment/hotel hybrid offers green working and meeting spaces, while boasting stunning rooftop views. Staying longer? Check out the regular events their Community Managers host.

De Kas restaurant

RESTAURANT DE KAS

EAT

Brasserie Ambassade Herengracht 339; brasserieambassade.nl. Sleek, smart and modern restaurant in a handsome old canal house. Offers an excellent French-international menu featuring the likes of lobster and *beurre noisette* or duck with onion, carrot, bacon and potatoes in a red wine *jus*.

Café Binnenvisser Bilderdijkstaat 36; binnenvisser.nl. A perfect choice for date night, this bustling candlelit café is in the heart of Amsterdam's Old West district. Come here for the extensive selection of natural wines and carefully curated tasting menu. Walk-ins only, so show up early to avoid disappointment.

Café 't Gasthuys Grimburgwal 7; gasthuys.nl. This traditional *bruine kroeg* (brown café) is one of the cosiest around. It's also one of the few spots in the city where you'll be able to have a cocktail for less than €8 and a bottle of wine for under €15.

Coba Schaafstraat 4; coba-taqueria.com. Across the IJ is the leading artisanal Mexican kitchen in town, serving up exquisite, delicately flavoured dishes. It's not a budget option – expect to spend at least €55 per person – but it's absolutely worth it. Continue your night at the nearby *Walhalla Brewery* at Spijkerkade 10.

De Kas Kamerlingh Onneslaan 3; restaurantdekas. com/eng/garden. Go all out at this lush Mediterranean-inspired glasshouse. Ranked the Best Organic Restaurant in the Netherlands, *De Kas* works exclusively with set menus, and has vegetarian and vegan options that even carnivores will go nuts for.

Leeman Döner Van Woustraat 160; leemandoner.nl. This unassuming hole-in-the-wall spot serves up some of the best Turkish döner. The bread is made on site, with tender, juicy meat. Best to grab and go.

Taste of Culture Korte Leidsedwarsstraat 139-141; tasteofculture-amsterdam.nl. Despite its touristic location, *Taste of Culture* offers authentic Cantonese cuisine in generous portions. Frequented by fine dining chefs, it's the spot for claypot rice (煲仔飯), though it's best to call a day or two in advance for this.

Canal boat parade during King's Day festivities

DRINK

Bar Buka Albert Cuypstraat 124; barbuka.nl. This relaxed lesbian bar serves a good selection of well-priced drinks, including lots of beers from women-owned breweries. It also hosts varied social events like queer crafting, tango, and speed dating, attracting a local and international crowd.

De Drie Fleschjes Gravenstraat 18; dedriefleschjes.nl. Cosy, antique and heartening tasting house for spirits and liqueurs – especially jenever, hence the long line of wooden barrels. Clients tend to be well heeled or well soused (or both).

Door 74 Reguliersdwarsstraat 74; finddoor74.com. On the Gay Street is a Prohibition-era speakeasy, the first of its kind in Amsterdam. If it's not too busy, chat with the knowledgeable bartenders about their extensive cocktail menu.

Labyrinth Amstelveenseweg 53; labyrinthamsterdam.nl. African-Caribbean soul food and craft cocktails can be found in this Black-owned bar just off the opposite end of Vondelpark. Stop by for one of the frequent spoken word, poetry, jazz, or open mic nights.

Prik Spuistraat 109; prikamsterdam.nl. This cheerful LGBTQ+ bar is famous for its bubbles (*prik*) on tap, but it also serves up a dizzying array of cocktails, G&Ts, beers, and other drinks. Lounge on the outside terrace, join for a karaoke night, or spend a Friday night dancing to the live DJ's tunes.

Rayleigh & Ramsay Multiple locations; rr.wine/en. A "candy store for adults", this wine bar offers 100 wines by the glass that visitors tap themselves. Load up a wine card with money and dispense wine in measurements of 25, 75, or 150 ml. There are three locations in town.

Taproom Oedipus Brewing Gedempt Hamerkanaal 85; oedipus.com. Slightly off the beaten path in Amsterdam North, Oedipus is the most colourful microbreweries around, providing experimental beers for sensible prices. Peckish? Try one of the award-winning burgers from the Beef Chief.

DANCE

Bitterzoet Spuistraat 2; Spacious but surprisingly cosy two-floored bar and theatre hosting a mixed bag of events: DJ sets, live gigs featuring European indie bands, plus occasional poetry and film nights.

Bloemenbar Handboogstraat 15; bloemenbar.nl. This *nachtcafé* is a popular spot among local students and is a kitschy dive bar you shouldn't miss for a cheaper night. Officially open as late as 5am.

Bourbon Street Club Leidsekruisstraat 6-8; bourbonstreet.nl. A former blues club that's a melting pot of locals, up-and-coming and more famous musicians, students and tourists, providing a constant line-up of the best soul, blues and jazz around, with even more genres popping up as of late.

Club NYX Reguliersdwarsstraat 42; clubnyx.nl. This three-storey queer-friendly club is best known for its 3X NYX parties, with each floor playing a different music genre. Weekend tickets can sell out, so purchase online and arrive right before midnight.

Exit Café Reguliersdwarsstraat 42; exitamsterdam.nl. Right next to *NYX* is *Exit Café*, a tiny gay bar that turns into one of the best places to go dancing around 1am. While it's open from early evening, *Exit* truly shines later at night and is the spot to end a night out.

Hotel Arena Gravensandestraat 55; hotelarena.nl/en. Hip club set in a restored chapel adjoining a deluxe hotel that used to be an orphanage and an asylum. Open for parties and special events. International DJs sometimes drop by – and there's a great cocktail lounge here too.

Pianobar Maxim Leidsekruisstraat 33; pianobar. online. Listen to live piano music seven days a week late into the night. Request top hits, and if you're lucky, the performer will play and sing it for you.

Shelter Amsterdam Overhoeksplein 3; shelter amsterdam.nl. Underground 21+ techno club in the iconic A'DAM Tower across the IJ behind Centraal Station, boasting an unrivalled sound system. With a 24/7 party license, most nights don't end until 8am at the earliest.

Museum Van Loon

The stunning façade of the Pathé Tuschinski cinema

SHOP

Albert Cupystraat Shopping Street Albert Cupystraat; albertcuyp-markt.amsterdam. Street tacos, fresh Dutch stroopwaffels, Columbian empanadas, and American brownies are just some of the foods you'll find on this iconic street. Wander for hours and browse groceries, clothes, and more.

Kalverstraat Shopping Street Kalverstraat; kalverstraat.nl. Stroll through nearly a kilometre of shops on one of the city's oldest streets; it dates back to the fourteenth cetury, when it was part of a cow market. Start at Dam Square and work your way down to Muntplein; if you go in the opposite direction, you can finish your trip at the Bijenkorf, a luxury department store just a five-minute walk from Dam Square.

Ten Katemarkt Ten Katestraat; tenkatemarkt.nl. This buzzing neighbourhood street market offers everything you need for daily groceries – and then some. Swing by the Hallen, which offers a fantastic food court, cinema and library.

DO

Mezrab Veemkade 576; mezrab.nl. This truly inclusive cultural centre is one-of-a-kind. Though focused on live storytelling (it offers storytelling classes), *Mezrab* hosts music, dance, and comedy nights, plus more innovative experiments like improv opera. Most events are free, so be sure to buy drinks to support them!

Pathé Tuschinski Reguliersbreestraat 26-34; pathe. nl/bioscoop/tuschinski. Step back into the 1920s in this stunning Art Deco/Art Noveau-style cinema, named the most beautiful in the world by Time Out. For an unforgettable experience, catch a movie in the Grote Zaal, then sip on movie-inspired cocktails afterwards in Bar Abraham.

Spiegelkwartier Nieuwe Spiegelstraat; spiegelkwartier.nl. This historic neighbourhood is a must-visit for art aficionados. Dozens of art and antique stores can be found in these typical Amsterdam houses, ranging from contemporary art to Egyptian antiques.

LISBON
Spring

Over the past decade, travellers and celebrities alike have flocked to Lisbon, and it's not hard to see why; you'll never get bored here. Lisbon doesn't have the sprawling streets and boulevards of other European cities; instead, it's a pedestrian-friendly capital where you climb hill after hill, finding neighbourhoods that retain their own unique personalities. Visit Bairro Alto, Graça and Indente and you'll find independently creative cultures, visible in the exciting array of bars, restaurants, cafés and shops that line the streets. From a historic planetarium to a world-renowned gay sauna, and from forest hikes to compact techno clubs, Lisbon has something excellent in store for you.

HISTORY

As one of the most important ports in history, trade, exploration, conquest and migration run through Lisbon's veins. The city has been inhabited since Neolithic times, with various Celtic, Greek, Carthaginian, Roman, and Moorish rulers. Crusaders conquered in 1147, creating the Kingdom of Portugal; the Inquisition brought persecution to non-Christians and sexual minorities, which affected Portuguese society acutely over the following centuries.

In the fifteenth century, Portugal became the world's prime maritime power, financing explorations by the likes of Vasco da Gama and Magellan, amongst others. It colonised most continents and extracted huge wealth from its colonies – often through using force against indigenous people.

This wealth helped Lisbon to develop its signature and very opulent style of architecture, known as the Manueline, until in 1755 it was struck by a historic earthquake and tsunami. Rarely has a sudden natural event had such an impact on a nation's history; 85 percent of Lisbon's buildings were destroyed, and tens of thousands were killed. Travellers today can still visit the ruins of the Carmo Convent, left standing as a reminder of the event.

Lisbon would undergo more tumult in the following centuries, including Napoleon's invasion and the court and capital's transfer to Rio de Janeiro (both in 1807), the end of the monarchy (1910) and the establishment of a right-wing autocracy (1926) which suppressed civil rights (including LGBTQ+ rights) for

decades. In 1974, though, Lisbon was the centre of the Carnation Revolution, which resulted in a return to democracy. The new constitution protected people from discrimination on the basis of their sexual orientation, still one of only eleven constitutions do so; other constitutions that do this include those of South Africa and Mexico. Post-colonial migration from Africa and Brazil continues to add to the city's music, nightlife and culinary cultures to this day.

Portugal joined the European Commission in 1986 which spurred economic development. Additionally, Lisbon hosted Expo '98, the 2004 European Football Championship Final, and the 2018 Eurovision Song Contest.

The Euro sovereign debt crisis of 2012 hit the whole country hard and the Portuguese government has promoted tourism and property acquisition as a means to recover. During the 2010s, Lisbon became *the* city for tourists, digital nomads and start-ups. Madonna and Michael Fassbender were amongst the big names who moved to the city and investors began redeveloping the decaying properties in the centre – but holiday lets and property speculation spread so fast that the population of central neighbourhoods like Alfama declined significantly as local tenants were priced out and pushed out Unfortunately, a scarcity of housing is the big story in Lisbon today – a city which still relies on tourism. It's for that reason that we have included more sustainable, regulated hotels as our suggestions for accommodation.

ICON

As Portugal's prime queer musical icon, Antonio Variações had a significant impact on how LGBTQ+ people are perceived in Portugal.

Born in Fiscal in 1944 in Portugal's rural north, Variações moved to Lisbon for work at the age of 12. After completing his military service in the mid-1970s, he travelled to London and Amsterdam, getting to experience the liberal edge of the 70s. He returned to work in Portugal's first unisex barbershop, before

setting up his own in Baixa.

Despite a lack of musical training, he began performing with the group Variações in *Rock Rendez-Vous*, a pioneering bar for rock and pop in newly democratic Portugal, and *Trumps*, still a popular queer nightclub. His New Wave style mixed elements of rock, pop, blues and fado (Lisbon's traditional style of singing backed by a guitar). His avant-garde style got him noticed, bringing him to the small screen in 1981,

dressed in rabbit and teddy bear pyjamas, and with his signature blonde, well-groomed facial hair.

As he released new material, he continued to play on television as well as at events across Portugal. His single *Canção de Engate* – a catchy-yet-bleak description of an amorous encounter – proved especially popular. But as the song was becoming more and more famous in spring 1984, Variações was admitted to hospital; his sudden passing from pneumonia the following June at the age of 39 shocked the country. Although his death was not officially attributed to HIV/AIDS, all of his clothes were burned after his passing and he is widely thought to have been one of Portugal's first AIDS-caused deaths, then an extremely taboo topic. His death greatly increased visibility and public discourse around AIDS.

After a period of being overlooked, he has now become a beloved figure in Portuguese culture, with supergroup Humanos covering his unreleased work in 2004, and the production of a polarising biopic called *Variações* (2019) which grossed higher than any other film in Portugal that year, as well as being awarded a Presidential honour in 2020.

Variações – a trendsetter of fashion, style and music – had long said he would go down in history, "even if only the history of a bathroom wall".

The grand Jeronimos Monastery

HIGHLIGHTS

CYCLE ALONG THE TAGUS TO BELEM

Rent a bike (or e-bike) from one of the city's dockless bike schemes and cycle from Praça do Comércio westwards, along the cycle path that hugs the Tagus. The ride is pleasant, flat and takes in Lisbon's waterfront attractions. You'll cycle under the buzzing, historic 25 de Abril Bridge, past several bars and restaurants, towards the futuristic Museum of Art Architecture and Technology and the Tejo Power Station, converted into the Museum of Electricity. With the dockless scheme, you're free to stop and start where you'd like. We suggest that you finish off at the landmark Belém Tower, have some *pasteis de nata* (custard tarts) from historic *Pastéis de Belém*, and when you're ready, make the most of being in the old port of Belém to visit its many sights. Highlights include the Maritime Museum in the grand Jeronimos Monastery, the Navy Planetarium, and the incredibly comprehensive and engaging National Museum of Contemporary Art.

A NIGHT OUT IN BAIRRO ALTO

Bairro Alto on a Friday or Saturday night really is a must if you're looking to get a grasp of the *Alfacinha* (Lisbon native) vibe. This raised neighbourhood is the nightlife centre of the city, with an array of bars to suit all tastes.

If you're after the gay bars, Rua da Barocca is the buzzing thoroughfare for you. Start your night around *Purex* after 10pm and go bar crawling up the street. Like most of the neighbourhood, the crowds spill out onto the cobbles. *Maria Caxuxa* has particularly good music, and *Side Bar* has an intimate, friendly vibe, ideal for meeting new people. Lisbon has a much heavier gay than lesbian bar scene, but *Purex* is a favourite for lesbian patrons; it has a dance floor and keeps buzzing long into the night.

Also on Barocca, and highly recommended for all LGBTQ+ people, is *Ze dos Bois*, where you can keep your cool at the bohemian bar on its rooftop with good views over the Bairro. It also houses the Ze Dos Bois Association, a queer-friendly cultural centre that puts on events and exhibitions. Check out what's

Belém Tower

on when you're in town at zedosbois.org. Elsewhere in the Bairro, *Associação Loucos e Sonhadores* is a particularly fun, quirky bar, often heaving with students – and if you feel like staying up after the bars close, head to the neighbouring Principe Real neighbourhood for clubs and drag until dawn.

If you can only get out on a weeknight, *Friends Bairro Alto* is the LGBTQ+ bar for you, with an appropriately friendly and vibrant mix of tourists and locals who dance until 2am every morning.

LISTINGS

STAY

Chiado Rua Nova do Almada 114; hoteldochiado.pt. Stylish hotel designed by Álvaro Siza Vieira with Eastern-inspired interior decor. The cheapest rooms lack much of a view, but the best have terraces with stunning castle vistas – a view you get from the bar terrace, too. Rooms are not huge but are plush and contemporary.

Heritage Avenida Av da Liberdade 28; heritage.pt. In a superb mansion, this hotel blends traditional and contemporary style. Though the dining area/bar is small (and the gym/plunge pool even smaller), the spruce rooms more than compensate for its diminutive size, with tiled bathrooms, retro taps and great cityscapes from those on the top floor.

The Late Birds Lisbon Tv. André Valente 21; thelatebirdslisbon.com. *Late Birds* is Lisbon's prime gay male hotel. It's hugely popular, with high-end touches including a swish pool, bar, and terrace to encourage mingling; there's even a desktop Mac in each room.

Lisbon Poets Privates Rua Nova da Trindade 2-5; lisbonpoetsinn.com. An arty hostel with a spacious lounge and a range of rooms, the best of which overlook the tram #28 route. Evening meals on request.

Lisbon Story Guesthouse Largo de São Domingos 18, Baixa; lisbonstoryguesthouse.com. Combining the best of hostel and hotel, *Lisbon Story* offers eight simple yet stylish private rooms with a Lisbon theme, a kitchen and a lounge stocked with travel books. Great breakfasts, too!

LX Boutique Rua do Alecrim 12; lxboutiquehotel.com. In a stylishly renovated old townhouse, *LX Boutique* is a popular small hotel with a chic restaurant right next to Cais do Sodré's hippest street. Its themed floors are named after Portuguese poets and fado singers, and the smart rooms are individually decorated, with shutters and tasteful lighting.

Costa da Caparica beaches

The Calouste Gulbenkian Museum

EAT

Beira Gare Pr D. João de Câmara 4. Lisbon's version of a fast-food diner is this stand-up or sit-down café-restaurant serving very good-value snacks and full meals on the cheap. It's constantly busy, which is recommendation enough!

Cantinho do Avillez Rua dos Duques de Bragança 7; cantinhodoavillez.pt. In a classy space, with tram #28 rattling by its door, this laidback canteen is the place to sample cuisine from Lisbon's top chef, José Avillez, but at affordable prices. Delectable main courses include the likes of scallops with sweet potatoes, and Alentejan black pork with coriander.

Cantinho do Aziz R. de São Lourenço 5; cantinhodoaziz. com. Perched on a hill in the Mouraria neighbourhood, *Aziz* is one of Lisbon's most exciting restaurants. Its Mozambican-Portuguese fusion dishes receive consistent rave reviews.

Celeiro Rua 1 de Dezembro 65. Just off Rossio in the basement of a health-food supermarket, this inexpensive self-service place offers tasty vegetarian spring rolls, quiches, pizza and the like. There's also a streetside café offering drinks and snacks.

Chapitô à Mesa Costa do Castelo 7; chapito.org. Multipurpose venue incorporating a theatre, circus school, restaurant and jazz bar. The restaurant is in an upstairs dining room, reached via a spiral staircase, and serves a range of imaginative mains such as mushroom risotto or black pork with ginger. The outdoor esplanade commands terrific views over Alfama.

DAMAS R. da Voz do Operário 60; facebook.com/ damaslisboa. You can't have everything, but *DAMAS* comes close to providing just that – at least everything you'd want on a night out. Women-owned, queer-friendly and unashamedly alternative, it offers some of the best modern takes on Portuguese food in Lisbon in a vibrant, informal atmosphere, on top of regular gigs in the adjoining suite.

Eleven Rua Marquês da Fronteira; restauranteleven. com. At the top of Parque Eduardo VII, this Michelin-starred restaurant hits the heights both literally and metaphorically. The interior is both intimate and bright, with wonderful city views. The haute cuisine here is expensive but not outrageously so for food of this quality. There's a great tasting menu, and for mains you can expect the likes of sea bass with chestnuts or suckling pig with passion fruit.

Landeau Chocolate Rua das Flores 70. You might smell this café before you see it! The dreamy scent of the devilishly good chocolate cake wafts into the street, drawing in a steady stream of locals and tourists.

Pois Café Rua São João da Pr 93–95; poiscafe.com. With its big comfy sofas and laidback ambience, walking into this Austrian-run café feels like eating in someone's large front room. A friendly, young crowd, light meals and home-made snacks.

Mini Bar Rua António Maria Cardoso 58; minibar.pt. There's certainly a theatrical element to the cuisine in this wacky restaurant-bar inside the Art Deco Teatro de São Luis. Various themed tasting menus feature innovative tapas-style dishes including Algarve prawns, tuna and mackerel ceviche, or beef croquettes. Some of top chef José Avillez's creations are decidedly Blumenthaleseque, including amazing edible cocktails and "exploding" olives.

Ribadouro Av da Liberdade 155; cervejariaribadouro.pt. The Avenida's best *cervejaria*, serving a decent range of grilled meat and fresh shellfish. If you don't fancy a full meal, order a beer with a plate of prawns at the bar. Very popular, so turn up early or book a table.

Varina da Madragoa Rua das Madres 34. Once the haunt of Nobel Prize for Literature winner José Saramago, this lovely, traditional restaurant with grape-embellished *azulejos* on the walls has a superb menu featuring Portuguese dishes such as bacalhau, trout and steaks.

Versailles Av da República 15A. One of Lisbon's most traditional cafés, full of bustling waiters circling the starched tablecloths. It's busiest at around 4pm, when Lisbon's best-dressed elderly dames gather for a chat beneath the chandeliers.

The Cacilhas ferry

DRINK

Alface Hall Rua do Norte 96. This quirky café-bar is in a former print works. Now part of a hostel and filled with retro chairs and artefacts, its high ceilings and comfy sofas make it an ideal place to hang out for live music, usually jazz or blues.

Casa Independente Largo do Intendente Pina Manique 45; casaindependente.com. At the heart of the bohemian Indente neighbourhood, *Casa Independente* is one of Lisbon's fantastic queer-friendly cultural centre-cum-bars. Come for a *vinho verde* (green wine) on the terrace; stay for a performance or exhibition.

Cinco Lounge Rua Ruben A Leitão 179; cincolounge. com. Run by an affable Brit, this New York-style bar has become legendary for its hundred-plus cocktails: choose from the classics to totally wacky concoctions. A great place to chill out.

Decadente Bar Rua de São Pedro de Alcântara 81; thedecadente.pt. Attached to a boutique hostel, this small, fashionable bar attracts a youthful, laidback crowd. It's best on Thursday and Saturday evenings when there is often live music, usually Latin or jazz.

Enoteca LX Rua da Mãe de Água; enotecalx.fitarias. com. Tucked into steps downhill from Praça do Príncipe Real, this extraordinary wine bar is set in the bowels of a nineteenth-century bathhouse and now serves upmarket wines and other drinks, along with *petiscos* (snacks).

Pavilhão Chinês R. Dom Pedro V 89; facebook.com/ pavilhaochines. With five rooms full to the brim with intriguing knick-knacks, *Pavilhão Chinês* is a memorable environment in which to grab a drink. Its splendid decor and the furnishings of a 1901 grocery store combine to give a sense of intrigue much more intensely than many other "curio-bars" around the world.

Portas Largas Rua da Atalaia 105; instagram.com/ portaslargasbar. Atmospheric, black-and-white-tiled adega with cheapish drinks, background music from fado to pop, and a varied, mixed crowd, which spills

out onto the street on warm evenings. Occasional live music, too.

DANCE

Finalmente Club R. da Palmeira 38; finalmenteclub. com. One of Príncipe Real's hugely popular queer nightclubs, *Finalmente* is more on the intimate side due to its compactness. If drag nights are your thing, this is the place to come to watch some of Lisbon's top queens perform.

LuxFrágil Armazéns A, Cais da Pedra a Santa Apolónia; luxfragil.com. This three-storey converted meat warehouse has become one of Europe's most fashionable places to be seen. Part-owned by actor John Malkovich, it was the first place to set up in the docks opposite Santa Apolónia station. There's a rooftop terrace with amazing views, a middle floor with various bars, comfy chairs and sofas, projection screens, and music from pop to jazz and dance, while the downstairs dancefloor can descend into frenzy.

Ministerium Club Ala Nascente 72, Pr do Comércio; ministerium.pt. The grand, historic buildings of the former Ministry of Finance partly make up the stylish backdrop to this hip club, mostly playing house and techno and attracting top-name DJs. It's not soley a gay club, but is queer-friendly, and there's a spacious dancefloor plus quieter zones and a great rooftop café-bar.

Povo Rua Nova do Carvalho 32–26. Hear fado from up-and-coming stars and DJs at this fashionable tavern in the heart of "pink street" (the tarmac is dyed pink).

Pride Burlesque Rua da Rosa 159. If you're not sure where the Burlesque name of this gay club comes from, just look to the heavy chandeliers hanging from the ceilings. Here you'll find regular drinks promotions and DJs at the weekend.

Trumps R. da Imprensa Nacional 104B; trumps.pt. Among the numerous Príncipe Real queer nightclubs, *Trumps* trumps the rest in history and size. After drinking in Bairro Alto, follow the crowd here to dance to live acts and international DJs until dawn, just as *Alfacinhas* have done since the 1970s. There are themed parties in the summertime and a year-round "hetero-friendly" policy.

The Late Birds Lisbon

A buzzy evening in the artistic Chiado neighbourhood

SHOP

Feira da Ladra Campo de Santa Clara; visitlisboa.com/en/places/feira-da-ladra-flea-market. Come on a Tuesday or Wednesday to Lisbon´s legendary flea-market to browse among the *azulejos*, antiques and vinyls, (as well as some completely unidentifiable knick-knacks!), to see if you can bag some bargain buys to bring back.

Lx Factory R. Rodrigues de Faria 103; lxfactory.com. This former textile plant under the 25 Abril Bridge is now one of the trendiest places to shop in Lisbon. Explore the many levels of the *Ler Devagar* bookstore, complete with wine bar, before grabbing a bite to eat and browsing the independent outfitters.

DO

Arraial Lisboa Pride Terreio do Paço; facebook.com/arraialpridelx. Portugal's largest LGBTQ+ event takes over the city's main square every June. Bars and a stage pop up on Terreio do Paço but Pride here tends to keep its political aims front and centre.

Cacilhas Ferry R. Rodrigues de Faria 103; lxfactory.com. Just before sunset, hop onto the Cacilhas commuter ferry at Cais do Sodré. Cross the Tagus to see the sun set behind the iconic 25 Abril Bridge and get a spectacularly different view of Lisbon. You can come straight back or spend some time in Cacilhas's vintage shops and visit the Christ the King statue.

Calouste Gulbenkian Musem Av. de Berna 45A, gulbenkian.pt/museu. Housed within the stunning Gulbenkian Gardens that combine Brutalism and nature, the museum exhibits an incredible, important and beautiful collection of Western and Eastern art, as well as high-quality modern exhibitions.

Costa da Caparica If Lisbon starts to reach scorching temperatures towards mid-summer, cross the Tagus to Costa da Caparica, an array of wide beaches facing the Atlantic. The most famous with the gay community is Praia 19 is a gay and nudist beach with high weekend footfall, while Praia da Mata is a popular, mixed-gender alternative with more amenities.

Start
Something
Priceless

18 SPECIAL SERVICE

OXFORD CIRCUS

mastercard.

9

A ROUTE 2 HIRE -
OUTEMASTER BUS HIRE

WHEEL
STEWARD

PRIDE IN
LONDON

WHEEL
STEWARD

403 CLT

LONDON
Spring

London is an ongoing cultural event, a whole world in one city, and the undeniable LGBTQ+ capital of Europe. Where else do Masters of the Universe stare down from their ivory skyscrapers across eleventh-century fortresses, two women hold hands on the Tube opposite an elderly man with a Harrods bag, stately homes peer majestically over picnics and parties in ancient parks, and locals ram the thousands of pubs after work for pints, pies and pickled eggs? All of life is in London – from West End stages to bright young things in Soho's twinkling bars to Cockney hecklers down Colombia Road Market – and it is magnificent.

HISTORY

Where do we start? No really – where? London pulsates with history. Roman walls in the City give way to glass, steel and FTSE 100 salaries, royal palaces host knights and nobility over gin cocktails in gilded ballrooms dripping with Old Masters' handywork, and streets of every architectural whimsy are peppered with blue plaques declaring which famous – or infamous – person used to live there. Literary geniuses, celebrated artists, icons of screen, stage and stadiums, innovators and revolutionaries, fashion legends, political visionaries, poets and paupers, princes, duchesses, ladies of disrepute, gentlemen of even more disrepute – these blue plaques are everywhere.

In London, you'll be pounding those same streets, propping up those same bars and strolling those same hallowed corridors as many an LGBTQ+ great. Oscar Wilde, Boy George, Virginia Woolf, Joe Orton, Noel Coward, Lawrence Olivier, George Michael, Francis Bacon, John Gielgud, Freddy Mercury, Vita Sackville-West, Ivor Novello, Derek Jarman, Siegfried Sassoon, EM Forster, names upon names upon names! You can take an LGBTQ+ tour of Soho – an underground haunt for many of those mentioned above before homosexuality in England was decriminalised in 1967, finally repealing Henry VIII's Buggery Act of 1533. Or you might choose to fill your boots at Queer Britain, the museum of British LGBTQ+ history in Kings Cross.

London (and the UK at large) is famous for its royal family, and there has been LGBTQ+ royalty aplenty. Edward II, whose coronation alongside Isabella of France took place at Westminster Abbey in 1308; James I, who commissioned Banqueting House on Whitehall and is immortalised in its ceiling paintings by Ruben; Queen Anne, portrayed gorgeously by Olivia Coleman in Yorgos Lanthimos's *The Favourite* (2018) and who lived at the Queen's Apartments at Kensington Palace, where Princess Diana plus William and Harry also lived. Then there are the Molly Houses of eighteenth century London, essentially the gay bars of their day where men would meet for discreet sex, drinking, and more sex. Records show that in the 1720s there were roughly 30 Molly Houses for a population of around 600,000 inhabitants; proportionally, that's the equivalent of London having around 450 LGBTQ+ venues now, in a population of almost nine million!

Queer culture is London, and London is queer culture. It has always thrived, and it is thrilling.

Highgate Ponds in Hampstead Heath

ICON

On 18th February 1895, the father of Oscar Wilde's lover Lord Alfred "Bosie" Douglas left his calling card at Wilde's private London club, the Albermarle. On it the Marquess of Queensberry wrote, "For Oscar Wilde, posing somdomite [sic]." Thus began the downfall of the greatest wit, playwright and man-about-town of his generation. Dodgy spelling aside, it was an incredibly hostile move towards world's most fêted Victorian cultural icon; homosexuality in Britain was then illegal. And Oscar Wilde was one notorious homosexual.

Quite how much the wider world was aware of Wilde's sexuality is debatable, but his inner circles – the liberal elite – were well aware. They, however, were more concerned with his all-round genius than with his sexuality: his comic masterpieces included plays *Lady Windermere's Fan*, *The Importance of Being Earnest* and *An Ideal Husband*, as well his only novel and pillar of queer literature, *The Picture of Dorian Gray*, and the most famous queer love poem of modern times, *The Ballad of Reading Gaol*.

Wilde was the walking, talking, shade-throwing poster-boy of the late nineteenth century Aesthetic Movement, which advocated beauty over political or moral pontification – "art for art's sake," in other words. Anyone who was anyone in London lived for his soirées at 14 Half Moon Street in Mayfair, where he occupied "bachelor chambers" among likeminded bohemians and where Algernon Moncrieff, hero of Wilde's play *The Importance of Being Earnest*, also resided. It is now part of The Mayfair Townhouse, a rather delicious hotel, and a short stroll to Café Royal on Regent Street where Wilde would knock back many an absinthe – you'd recognise the brown floppy curls, the patent shoes, the garments made of the fur of at least two different animals – and Burlington Arcade, where he would buy green carnations for his buttonhole. A party wasn't a party without Wilde.

But his whole camp and glamorous world came tumbling down in a very public trial. There's a plaque on the house where Wilde lived when he was arrested,

34 Tite Street in Chelsea, where he resided with his wife and two children. The smoke and mirrors the age demanded had been shattered, all because of "a love that dare not speak its name".

HIGHLIGHTS

HIGHGATE PONDS

Perhaps on of the most unexpected things in all of queer London... a swathe of bathers lying out in the sun, drinking, dancing, flirting and popping into the ponds to take the edge off the summer heat. Up on the fringes of the beautiful Hampstead Heath, which is a slice of English countryside just north of central London (explore at any time of the year and finish up with a beer in Hampstead Village), you'll find Highgate Ponds. The name is misleading; they are not actually ponds, but rather where the ancient River Fleet hits the surface, meaning the water may be a bit on the murky side even though it's very fresh... even if you suspect that duck swimming past may have had a comfort break in the water. The Men's Pond, with its diving board and changing room area where you can sunbathe nude, is a favourite with gay men, as is the strip of grass outside (it's especially rocking on a sunny Sunday) while the women have the aptly named Women's Pond, a female-only space for wild swimming and sunning, all within the glorious, bucolic surrounds that once hosted Henry VIII's hunts.

MIGHTY HOOPLA

In the olden days of London's Gay Pride (before it became Pride in London), after the March, the festivities would commute out to one of London's many parks – Hyde Park, Clapham Common and Brockwell Park are all good examples. That ground to a halt, and people began to miss the atmosphere of giddy celebration, with famous pop performers, drinks stalls churning out shots, crowds lazing around on the grass with mates old and new, wandering from stage to stage and dance tent to dance tent, trying your best

The Duke of Wellington in Soho

to wangle entry into the VIP area where the celebs don't even have to queue for their booze... and thus, Mighty Hoopla was invented! This two-day festival that comes round every summer brings the poppest of pop acts – former performers have included everyone from Eurovision favourites to ex-Spice Girls – to a very sparkly crowd and more fairy wings than it's surely safe to have in one space. How they get the glitter out of the grass afterwards is anyone's guess...

FLARE

The highly respected BFI (British Film Institute) runs not only the London Film Festival for all the big-hitters in the Autumn, but also FLARE, the biggest LGBTQ+ film festival in Europe, every spring. It attracts major stars, queer directors, big films, and a lot of underground films and shorts that you might not get to see anywhere else, as well as talks, conferences, panels and – more importantly! – parties galore! With movie tie-ins, themes and plenty of opportunities to get dressed up to the nines – or even the tens – it's a festival that is deadly serious... without ever taking itself too seriously.

Oscar Wilde (1854-1900)

LISTINGS

STAY

Art'otel Battersea 1 Electric Boulevard, SW11 8BJ; artotellondonbattersea.com. The only hotel to blag its way into the extraordinary redevelopment of London's iconic Battersea Power Station (which, pop-pickers, you'll recognise from the cover of Pink Floyd's *Animals* album), *Art'otel* doesn't half strike a pose. For starters, there's a rooftop pool with views wonderful enough to make your jaw drop, a destination restaurant, *JOIA*, with food by Michelin-starred Portuguese chef Henrique Sá Pessoa, and a café in the grand European style that's always totally rammed.

Kingsland Locke 130 Kingsland High Street, E8 2LQ; lockeliving.com/kingsland-locke. Locke – who have cornered that coveted market of very affordable yet utterly gorgeous apart-hotel living with incredible food and drink thrown in – is all about living like a local. This very LGBTQ-centric locale of Dalston (here's looking at you *The Glory*, *Dalston Superstore*, *Spurstowe Arms*!)

is cooler than your average cucumber, with nearby bars, pubs, clubs, cinemas, restaurants, markets, bakers and matchstick-makers (really!) that'll have every hour of your day covered.

The Mandrake 20-21 Newman Street, W1T 1PG; themandrake.com. Sexy and secluded – it's a mission to even find your way in – *The Mandrake* is that rare thing in hotels of this calibre – utterly independent. Down an almost pitch-black catwalk (once you've found it, that is), you emerge into a fantastical world of glamour and good times. There's *Jurema*, which might just be the most unique (and beautiful!) sun terrace in the whole of London, and *YOPO*, which is all about South American food and long, drawn-out cocktails. Expect eccentrically decadent rooms where your shower comes with a red button; press it, and if the guest next door has reciprocated, the glass wall between you turns clear (you have to sign disclaimer for this very reason when you check in). From this to the impressive art on the walls (yes, that is a Warhol), *The Mandrake* has hedonism written into its DNA.

One Hundred Shoreditch 100 Shoreditch High Street, E1 6JQ; onehundredshoreditch.com. *One Hundred Shoreditch* has nailed the sparkly sophisticated brief so hard they're going to have to get considerably bigger nails. East London's hot-hot-hottest hotel by far, it's a wonderland of art- and installation-led design, has one of the sexiest rooftops in all of London Town and, right down in the basement, you'll find yourself in *Seed Library*, a scarlet beauty of a cocktail bar brought to you by Ryan "Mr Lyan" Chetiyawardana, one of the world's most influential Misters in the business of glamorous drinking.

The Standard 10 Argyle Street, WC1H 8EG; standardhotels.com/London. This is the kind of hotel that crushes are made of. Bold and beautiful and all kinds of fun, *The Standard London* is not only a doddle to get to – it's right in front of St Pancras International Station – but also very welcoming to LGBTQ+ people. The décor is punch-drunk 70s glam fantasia, the rooms are what is known in the business as stunning, there are five bars and restaurants to choose from, and the lighting is the flattering kind that make for really successful dates.

EAT

Balans No.60 60-62 Old Compton St, W1D 4UG; balans. co.uk/locations/soho-no-60. People go bananas for "Big Balans" (there's another "Less Big" Balans two minutes' down the road) – and who can blame them? Open almost 24/7 (well, until 6am of a weekend, which is when it matters most) and a whole load of fun for most of said hours, Soho's original LGBTQ+ restaurant is where you go to line your stomach before clubbing, for sobering stodge after clubbing, to spot Lady Gaga gossiping with her dancers over cocktails in the booths out back, and boozy brunches that last for days (mostly because you're busy flirting with the staff).

Café Boheme 13 Old Compton Street, W1D 5JQ; cafeboheme.co.uk. One of the great joys of Soho is

London Pride's 50th anniversary in 2022

people-watching. This neck of the West End attracts the most wonderful, eccentric, bizarre and, well, drunkest of all of London's – and the world's! – characters. A seat at *Café Bohème* is akin to sitting on the front row for this spectacle. Taking up a covetable corner of Old Compton Street, it is first and foremost a very lovely French-inspired bistro, beloved of LGBTQ+ locals as well as those who work in local late-night hospitality who come here for garrulous after-hours downtime. Grab one of the outside tables at any given minute and boom – you're right in the thick of Soho's addictive action.

Mildred's Soho 45 Lexington Street, W1F 9AN; mildreds.co.uk/soho. Latest estimates suggest that *Mildred's* has been around since 1988, which is quite the accolade for a vegetarian – now 100% plant-based – restaurant that took root during a decade that held rare steak in such high regard. Nowadays, this Georgian Soho beauty is the go-to for comfy, delicious, traditional dishes, whether they be British or Indian or Japanese, in a welcome-to-all atmosphere where making friends is just as important as food that doesn't cost the earth. Literally.

Paradise 61 Rupert Street, W1D 7PW; paradisesoho. com. It's tough establishing yourself as a must-eat in Soho. Which is why we really have to talk about *Paradise*. Small-plated, plant-focussed Sri-Lankan delights, each one more delicious than the next, in the most minimalist of minimal spaces (think of a concrete cube, and you're pretty much there). The staff are joyous, helpful, and fun, and you're just seconds from Soho's most notorious LGBTQ+ joints.

The Wolseley 160 Piccadilly, W1J 9EB; thewolseley. com. Is that Joan Collins over there? Dame Judi? Aunty Jean out on the night of her life? Or, you know, thingy from that film, the one that won, you know, all the Oscars? Or perhaps someone of royal ilk who's popped in for an Eggs Benedict, seeing as Buckingham Palace is just ten minutes' walk away across Green Park? *The Wolseley* is as institution as restaurants in the Grand European tradition get, with food that's rarely shy of

Sweet treats at Broadway Market

London. She took over this gorgeous Georgian pub, but maintained its Tiki décor and created the friendliest, most fun LGBTQ+ boozer possible with trash DJs, pub quizzes, strong cocktails and very flirty staff.

The Duke of Wellington 77 Wardour Street, W1D 6QA; dukeofwellingtonsoho.co.uk. In the heart of big old gay old Soho is this seemingly ordinary London pub – "The Welly" to those who know it well – packed to the rafters with gay men of all ages enjoying big beers, gay bingo, cheesy dance music and, in summer, a bumper-to-bumper outdoor space where you can wave across to cast members from *Les Miserables* having a half-time cigarette outside.

The Glory 281 Kingsland Road, E2 8AS; theglory.co. Come to Hackney and discover two floors of madness in London's glittering East End thanks to drag legend Jonny Woo and his assorted ragtag bunch of pals. Expect a basic London boozer atmosphere but with a crazy showtime; here you'll find performances from DJs like veteran nightclub legend Princess Julia, cabaret of the very surreal kind and a crowd of queer trendsetters of all ages. Big fun guaranteed. The biggest, in fact.

The Royal Vauxhall Tavern 372 Kennington Lane, SE11 5HY; vauxhalltavern.com. We don't use the term "institution" lightly, but this Grade II listed pub is truly part of London's LGBTQ+ culturescape – it even has a protection order to prove it, so it will live on forever (or hopefully even longer). Expect the maddest cabaret, the daftest DJs, and the most raucous clientele, all in a venue that is the epitome of the London boozer. Don't be surprised to pop down for a few on a Friday night and not emerge till Sunday. It is rumoured that Princess Diana once came in disguised as a man on the arm of Freddie Mercury.

perfect, in a room that echoes with history and very good taste. Lucien Freud – an artist who could have paid off a hundred mortgages with a two-second doodle on a napkin – ate here every day of his life at the table in the corner that has the best views of everyone coming in. You can feel – and taste – the elegance.

DRINK

JAKE jakeldn.com. Think of it as a roving members' club for gay men (though everyone is, of course, welcome), one they like to call "the best gay bar in town tonight". *JAKE* takes over the loveliest venues across London – *Somerset House*, *The Ivy Club*, *One Hundred Shoreditch* – and turns them into the buzziest of queer happenings for one night only. The friendliest (and most glamorous) LGBTQ+ night in London? Could be!

The Cock 340 Kennington Road, SE11 4LD; thecocktavernlondon.com. Having ruled the roost at *Nelson's Head* back when Shoreditch was much gayer than it is today, landlady Farika decamped to south

DANCE

Adonis instagram.com/adonis.adonis.adonis. Imagine, if you will, a big LGBTQ+ blow-out, bobbing across various cavernous north and east London venues, where a huge crowd of sexy and sexied-up queer and mixed revellers do their thing in fabulous and often bonkers outfits until the sun comes up. Turns out you're imagining *Adonis*. They keep their roving rotation pretty schtum until the last minute, so keep an eye on their Instagram page.

Feel It Omeara, 6 O'Meara Street, SE1 1TE; omearalondon.com; instagram.com/feelitparty. You can thank superstar drag DJ Jodie Harsh and queer party people Little Gay Brother for this occasional jumping Friday-nighter that takes over this multi-space venue. These nights fill the terrace, the bar and the gorgeous main room – all peeling paint and proscenium arch – with jumping, often shirtless men. Chill outside, grab a drink or get sweaty on that heaving dancefloor, the choice is yours.

G-A-Y at Heaven Charing Cross Arches, Villiers Street, WC2N 6NG; heavennightclub-london.com. It's the coming together of two gay mega-brands: *Heaven*, the biggest gay nightclub in Europe since the 70s, and *G-A-Y*, the Soho bar with a very pop sensibility. Together they make a whole lot of fun, the kind of fun that's especially popular with a young queer crowd who come to enjoy everything from live legends – think Cher, Kylie, and RuPaul – to specialist nights and "Porn Idol", which is just as entertaining and naughty as it sounds. Even Adele has turned up to judge the proceedings.

Horsemeat Disco The Eagle, 349 Kennington Lane, SE11 5QY; eaglelondon.com. Come a sultry Sunday evening, people queue round the block to get into this fabled club night. You could be waiting for hours, but even the queue itself is a whole bunch of fun, with people bringing along bottles of plonk to pass the time. The schtick is simple; the most *recherché* disco music from DJs like Severino and Jim Stanton in a basic London pub on a Sunday night, with a slightly dishevelled outside garden selling burgers and chips. But that barely scratches the surface of how fun and glamorous *Horsemeat* is; you don't become a global brand unless you know what you're doing! There are plenty of other superstar nights to check out at this great little south London hotspot, too.

Roast Electrowerkz, 7 Torrens Street, EC1V 1NQ; facebook.com/roast.club.ldn. So popular has this new men-only night for bears, cubs, chubs, chasers and muscle bears been that they've had to go twice monthly just to deal with demand. Having filled a niche in London's queer nightlife, *Roast* takes over a huge venue in east London for regular testosterone-heavy all-nighters. Expect a beefed-up masculine crowd enjoying rooms of techno, pop and all things in between.

SHE Soho 23a Old Compton St, London W1D 5JL; instagram.com/shesohobar. Believe it or not, *SHE Soho* is still London's only womxn-priority bar. It's a cosy underground space dedicated to queer women and non-binary folk, as well as their guests. Through the doors and down a small staircase inside, you'll find a kind of modern bunker with a bar, a dance floor, and several intimate seating areas; there's always really inclusive and welcoming vibe, with hot new DJs and karaoke nights as well as regular social events. The only downside is that it's all in a very small space; you'd be well-advised to arrive by 10pm to be sure to get in. Otherwise, be prepared to queue!

SHOP

Columbia Road Market Columbia Road, E2 7RG; columbiaroadmarket.co.uk. A Sunday morning tradition since the late 1800s, this beautiful flower

Haute couture by John Galliano for Dior at The Victoria and Albert Museum

The Rainbow Flag flies alongside the Union Jack on Tower Bridge in support of Pride

market is more than just somewhere to buy potted plants. The whole area comes alive on Sundays as those after a horticultural bargain rub shoulders with A-list Hollywood movie stars. If you don't have the greenest of fingers, no matter; come too for the artisan coffee, street food and the quaintest of quaint pubs. Speaking of which, check out *The Nelson's*, two minutes' away on Horatio Street, which clings on to its LGBTQ+ status with gay abandon.

Gay's The Word 66 Marchmont Street, WC1N 1AB; gaystheword.co.uk. This pocket-size LGBTQ+ bookshop within walking distance of the glorious (and free to enter!) British Museum isn't just a well-stocked store, it's an institution. The staff are experts in their field and very happy to answer questions and give recommendations, and any queer author worth their salt has done a reading here – while up the stairs is where the monumental collaboration between striking miners and the LGBTQ+ community, made famous in the film *Pride* (2014), was forged during the 1980s.

Liberty Regent Street, W1B 5AH; libertylondon.com. Is this the most beautiful department store in the world? An 1885 Tudor-revival belle-of-the-West End just off the beauteous Regent Street, Liberty is a wonderland of the most gorgeous objects your hard-earned money can buy. Step inside and enter a masterclass of craft and engineering, with three atriums created from the timbers of two ancient battle ships. So far, so amazing. Then there's the stuff that's on sale, from *objets d'art* to extraordinary homeware via high-end clothing and all the right colognes, not to mention *Liberty*'s world-coveted fabric collection.

Selfridges 400 Oxford Street, W1A 1AB; selfridges.com. The *grande dame* of British department stores, this huge West End emporium is no way stuck in the past. Cool, funky and with famously fabulous window displays at Christmas, it houses the *crème de la crème* of global brands with 21 food and drink outlets of only the most glamorous kind to offer some respite from the hard-core shopping experience, plus an intriguing roster of events.

DO

Broadway Market Broadway Market, London Fields, E8 4PH; broadwaymarket.co.uk. A very busy, very buzzy Victorian street market – just a ten-minute walk from Columbia Road Flower Market – that can be traced back to 1,000 years BC, Broadway Market comes alive at the weekend with food stalls selling everything from oysters to vegan cheese, while the shops that line the street range from luxury brands like Aesop to very clever, very LGBTQ-friendly bookshops. There's no end of bars, restaurants and good old English pubs round here too, all the better for refueling after all that walking! Afterwards check out adjoining London Fields, London's coolest stretch of verdant park, which fills with picnicking locals as soon as the weather gets warm enough (and even a little bit before).

Queer Britain 2 Granary Square, N1C 4BH; queerbritain.org.uk. The UK's first – and so far, only – dedicated LGBTQ+ museum is a celebration of queer culture, people and history, with exhibitions, panels and the odd champagne reception to keep all of us – queer or otherwise – on our toes. Free to enter, you'll find *Queer Britain* among the hubbub of Kings Cross. As you're here, stop off for dinner at *Coal Office* just the other side of Granary Square for its sumptuous Middle Eastern menu and delicious Tom Dixon interiors.

Victoria & Albert Museum Cromwell Road, SW7 2RL; vam.ac.uk. Known simply as "The V&A", this huge applied and decorative arts museum – the world's largest! – contains everything from Tudor headwear to padlocks, priceless jewellery to stained glass, theatrical scenery to plaster casts of the world's most famous monuments – with world-leading fashion exhibitions from Westwood and McQueen to Bowie and Kylie thrown in for good measure. Then there are the educational courses, late-night openings with lashings of champagne, live catwalk shows, an Italianate garden and the building itself – just look at it! – and you have one of the globe's greatest cultural experiences.

PARIS
Spring

Ah, Paris. The city that clichés were built on, that metropolis of lights and marriage proposals, of sunset strolls along the Seine, of bistros and *pâtisseries* and cute terraces made for people-watching and half-smoked Marlboro Lights, of boulevards and boutiques, of fashion weeks and the Folies Bergère, of dusty salons where the *bons mots* of cultural luminaries still hang in the air – or maybe that's the *pot-au-feu*. Throw in an LGBTQ+ scene that refuses to quit – they don't call it 'Gay Paree' for nothing – and you'll find a city that really ought to be on everybody's lips.

The ornate main hall of the Musée d'Orsay

HISTORY

You could close your eyes and drop a pin on any period of Paris's LGBTQ+ history and find yourself in a rabbit hole, and probably a very chic one at that. France was, after all, the first modern country to decriminalise homosexuality in 1791, during the French Revolution. Even Napoleon Bonaparte was pretty *laissez-faire* about the whole thing, failing – refusing, perhaps? – to renegue on the 1791 decriminalisation while acting as Emperor of the French Republic. Symbolically, this was a big deal, as it meant that from the French Revolution onwards LGBTQ+ people could go about their business without much to-do; enter stage left Oscar Wilde, James Baldwin, Gertrude Stein. It meant that native LGBTQ+ writers such as Marcel Proust and Jean Cocteau could thrive.

It was also a very big deal for another French writer, a woman who scandalised French society with her sexual 'deviancy' and gluttony for life. Colette lived out her final decades at the Palais-Royal, during which she produced the sapphic masterpiece *The Pure and the Impure*, receiving a state funeral in 1954. Her gallivanting also took in another fascinating period of Parisian history, the Jazz Age, also referred to as "*Les Années Folles*" – the "Crazy Years", or the "Roaring Twenties" to English-speakers. World War I was over and fun was very much back on the agenda. What made Paris stand out by a hot mile – certainly compared with, say, New York – was its attitude towards race and sex, namely that nobody gave a hoot how you buttered your bread. The arts flourished, American expat and collector Stein opened her house at 27 Rue de Fleurus to Fitzgerald and Hemingway, Picasso and Matisse, and queer icon Josephine Baker fled racial apartheid in her native USA for the brighter lights and enlightened audiences of the Folies Bergère. It's this flamboyant and bohemian spirit that is still evident in the atmosphere of *le gay Paris* today.

Born Freda Josephine McDonald in St. Louis, Missouri in 1906 in a racially segregated USA, Josephine Baker did not have what could be called an easy childhood. Her mother was a frustrated music hall dancer, but worked as a laundress, and against the background of the rampant racism of the early twentieth century, Baker was sent to work as a live-in maid aged eight and was horrifically abused by her employer. By age 13, she had entered into her first marriage; however, the unhappy union didn't last long, and she was married a second time, this time aged 15, to the man who bestowed her with the name Baker. For Baker, the USA represented "that terror of discrimination, that horrible beast which paralyses one's very soul and body." Add the fact of her bisexuality into the mix – and this at a time when attraction to more than one gender didn't even have a name – and it becomes clear with hindsight that trouble could never have been far off.

So it was that in 1925, the talented, charismatic and queer Baker made her way to Paris as part of *La Revue Nègre*, an all-black performing group. At the time, Paris was a city besotted with black art and culture, albeit through a colonial lens – you couldn't move in the cooler cafés for the jazz beats, and Picasso was *all* about African masks. Here, in a libertarian Paris that wasn't as beholden to bigotry as her birthplace, Baker could finally breathe.

Baker was a phenomenally original dancer, singer, dresser and innovator, as well as being a striking and beguiling individual. When she moved to Paris, a star was born. The biggest star in France, in fact. Her *Danse Sauvage* – wild, frenzied, sexy – in the now-iconic banana skirt at the Folies Bergère bewitched Parisians' they couldn't get enough of her. News of Baker's fame quickly found its way back to her native USA, where rampant racism would have meant that she would only be allowed in through the back door of venues she herself had sold out. She was the embodiment of the Jazz Age and France declared her "the Bronze Goddess".

Such was her talent and charisma, Baker stood out like an exclamation mark. She was enlisted as a spy for the French Resistance during World War II as the perfect double-agent who could snoop in plain sight while entertaining the world onstage. She had become the biggest black star on the planet, and was the first black woman to play the lead in a major motion picture, *Siren of the Tropics*, in 1927. She adopted twelve children from disadvantaged backgrounds around the world into what she called her "rainbow family", and her political activism and bold criticism of American segregation rattled the US government to such an extent that she was arrested as a suspected Communist.

When she died in Paris in 1975 aged 68, her funeral was accompanied by a 21-gun salute and over 20,000 mourners lining the streets to pay their respects. Josephine Baker now lies in state at the Panthéon, the only black person ever to have been given that most Parisian of honours. Now, seriously, someone needs to make this film.

Oscar Wilde's grave at Père Lachaise Cemetery

Pride in Paris

HIGHLIGHTS

PÈRE LACHAISE CEMETERY
16 Rue du Repos, 75020

It might sound odd to suggest that you hang out in an old cemetery, but Père Lachaise is truly the Hollywood Hills of necropolises. Just east of Paris's top tourist must-sees in and around Île de France, Père Lachaise is a glorious homage to the even more glorious dead. Doubling up as the largest landscaped garden in the city, it makes for a real who's who of the past. From the LGBTQ+ contingent there's Marcel Proust, Balzac, Colette and Rosa Bonheur. Gertrude Stein shares a tomb with her life-partner Alice B. Toklas, bound together in romantic, dreamlike perpetuity. Jacques Régis de Cambacérès, the gay aristocrat who made it through the French Revolution head intact, then becoming second consul in Napoleon's republic has the fanciest of tombs, so large it actually has a door in it (though it is of course not open to the general public). There are also cherished icons including Édith Piaf, Maria Callas and Gioacchino Rossini. But top spot must go to Oscar Wilde, whose tomb is (literally) to-die-for. Designed by the American-British sculptor Sir Jacob Epstein and taking ten months to complete, it is covered in scarlet kisses; the tomb itself is now protected by a huge screen to stop any more damage from admirers' lipstick (though the screen itself is also covered). Paris and London have a shared history when it comes to Wilde, but his time – and death in 1900 aged 46 – while exiled in the latter was defined by poverty, illness, and loneliness. There's a wonderful film by (and starring) Rupert Everett as Wilde about these last years called *The Happy Prince* (2018). Fittingly, *Les Mots à la Bouche* – a delightful LGBTQ+ book shop that really ought to be on your agenda – is a few minutes' walk away, via L'Atelier des Lumières.

ROSA BONHEUR

1 Rue Botzaris, 75019

www.rosabonheur.fr

Named in honour of one of the most successful artists and sculptors of the nineteenth century, Rosa Bonheur, this party's pretty left-field; just what you'd expect from a gathering named after a woman who was openly lesbian, wore her hair short and smoked cigarettes (gasp!) as well as living openly with her female partner for over 40 years.

The parties themselves take place in the eponymous restaurant in Buttes Chaumont – itself one of Paris's more idiosyncratic parks, built to look like a romantic English garden. At the top of the hill you'll find the *Rosa Bonheur* restaurant, a stunning white and green building (the walls inside are pink!) sitting in dappled shade and surrounded by chestnut trees. A more bucolic setting you could not find.

During the long, languid Parisian afternoons, the restaurant makes for the perfect place to stop for a quick round of tapas and a glass of wine while families stroll lesuirely past; but on Sundays, it is here that the Rosa Bonheur party starts, taking its cue from the city's queer tea parties.

The gathering starts early and will allow you to party till your heart's bursting while still getting to bed at a decent (ish) hour for those who have work in the morning – or not, for the lucky ones that don't! Crowds start to gather from the early afternoon, and are a mixed bunch – of course, the parties are popular with a the city's hip lesbian contingent, but the atmosphere is very laid-back and everyone is welcome. The music goes up several notches around 8pm (think queer anthems and lots of Madonna), and drinks are cheap – for Paris, anyway.

In spring and summer you'd be well advised to arrive early to be in with a chance of getting anywhere close to the building itself. If you do, you'll probably hear the LGBTQ+ choir rehearsing next door before they too get in on the action. Surreal!

The Palais Bourbon decorated with the rainbow flag to celebrate Pride

ASSEMBLÉE NATIONALE

LISTINGS

STAY

Hotel Dame des Arts 4 Rue Danton, 75006; damedesarts.com. A *Rive Gauche* superstar with all the right Latin Quarter credentials, *Dame des Arts* lives up to its name. Beautiful, classy and sassy, the Raphael Navot interiors are seductively laid-back, the suites looking gorgeous and come-hither with their handsome natural materials, expertly-chosen artworks and views towards the Eiffel Tower. Up top we have one of Paris's marvellous rooftop bars, down below the loveliest of secret gardens, and a restaurant brought to you by Othoniel Alvarez Castaneda, who's keen on feeding you as sustainably as possible. *Oui, s'il vous plaît!*

Hôtel du Petit Moulin 29 Rue de Poitou, 75003; hoteldupetitmoulin.com. This teeny hotel in a former *boulangerie* in Le Marais is all about Christian Lacroix – in that he designed the rooms, and they're just as bonkers-fabulous as you'd expect. There are only 17 of them, and each is unique. Venetian fantasia, much? Or how about a galaxy of stars above your bed? Sexy-luxe with maximalist wallpaper and come-to-bed couture throws? Now we're talking. Given the hotel's diminutive size, the only refreshment options are a stylish little honesty bar and a breakfast spot that's as cute (and *petit*) as your average button. Victor Hugo got his bread from here back in the day.

Hôtel Lutetia 45 Boulevard Raspail, 75006; hotellutetia.com. The only *grand palace* hotel on the Left Bank, and hot-damn is it beautiful. It's not as on-the-radar as other Parisian hotel showstoppers, meaning the clientele here really know their *oignons*; if you like little-black-book on a grand scale, step right in. It's also home to one of the best bars in Paris, *Josephine*, named after LGBTQ+ hero and erstwhile *Lutetia* regular Josephine Baker. Just over the road you'll bump into *Le Bon Marché*, an enormous and gorgeous department store.

Mama Shelter Paris East 109 Rue de Bagnolet, 75020; mamashelter.com. Rambunctious, friendly and very good value, *Mama's* in the Belleville does quirky-stylish in the way you'd expect from the mini-hotel chain co-founded by the *enfant terrible* of design, Philippe Starck. It's only 15 minutes into tourist-central, and five to the gloriously spooky Père Lachaise cemetery.

Sinner 116 Rue du Temple, 75003; sinnerparis. com. Lapsed Catholic is the schtick, Le Marais is the location, and high-concept ecclesiastical fantasy is the in-your-face reality. Dry ice is pumped into the lobby every evening which makes entering feel much like swishing into a Cher video, the restaurant is one of the hottest spots in Paris, and the rooms are deliciously lavish.

EAT

Anne Pavillon de la Reine, 28 Place Des Vosges, 7500e; pavillon-de-la-reine.com. Received wisdom is that hotel restaurants aren't worth the bother, but to pass up on *Anne* in the divine *Pavillon de la Reine* on the Place des Vosges – which is all your Parisian dreams come true, especially on a summer's night when the lawn is littered with wine-drinkers – would make you the most foolish of fools. The décor inside and in the courtyard is exquisite, but even that has nothing on chef Mathieu Pacaud's culinary creations, which put the class right back into classic French cooking. Simply enchanting.

Derrière 69 Rue des Gravilliers, 75003; derriere-resto. com. Cheeky by name, cheeky by nature, *Derrière* is a Le Marais staple and a masterclass in irreverent gastronomy. Down an alley and into a courtyard and then the restaurant proper, *Derrière*'s ramshackle appearance – mismatching tables and chairs, bric-à-brac strewn all over the place, piles of books, the odd ping-pong table, the sort of furniture your Nana would've thrown out years ago – belies the world-class food and general elegance of the place. Bad behaviour is encouraged, especially after a few vodka martinis.

Georges Place Georges Pompidou, 75004; restaurantgeorgesparis.com. This is event dining. A restaurant plonked on top of Renzo Piano and Richard Roger's (in)famous inside-out Centre Pompidou like it just doesn't care, the views are to die for. Inside, it's a story of crisp, streamlined design, with a central room that we can only describe as an amorphous alien pod, inside which you'll find the toilets and kitchen.

The food is modern French with some Italian thrown in, and at night it becomes Instagram-heaven, with perfect hair and camera flashes at every turn.

Ora 12 Rue Philippe de Girard, 75010; ora-paris.co. Paris is really beginning to cotton on to vegetarian and vegan diets, for which we salute them. *Ora* is a beautiful space just made for hanging out in and putting the world to rights; the food, which is plant-based and of the healthy and delicious variety, is favoured by Parisians who like a slice of conscience with their sustenance. It's also very good value for money.

DRINK

Bar Josephine Hôtel Lutetia, 45 Boulevard Raspail, 75006; hotellutetia.com. There is certainly no shortage of wow-factor at this *haute*-bar dedicated to the memory of French-American LGBTQ+ icon Josephine Baker, who used to frequent this gorgeous spot inside the equally delicious *Lutetia* hotel – the only palace hotel on the Left Bank. The ceiling is exquisite (as are the martinis!), the bar is a thing of such beauty you

may forget to even give your date the time of day, and the well-Manolo-Blahnik-heeled, mixed crowd only adds to the air of all-round sophistication. *C'est très, très chic.*

Le Bonjour Madame 40 Rue de Montreuil, 75011; facebook.com/bonjourmadame.paris11. This women-centred, queer bar is on a mission, and a feminist one at that. Entertaining in a safe space for women and their friends is a wonderful thing, but *Le Bonjour Madame* also put themselves out there to make the world a better place – just take a look at their roster of activism, taking on equal rights and climate change and amongst other worthy causes – making this legendary spot an essential part of Paris's LGBTQ+ landscape. They also know how to throw a really good party.

Cox 15 Rue des Archives, 75004; cox.fr. Alexander McQueen's favourite bar back when he was doing his thing over at Givenchy, this boutique gay bar gets so busy that, if the weather is good, the street outside becomes road-blocked with a cross-section of good-time gay gentlemen. Big-name DJs are one

Anne, the upmarket restaurant in the Pavillon de la Reine

The terrace of the *Rosa Bonheur* restaurant in the Parc des Buttes-Chaumont

of the draws, but mostly *Cox* is a busy, buzzy LGBTQ+ bar where the only thing on the agenda is fun and the crowd is a heaving mish-mash of every which way of gay.

Le Syndicat 51 Rue du Fabourg Saint-Denis, 75010; domainesyndicat.com. The entrance to *Le Syndicat* isn't much to look at; it's an unprepossessing, run-down-looking wall of peeling posters beside a door that's been graffitied a hundreds of times over; step inside, though, and you'll find one of Paris's hottest bars, where the soundtrack is mostly hip-hop and the cocktails are made using only French spirits. The staff are wonderfully friendly and always on hand to help you decide which drink to go for next. *Le Syndicat* has been named among the world's best 50 bars so many times, it's almost embarrassing.

DANCE

BigWolf bigwolf.fr. There's a clue in the name of Paris's finest curators of same-sex-oriented mega-parties.

BigWolf put on huge circuit-style parties across the city, each one better than the last. With big-name DJs and a lot of shirtless (mostly male) action, they also have a penchant for putting on spectacular events around Halloween, Christmas and New Year.

La Boîte à Frissons 13 rue au Maire; boite-a-frissons.fr. Unpretentious (and inexpensive) LGBTQ+ club in a retro 1930s dance hall, with a traditional Sunday-afternoon tea dance from 6pm. Friday and Saturday nights also begin with couples of all sexual orientations dancing traditional *danse à deux*, until the legendary "Madison" line dance at 12.30am, after which it's pure fetish costume and disco.

Doctor Love doctorlove.fr. This monthly queer night is a whole lot of grass-roots fun. What started out as a few friends just doing their thing is now one of the biggest parties in town. They like a theme, which only adds to the drama and gives party-goers the opportunity to dress themselves silly. Keep an eye on the ever-changing location.

Raidd 23 Rue du Temple, 75004; facebook.com/leraiddparis. A warning to those of a sensitive disposition: there will be nudity. In fact, that's the reason most people come to *Raidd*, to see the famous shower dances where gentlemen get squeaky clean in the most public way possible. The crowd is mostly male and the surroundings more salubrious than you might imagine with such a boisterous crowd.

SHOP

Le Bon Marché 24 Rue de Sèvres, 75007. Paris's – and indeed the world's – first department store, *Le Bon Marché* is still the city's smartest (although *Galleries Lafayette* give it a run for its money), and the escalators alone make it worth a visit. This beauty, that started small in 1838 and is now owned by LVMH, also doubles up as a gallery with rotating installations from newsworthy global artists; it has been thrilling senses and pulling at right purse strings since Louis-Philippe I was King of France. Read all about it in Zola's unexpectedly gripping *Au Bonheur des Dames*.

Fleux 39 Rue Sainte-Croix de la Bretonnerie, 75004; fleux.com. Homeware doesn't get more delicious than this. Clearly curated by people who know what they're doing, *Fleux* sets the standard when it comes to showing off one's home. There are – thankfully – a few *Fleux* outlets across town, but seeing as this is Paris and we're looking for a good time, swing by the one in Le Marais. You'll be glad you did.

Merci 111 Boulevard Beaumarchais, 75003. You'll find curated clothes from *NNO7*, *OrSlow*, *Autry*, and *Xirena*; recherché books and magazines to make your coffee table pop; pretty stationery (because who doesn't love pretty stationery?); and the cleverest collection of knick-knacks for the home you ever did covet, lots of them bafflingly affordable. Now pop to *Merci*'s super cute *Used Book Café* to congratulate yourself on your purchases with a luscious *gâteau clémentine*.

Les Mots à la Bouche 37 Rue Saint-Ambroise, 75011; motsbouche.com. There was a huge outcry when this beloved establishment shut up shop in Le Marais, but luckily *Les Mots à la Bouche* has relocated to the

The stunning interior of the *Hotel Lutetia*

The Bourse de Commerce in the Halles district

eleventh arrondissement – and what a joy it is too. As well as stocking every LGBTQ+ book and magazine you've ever wanted (as well as some you didn't know you wanted yet), it has its own programme of events while also being a bit of an oracle when it comes to other LGBTQ+ goings-on across town.

DO

Bourse de Commerce, Pinault Collection 2 Rue de Vairmes, 75001; pinaultcollection.com. Paris has always been good at reinventing spaces in the interest of art. Take the Musée d'Orsay, once a railway station, now arguably the most beautiful art gallery in Paris. Until the Bourse de Commerce came along, that is. The beautiful circular ex-Stock Exchange is now a stunning art space where the building is as big a star as the work on show. Specialising in art at the edgier end of the spectrum, it's somewhere you should visit even if you're less interested in the exhibition. Plus, there's a cool little souvenir shop to boot.

Marche des Fiertés en.parisinfo.com; Formerly known as Paris Pride, the rebranding of the biggest celebration of LGBTQ+ life Paris has ever known has given it a new lease of life. Doing its thing since 1977, here you'll find the biggest queer party in all of France. It takes place in June which means the weather's usually sunny, and it ropes in a good half a million people whose focus is mostly on having a good time.

Free First Sundays en.parisinfo.com. With 130-odd museums, Paris isn't just showing off, it's putting a walloping big hole in your culture budget. Every first Sunday of the month, though, a bunch of said museums are free to visit. Big-hitters include The Louvre, Musée National d'Art Moderne at the Pompidou, Musée d'Orsay and Versailles, but it's best to check out which lesser-knowns will give you free reign closer to the time.

REYKJAVÍK
Spring

Those who've been to Iceland before will be familiar with the country's uniquely beautiful melancholy aesthetic, which makes for a great driving companion on scenic car journeys around the Golden Circle, venturing past breath-taking sights of waterfalls and geysers. In the southwest, on the southern shore of Faxaflói bay, you'll find Iceland's quirky and colourful capital city, Reykjavík – the perfect base from which to explore Iceland's rugged wilderness. Small as it may be, this charming cosmopolitan spot has far more to it than you'd ever assume from a city of its size, including an abundance of cultural gems and wild nightlife, particularly for the LGBTQ+ community.

Reykjavík Pride Parade

HISTORY

It is traditionally believed that Reykjavík (or "Smokey Bay") was founded in 874 by Norseman Ingólfr Arnarson. In its early days as a fishing village and trading post, Sheriff Skúli Magnússon, also known as the father of Reykjavík, opened wool mills to modernise Iceland's economy; it was in this way that Reykjavík began its modern urban development. It was then granted municipal powers and was designated the administrative centre of the Danish-ruled island in 1786. The twentieth century was a period of rapid urbanisation and as agriculture and fishing became less crucial to the growing nation, many young people moved to the city. It then became the capital of a self-governing Iceland under the Danish king in 1918, and finally became independent from Denmark in 1944.

Iceland was the first country to have a female president, Vigdís Finnbogadóttir, elected in 1980. It also has the world's first female and openly gay head of government, Jóhanna Sigurðardóttir, who was elected prime minister in 2009. Iceland legalised same-sex marriage on 27th June 2010, and as such was amongst the first ten countries to do so; the government also passed a bill that provided a gender-neutral marriage definition, and not one person in parliament voted against it. The general Icelandic public were also mostly in support of the bill.

Today, Reykjavík is the world's northernmost capital city with 200,000 inhabitants, two thirds of Iceland's entire population. Since the financial crash of 2008, it has reinvented itself as a bustling tourist hub. It also has a powerful reputation as a progressive, forward-thinking city that welcomes the LGBTQIA+ community. Every year Reykjavík Pride has a theme, and 2022's was "Beauty of Freedom", a theme to celebrate post-Covid-19 life as well as the freedom to be themselves that LGBTQ+ people in Iceland enjoy.

ICON

Jóhanna Sigurðardóttir is a trailblazer in more ways than one. Not only did she make history as the first female prime minister of Iceland, she was also the first openly gay head of government in the world. Born in 1942 in Reykjavík, Sigurðardóttir had a long and accomplished career in politics before becoming prime minister in 2009.

Sigurðardóttir initially worked as a flight attendant and was active in the trade union movement. She went on to hold various positions in government and was a champion for the rights of marginalised communities, including women and the LGBTQ+ community; she was a key figure in passing legislation that aimed at improving their quality of life. In 2002, she and her partner Jónína Leósdóttir entered into a registered partnership, which was converted into a marriage when same-sex marriage was made legal in Iceland in 2010. This helped pave the way for other LGBTQ+ individuals who wanted to do the same.

As prime minister, a position she held between 2009 and 2013, Sigurðardóttir prioritised stabilising the Icelandic economy after the 2008 financial crisis and worked towards creating a more sustainable and equitable society. Under her leadership, Iceland became a leader in renewable energy, with an ambitious plan to transition to 100% clean energy by 2050. She also championed gender equality and worked to improve the lives of women in Iceland.

Sigurðardóttir's lasting legacy is one of courage, determination and progress. She broke down barriers for the LGBTQ+ community and paved the way for other leaders to follow in her footsteps. For LGBTQ+ travellers visiting Reykjavík, her story is a testament to the country's progressive attitudes and its commitment to creating a more inclusive society. In recognition of her contributions, Sigurðardóttir was named as one of Forbes's 100 Most Powerful Women in the world in 2009. She continues to be an inspiration to people around the world, and her legacy will continue to be remembered as a beacon of hope and progress.

The Blue Lagoon

HIGHLIGHT

There are so many wonderful things to do if you're staying in Reykjavík, including relaxing at the Blue Lagoon, taking a day trip to Gulfoss waterfall, or, if you're lucky, catching a glimpse of the Northern Lights on a nighttime excursion. For the full Icelandic experience, though, visiting the Golden Circle in spring makes for a magical adventure for any visitor to Reykjavík. The off-season offers a uniquely peaceful atmosphere with fewer crowds, and is the perfect time to witness the Golden Circle's breathtaking natural beauty. As the land thaws in the increasing hours of sunlight, the landscape bursts into life, treating travellers to hundreds of shades of green.

The whole Golden Circle route can easily be done in half a day by car or on a tour; the journey typically covers around 300 kilometres. Begin your journey with a visit to the historic Thingvellir National Park, which is located a short drive east of Reykjavík. This is the boundary where the North American and Eurasian tectonic plates meet, creating a dramatic landscape of rocky cliffs and fissures. In the spring, the park is blanketed with wildflowers. Explore the idyllic landscape by way of a guided hike, which will allow you a deeper understanding of the park's history and geology.

The next stop is the majestic Gullfoss waterfall, one of Iceland's most iconic and popular attractions. The waterfall is at its most powerful in spring as the glacial waters thunder down the cliffs into the pool below.

Another must-see on the route is the Geysir geothermal area, a hot spring paradise in Haukadalur valley. Here you will find a series of geysers, hot springs, and bubbling mud pools that are an otherworldly marvel to behold. In spring you will find vibrant green moss covering the surrounding area, which further adds to the site's luscious beauty.

The Golden Circle is one of Iceland's real treasures, and Reykjavík is your best port of call from which to explore it all. It's a remarkable adventure that will mesmerise any traveller.

Replica of a traditional room inside the National Museum of Iceland

LISTINGS

There are a few things to bear in mind when planning your trip to Reykjavík. Iceland is a country of extremes, so depending on what time of year you travel, you may have limited daylight, which could significantly impact your plans. In spring you will have more hours of daylight, so if you're planning anything that includes good views, make sure you go at the right time of day so that you can make the most of your experience.

It's also a good idea to make bookings in advance. Iceland is a small country with limited spaces on tours, so plan ahead to make sure you're not disappointed!

Another key thing to note about Reykjavík is that alcohol is incredibly expensive, both in supermarkets and in restaurants and bars. If you're someone who likes a tipple, you'd do well to make use of the tax-free booze available at the airport as this will help you save money for other elements of your trip, particularly if you choose a self-catering accommodation option.

STAY

CenterHotel Plaza Aðalstræti 4- 6; centerhotels. com/plaza. The style in this tastefully renovated old building a stone's throw from Austurstræti is Nordic minimalism meets old-fashioned charm, with the heavy wooden floors, plain white walls and immaculately tiled bathrooms complementing the high-beamed ceilings. Ideally located for exploring the city, rooms are basic but roomy and clean, and the beds are particularly comfy.

Holt Bergstaðastræti 37; holt.is. Over three hundred paintings by Icelandic artists adorn the rooms and public areas of this luxury, centrally located place which first opened its doors in 1965. The sumptuous rooms here are of the Persian-carpet, dark-wood-panelling, red-leather-armchair and chocolate-on-the-pillow variety.

Hotel Borg Pósthússtræti 11; keahotels.is/hotel-borg. Located in downtown Reykjavík, the 99-room Art Deco *Hotel Borg* has set the standard for Reykjavík's luxury hotels since it opened in 1930.

Hotel Fron Laugavegur 22A; hotelfron.is. A luxury hotel in the heart of the city, close to all the main bars, shops, restaurants and museums. In addition to regular double rooms, it offers stylish studios and larger apartments, each with bath, kitchenette and TV.

Icelandair Reykjavík Marina Mýrargata 2; icelandairhotels.com. Bold, bright and refreshingly quirky, this harbourside hotel not only enjoys terrific views of the trawlers in dry dock right outside, but its rooms also have a maritime feel with a twist of chic.

Klöpp Klapparstígur 26; centerhotels.is. This amusingly-named hotel is one of central Reykjavík's best; modern throughout, with tasteful wooden floors, oak furniture and wall panelling in all rooms. The breakfast room is a little cramped, though.

Kex Hostel Skúlagata 28; kexhostel.is. This renovated biscuit factory offers a range of stylish accommodation options, including private doubles with en-suite bathrooms and ocean views. There are dorms with shared kitchens available too, where fresh free food is often left by other travellers for you to help yourself to. The shared facilities are kept sparklingly clean.

Kvosin Downtown Hotel Laugavegur 36; kvosinhotel.is. A boutique hotel in the heart of Reykjavík's shopping district, located within easy walking distance of several good bars and restaurants.

Leifur Eiríksson Skólavörðustígur 45; hotelleifur.is. With a perfect location overlooking Hallgrímskirkja, this is a small, friendly and neatly furnished place; the top-floor rooms, built into the sloping roof, are particularly worthwhile for their excellent views.

Radisson Blu 1919 Hotel, Pósthússtræti 2; radissonhotels.com/en-us/hotels/radisson-blu-Reykjavík-1919. Set in a century-old building in the heart of downtown Reykjavík, this hotel is within easy walking distance to visitor attractions like the Harpa concert hall and Reykjavík Art Museum, as well as the city hall, parliament and the prime minister's office.

Harpa Concert Hall

EAT

101 Reykjavík Street Food Skólavörðustígur 8; 101Reykjavíkstreetfood.is. Classic cockle-warming Icelandic dishes like fish stew and lobster soup are superb value at this unpretentious, friendly, and always popular restaurant.

Brauð & Co Frakkastígur 16; braudogco.is. You can't miss this modern Reykjavík institution, housed in a building colourfully adorned with pastel paints. The pastries are unforgettable – the cinnamon rolls and pain au chocolat come particularly recommended – and the self-serve coffee is good too.

Café Babalú Laugavegur 36; babalu.is. A cute and stylish café serving specialty coffee and light bites. Word on the street is they have a delicious soup and grilled cheese that makes it a perfect stop for lunch.

Dill Restaurant Sturlugata 5; dillrestaurant.is. A fine dining restaurant serving contemporary Icelandic cuisine, *Dill* was the first restaurant in Iceland to be awarded a Michelin star in 2017.

Kaffibarinn Bergstaðastræti 1; kaffibarinn.is. This trendy café is known for its diverse, mostly queer crowd and lively atmosphere.

Matur og Drykkur Grandagarður 2; maturogdrykkur.is. Inside the Saga Museum building, this inventive restaurant, plainly decorated with a concrete floor and wooden tables, has a truly unusual menu, featuring everything from an entire baked cod's head (complete with throat muscles) in batter, to cured salmon with dill skyr on oat-and-beer flatbread.

Sjávargrillið Skólavörðustígur 14; sjavargrillid.is. The restaurant owner Gústav has designed a really special menu that is both uniquely Icelandic and international. This is more than a restaurant; it's a true Icelandic experience.

Stofan Café Vesturgata 3a; stofan.is. This cosy café has a laid-back atmosphere and a range of delicious treats and beverages.

Tapas Barinn Laugavegur 20b; tapasbarinn.is. This contemporary tapas restaurant in central Reykjavík offers an exquisite eating experience, with over 50 meat, fish and veggie options on offer.

Dishes at *Matur og Drykkur*

Hotel Leifur Eiríksson

DANCE

Bravó Laugavegur 22; bravo.is. A well-known club playing a mix of electronic, hip hop and pop music. While it might not really look like the sort of place from the outside, it actually features the longest happy hour in Reykjavík!

Broadway Ármúli 9. Inside the *Ísland* hotel, this is the country's biggest nightspot, with room for over 2000 punters, and is popular with people of all ages, from teenagers to pensioners. It's prone to Vegas-style singing-and-dancing shows.

Gaukurinn Tryggvagata 22; gaukurinn.is. This is a great club and live music venue with a strong LGBTQ+ following, hosting concerts and events, featuring local bands as well as hosting karaoke and drag shows in this lively yet relaxed venue.

Húrra Tryggvagata 22; hurra.is. This live music venue and club hosts both local and international acts and is a great place to spend an evening of drinks, music and dancing. Here you'll find live jazz, a great selection of

wines and craft beers, and an achingly cool adjoining clothing boutique.

Kaffibarinn Bergstaðastræti 1. With an unmistakable frontage emblazoned with the London Underground logo, this tiny bar trades on the rumour that Blur's Damon Albarn owns it, however unlikely that may be. It's still your best chance of a great night out in Reykjavík, though, and is a legend on the scene.

Kiki Queer Bar Laugavegur 22; kiki.is. The home of Reykjavík's queer scene, *Kiki Queer Bar* is popular bar catering to the LGBTQ+ community; it has a fun and inclusive atmosphere and hosts all kinds of events.

Paloma 1-3 Naustin; en-gb.facebook.com/palomarvk music. This contemporary club and live music venue in central Reykjavík offers a somewhat strange mixture of music that ranges from reggae to electronic, with a big underground dancefloor.

Prikið Kaffihús Bankastræti 12; prikid.is This cosy spot is a popular bar and club featuring live music and DJs as well as brews on draft and pub grub.

DRINK

The Laundromat Café Austurstræti 9; thelaundromatcafe.is. A café and bar with a welcoming and inclusive atmosphere, offering a range of drinks and light bites.

Lebowski bar Laugarvegur 20a; lebowskibar.is. This is one of Reykjavík's highlights, and the best place in town for a White Russian! A bar for true fans of *The Big Lebowski* – and if you weren't a fan already, you'll certainly be going home as one.

Pablo Discobar Veltusund 1; pablodiscobar.is/en. This vibrant and kitschy cocktail bar is a great place to party. It hosts regular DJs as well as offering Latin American entrées and cocktails.

Skúli Craft bar Aðalstræti 9; facebook.com/skulicraft. Another fan favourite for locals and tourists alike. Here you can find 14 different craft beers on tap and most of them should be Icelandic.

SHOP

Geysir Laugavegur 33; geysir.is. This apty-named store specialises in high-quality Icelandic design products, including clothing and home goods. It takes inspiration from Nordic city life and culture, as well as from Iceland's long history of craft and knitwear.

Kolaportið Flea Market Tryggvagotu 19; kolaportid.is. This indoor market is Iceland's only flea market, selling a variety of interesting things including souvenirs and second-hand items. It takes place close to the harbour on weekends and, if you dare, is a great place to sample the local delicacy – fermented shark. It makes for an fascinating wander.

Rammagerðin Skólavörðustígur 22; rammagerdin. com. This iconic gift shop is one of the oldest in Iceland; it has been home to Icelandic crafts since 1940. Here you can find a variety of crafts by Icelandic craftspeople and designers, particularly woollies.

The Sun Voyager sculpture at sunset

Perlan Nature Exploratorium

DO

Blue Lagoon Nordurlijosavegur 9; bluelagoon. com. This iconic Icelandic spot is not one to miss. A geothermal spa located south of Reykjavík, its azure blue waters are said to have healing properties; people have been taking dips in this otherworldy pool since 1981. It is recommended to visit the Blue Lagoon on your travels between Reykjavík and Keflavik airport.

Hallgrímskirkja Hallgrímstorg 1; hallgrimskirkja.is. This iconic landmark is a parish church. At 74.5 metres tall, it is the largest church in Iceland and among the tallest structures in the country, reaching majestically up towards the heavens.

Harpa Concert Hall Austurbakki 2; harpa.is. A stunning building and world-class concert hall and conference centre housing concerts, operas, and other events. It is home to the Iceland Symphony Orchestra.

Iceland Airwaves icelandairwaves.is. This annual music festival held in early November is an immersive, multi-genre experience with a diverse lineup, featuring many LGBTQ+ artists and held across a multitude of venues in Reykjavík.

Perlan 105 Reykjavík; perlan.is. This is a Nature Exploratorium and one of Reykjavík's main landmarks, where you can learn all about Icelandic nature in fun and interactive ways. They also have a restaurant and cocktail bar in its futuristic revolving glass-dome.

Sun Voyager Sæbraut, 101 Reykjavík; sunvoyager. is. This wonderful sculpture by Jón Gunnar Árnason is located next to the Sæbraut road in Reykjavík. It is described to be a dreamboat, or an ode to the Sun. The artist intended it to convey the promise of undiscovered territory to onlookers; a dream of hope, progress and freedom.

The National Museum of Iceland Suðurgata 41; thjodminjasafn.is This museum showcases the rich history of Iceland from its early beginnings right through to modern times.

The Reykjavík Art Museum Fríkirkjuvegur 7; listasafnReykjavíkur.is. A museum displaying contemporary and modern Icelandic art. Reykjavík Art Museum is the largest visual art institution in Iceland and occupies three locations in Reykjavík; Hafnarhús by the old harbour, Kjarvalsstaðir by Klambratún and Ásmundarsafn in Laugardalur.

SITGES
Spring

Sitges is a famously liberal seaside town that, like many LGBTQ+ destinations, has its roots in residents who were fleeing oppression elsewhere; Sitges today is a monument to liberal freedoms which attracts everyone from the 2am clubbers to the 7am beachgoers, from the shoppers to the coffeeshop people-watchers to the wine-sippers. Although best known for its summer Pride celebrations, Sitges is also a perfect place to visit for a quieter trip during the spring to take advantage of the freshly opened venues and cooler temperatures.

Despite being just a short drive from Barcelona, Sitges is one of those places that people have either never heard of, or alternatively, when you mention it the stock response is likely to be; "Oh, the gay place in Spain?". Traditionally famous with the gay male community, Sitges has broadened its audience in line with the LGBTQ+ community's continuously growing visibility, and has become an inclusive, safe and welcoming space for all.

Although settlements can be traced back to the fourth century BC, it can be argued that Sitges came into its own during the eighteenth and nineteenth centuries. As lucrative trade routes opened up between Catalonia and the Americas, the traditionally fishing-focussed town saw wealth from both the inhabitants of neighbouring Barcelona and the town itself being invested into renovations and the building of summer houses.

With a common parallel found in the histories of other creative and LGBTQ+ locations, it didn't take long for the beauty and beaches of Sitges to attract those who would become famous cultural and artistic icons in the years to come. Artist Santiago Rusiñol arrived in Sitges in 1891, and with his residency the town soon became the centre of the Modernist movement. He was quickly followed by members of the Bohemian and LGBTQ+ community of Barcelona and beyond, including such famous names as dancer Nijinsky (who was also reportedly Rusiñol's lover), composer de Falla, playwright Lorca and painter Salvador Dali. This influx meant that Sitges soon became the Bohemian artists' retreat which it remains, in part, today.

"In the dark days of Franco's dictatorship, Sitges became an almost secret haven for gays who felt safe here, although they still had to behave discreetly." – Brian Butler, gay Sitges film director

During the Franco dictatorship in the mid-twentieth century amid rumours of the gay sons of the Barcelonian elite being sent to Sitges to avoid the embarrassment of their families (with their friends often tagging along for the advenure), Sitges became one of those beautifully rebellious communities that begin with exile, yet blossom into a creative, open and accepting home for those considered to be somewhat outside of 'the norm'.

Soon, increasing numbers of film shoots and relocating film stars sparked the initiation of the first Sitges Film Festival in 1968. Now one of the most prestigious film award ceremonies in Europe, the festival, which is dedicated to the fantasy genre, attracts thousands of visitors every October. During the festival, actors, directors and fans come together for five days of film screenings, parties, talks and celebrations.

Sitges's draw for those within the LGBTQ+ community remains strong to this day. After international star Antonio Amaya opened the first explicitly gay club in 1980, Sitges now boasts over 40 LGBTQ+-owned establishments, many to be found on along Carrer 1er de Maig, more commonly referred to by locals as the "Street of Sin".

ICON

In the 1970s and 1980s, Sitges was frequently visited by the Spanish LGBTQ icon and historical figure of the art and resistance movements, José Pérez Ocaña, better known as simply "Ocaña". Like many LGBTQ+ historical figures, the establishment has largely forgotten their work and activism; however, dig deeper and you will find that Ocaña represents a streak of rebellion within the creative world which helped bring LGBTQ+ rights to where they are today.

Forced to leave their rural village home in 1971 after refusing to hide their homosexuality, Ocaña found themselves at home in the more liberal and art-focused Barcelona. Although Barcelona may have been a slightly more accepting location than their birthplace, 35 years of LGBTQ+ persecution under Francisco Franco's military dictatorship had seen homosexuality made illegal, with those suspected sent to internment camps, jail or simply killed. Before

LISTINGS

STAY

Eurostars Sitges Cami del Miralpeix 12; eurostarssitges.com. As far as resorts go, this is a good one. Though sprawling, it still feels personal, with warmly decorated rooms and an intimate spa. Plus, the resort is equipped with several pools and a range of breezy restaurants, most specialising in Mediterranean cuisine, along with sleek bars and lounges.

Hotel Medium Romantic Carrer de Sant Isidore, 33; mediumhoteles.com. Centrally located and just 100m from the beach, *Hotel Medium Romantic* fulfils all of your needs for a great-value trip to Sitges. 60 well-kitted-out rooms and breakfast included will set you up well for your day at the beach or of sightseeing.

Hotel Subur Passeig de la Ribera; hotelsubur.com. One of the first hotels ever built in Sitges in the early 1900s, *Subur* has been a recognisable landmark of the town ever since. Facing the beach, its large sign and elegant building are unmissable. Stylishly decorated with its well-reviewed restaurant, *Hotel Subur* is a true Sitges institution.

MiM Av. Sofia, 12; mimhotels.com. If modern is more your style, *MiM* has you covered. One of the few modern purpose-built hotels, it boasts understated yet slick rooms and the highest bar in Sitges with incredible views, and all just a couple of minutes' walk from the beach.

Royal Rooms Carrer de Francesc Guma, 17; sitgesroyalrooms.com. Experience Sitges as it might have been at the very beginning of its life as a tourist destination in the early twentieth century. With nine rooms housed in a lovingly restored mansion built in the 1910s, *Royal Rooms* is the epitome of vintage luxury, complete with breakfast in the walled garden and a lavish collection of antiques. Fear not for your creature comforts; coffee machines and pleasantly furnished balconies round out the perfect stay.

The beaches and seafront promenade of Sitges

EAT

Alfresco C/Pau Barrabeitg 4; alfrescoestaurante. es. This welcoming restaurant serves superb Catalan cuisine with Asian touches, like Thai marinated lamb salad and grilled octopus with spinach.

Bar Tomeu Carrer Jesus, 8; bartomeusitges.com. Right in the hubbub of the main street, *Bar Tomeu* serves up traditional Catalan tapas and drinks. With an all-day kitchen, they will make sure you're well taken care of no matter what time you stumble off the beach (or out of bed). Try to grab an outside table to people-watch as you sample their delicious small plates.

El Cable C/Barcelona 1; elcable.cat. With its lively social scene, Sitges is a tapas town at its heart – and the long-running, amiable *El Cable* is one of the best tapas places you'll find. Feast on patatas bravas, ham croquettes and spicy sausage.

Café-Bar Roy C/les Parellades 9. An old-fashioned café with dressed-up waiters and marble tables. Watch the world go by from its prime streetside perch, over a glass of cava or a fancy snack.

Can Laury Av. del Port d'Aiguadolc, 49; canlaury. com. Find your way past the church and coves to the Aiguadolç marina and your best bet for fresh seafood is *Can Laury*. A favourite of visitors and locals alike, try their monkfish casserole or *fideuà* (a rice dish similar to paella) as you sit watching the boats come and go.

Chiringuito Passeig de la Ribera, 31; facebook.com/ chiringuitositges. Built in 1914, *Chiringuito* is Spain's first recorded beach café. Catering to a mix of sandy-footed sunbathers and those taking a coffee break from the shops, it serves a basic yet filling mix of traditional Catalan tapas, sandwiches, wine and coffee. Perfectly located for a quick break from your lounger, or for taking respite from the midday sun.

Make Me Cake Carrer d'Espalter, 41; makemecake.eu. The German-owned café *Make Me Cake* may be tucked away on a backstreet, but their ingenious creations make them well worth seeking out. Everything from seasonal bakes to traditional gateau are available, alongside great coffee and excellent gluten-free and vegan options.

Mare Nostrum Passeig de la Ribera 60; restaurantmarenostrum.com. Long-established fish restaurant on the seafront, with a menu that changes according to the catch and season. Expect to spend around €40 a head.

Maricel Passeig de la Ribera, 6; maricel.es. Sitges's only Michelin Star restaurant combines traditional Catalan flavours with modern presentation and excellent service. Expect complimentary gazpacho with more flavour than you thought was possible to pack into a shot glass, followed by perfectly cooked meat or seafood. One of the pricier options in town, *Maricel* is well worth it for a special occasion.

La Nansa C/Carreta 24; restaurantlanansa.com. A *nansa* (fishing net) hangs in this amiable, family-run restaurant, which has wood-panelled walls, brass lanterns and maritime paintings. The top-notch seafood- and fish-focused menu includes the regional favourite, *arroz a la Sitgetana* (rice with meat, prawns,

clams and a generous splash of Sitges Malvasia wine).

Olivier Carrer de les Parrelades 43; instagram.com/gelateriaolivier. You can find ice cream on most corners in Sitges, but *Olivier* has a certain something that will keep you coming back for more. A wide selection of handmade gelato alongside sorbets and fresh fruit ice lollies, you can choose from one to multiple scoops of ice cream – or even take away a few litres to enjoy in your apartment at leisure.

La Picara Carrer de Sant Pere, 3; lapicarasitges.cat. *La Picara* serves Catalan and Riojan specialities as well as a long list of freshly prepared seafood and other dishes, all with locally-sourced ingredients. With a relaxed and friendly atmosphere, they are open most days from midday for lunch, dinner and drinks.

La Salseta C/Sant Pau 35; lasalseta.com. Classic, unpretentious Catalan dishes (including cod with garlic confit, seafood paella and plenty of vegetarian options), cooked with slow-food attention and using locally sourced ingredients, keep this cosy little dining room filled with tourists and locals alike.

An aerial view of Sitges at sunrise

Dinner at *Bar Tomeu*

DRINK

Cocteleria Factor VI Carrer Bonaire, 25; instagram. com/factorvi. Slick and sexy, *Cocteleria*'s dark and chic interior matches their well-made classic cocktails and excellent wine list. Great for a drink, or if you're ready to eat try their chef's choice plates with wine pairings – you won't be disappointed!

Parrots Placa de la Industria, 2; parrots-sitges.com. A Sitges institution, *Parrots* is the centre of Sitges's LGBTQ+ street (or "Street of Sin", as it is affectionately known to locals). Two bars on opposite sides of the street with outside seating and umbrellas make for excellent people-watching as you sip cocktails from a full newspaper of options. With drinks to suit anyone's palate, including plenty of non-alcoholic options named after Hollywood starlets for extra camp, *Parrots* is buzzing at all times of the day. Grab a seat if you can find one and settle in during the early evening for "*el aperitivo*", obligatory sassy waiters and occasional street performers.

Sky Bar Av. Sofia 12; hotelmimsitges.com. Toast the night at this soaring bar that crowns *Hotel Mim Sitges*. The star here is the spectacular view, but the cocktails also hold their own, including potent mojitos, as well as sparkling cava. Hours vary and are weather-dependent, so if you're not sure, it's a good idea to call ahead.

Vivero Beach Club Av. Balmins s/n; elviverositges. com. With arguably the best views of any terrace in town, *Vivero* is a typical southern Spain beach club with a high-class atmosphere. Enjoy cocktails or champagne (they have some great non-alcoholic options too) on their sunbeds up top, or take the steps down into the clifftop below for a glass of wine overlooking the ocean. Book ahead for sunset for a really special experience.

Voramar C/Port Alegre 55; pub-voramar.com. Charismatic, old-school seafront bar, away from the main crowds, just right for an ice-cold beer or sundowner cocktail.

DANCE

New Ricky's C. de Sant Pau, 25; instagram.com/newrickys. A lively nightclub in central Sitges, popular with locals and visitors alike, *New Rickey's* often runs themed nights and is open until the early hours.

Parrots Placa de la Industria, 2; parrots-sitges.com. Our favourite gay bar also has a dancefloor; it's open late and blasts camp tunes almost every night.

Pachito Carrer Primer De Maig, 5; instagram.com/pachitosites. Created by the founder of the famous *Pacha* nightclub in Ibiza, *Pachito* brings a mixed crowd together for house and electric sets.

Queenz Cabaret Carrer d'Espalter, 2-4; queenzdinnershow.com. Sitges's most famous dinner cabaret brings together the best of southern Spain's drag performers and singers. Not to be missed.

Zak Rendezvous C. de Sant Pau; zakrendezvous.com. Bringing together dinner and live music, *Zak* offers a four-hour extravaganza of curated food and performances.

SHOP

Ametller Origen Avinguda d'Artur Carbonell, 24; ametllerorigen.com. Spain's answer to *Whole Foods* is worth a visit for a restorative smoothie after a night of dancing and cocktails, or to sample some of the local produce for a picnic on the beach.

Cincos Elementos Carrer Jesus, 25; cincoselementosbcn.com. Representing the eclectic nature of Sitges, this tucked-away shop sells clothing from unique Spanish designers, unusual jewellery and one-of-a-kind homewares.

Eleven Carrer de les Parrelades, 12; elevenmensjewlry.com. An all-men's jewellery store with some unique pieces, great for gifts to take home or a few holiday treats for yourself.

Prowler Carrer d'Espalter, 37; prowlersitges.com. London and Barcelona's famous gay store has its own Sitges branch (but of course!). Here you'll find clubwear, kitschy gifts and a saucier section too if that should take your fancy.

A room at *Eurostars Sitges*

Nicolas Cage makes a speech during Sitges Film Festival

DO

Beaches Sitges's beaches are its most recognised attraction for good reason. Golden sand and invariably clear and shallow waters make them worth at least a few days of your trip. With several to choose from, your options range from the central family-friendly Platja Del Sitges with pay-to-play loungers and umbrellas available during the high season to the optionally nudist beach Platja del Balmins closer to the marina. In the busy summer months, head south from the town to reach quieter stretches.

Rainbow Sitges Tour Enjoy the history of Sitges with an LGBTQ slant. Walk in the footsteps of its previous inhabitants, ending with a glass of Cava at the LGBT centre. Visit the Colours website for timings (colorssitgeslink.org/en).

Take in some culture at the Sitges museums Sitges has no fewer than five museums. Perhaps the most well-known is the Cau Ferrat museum, founded by Santiago Rusiñol and set in their workshop. Today it houses much of Rusiñol's work and collections of other artists from around the world. If architecture is more your thing, Palau de Maricel will wow you with every room.

Take a day trip to Barcelona It's so easy to get into Barcelona from Sitges that it would be a shame to miss it during your trip, especially if you happen to have a rainy day when the beaches are a no-go. Pick up the bus by the Escultura Sitges de Subirachs or the train from the main station in Sitges, both of which will land you in central Barcelona for a day of Gaudi sightseeing or shopping. Though it boasts outstanding Gothic and Art Nouveau buildings, and some great museums – most notably those dedicated to Picasso, Miró and Catalan art – Barcelona's main appeal lies in getting lost in the narrow side streets of the Barri Gòtic (Gothic Quarter), eating and drinking late, lazing in the parks, and generally soaking up the atmosphere before heading back to the tranquility of the ocean.

BRIGHTON

Summer

Established as one of the queerest and most diverse cities in the world, Brighton is special in so many ways – from attracting hundreds of thousands of people to its annual Pride weekend to frequent independent events run by young LGBTQ+ people. Pop culture that celebrates queer stories – including the TV show *Sugar Rush* (2005) and more recently the film *My Policeman* (2022), both set in Brighton – allow residents and visitors to feel a part of a proud LGBTQ+ community. The remarkable Trans Pride march, which began in 2013 and now takes place every July, is a reminder that Pride was originally a protest, and that the LGBTQ+ community and its allies still have rights to fight for.

HISTORY

Brighton has been a magnet for day-tripping Londoners since the Prince Regent (later George IV) started holidaying here in the 1770s with his mistress, thereby launching a trend for the "dirty weekend". Since then, the city has emerged from seediness to embrace a new, fashionable hedonism, gaining a reputation as one of the country's queer-friendly places.

For centuries, Brighton has been known as a safe haven for outcasts and rebels, and non-conformists, including many well-known LGBTQ+ figures; famous names such as Oscar Wilde and Anne Lister were known to have escaped to this liberating city in order to spend time with secret lovers.

Notorious landowner and diarist, Anne Lister – also known as "Gentleman Jack" – visited Brighton with her lover Mariana Lawton for three days in 1826. Whilst staying in the Royal York Hotel, Lister wrote coded entries in her diary that covered the events of their visit. Likewise, famous wit and playwright Oscar Wilde visited the south coast with his lover Lord Alfred Douglas where they stayed in the *Metropole Hotel*, now known as the *Hilton*. During his stay in 1884,

Wilde visited the Royal Pavilion to present two popular lectures on art and life.

Throughout the 1900s a number of meeting places for working class gay men opened and closed, especially in Kemptown, which is where the majority of queer spaces are still found today. Another popular place for queer people to meet and find community was bookshops, such as *The Unicorn Bookshop* which was open from 1966-1973 and owned by openly gay writer, Bill Butler. In 1975 The Lavender Line – an LGBTQ+ helpline now known as Switchboard – opened with just one phone in order to offer support queer people in crisis.

In 1988, the introduction of Section 28 – a series of laws that prohibited the so-called "promotion" of homosexuality – outraged LGBTQ+ activists, with regular marches starting between Brighton and Hove town halls. Moreover, in 2013 Trans Pride was founded by Fox Fisher and Sarah Savage and was the first Trans Pride event in Europe; it remains the largest in the UK. This event is both a political march and a colourful celebration of trans empowerment that aims to uplift trans voices and bodies.

ICON

Virginia Woolf is widely accepted as one of the most influential writers of the modern age, and has many connections to Brighton and its surrounding areas. Her popular works of fiction have had a large impact on queer literature, in particular *Orlando*, a book that could be seen as the most romantic love letter in history. The novel is about the eponymous gender-non-conforming poet and was inspired by Woolf's lover, Vita Sackville-West; the majority of the book was written in Brighton, where Woolf and Sackville-West would meet in the *Marlborough Hotel* throughout the 1920s. After one visit to Brighton, Woolf wrote that it was "the most beautiful town in the world", conveying the joyous freedom she felt whilst there. Indeed, the women continued to inspire one another's creative work throughout both their lifetimes.

Woolf and Sackville-West's romantic and sexual

relationship was documented through their published diaries; Sackville-West would mark an X on the days when they made love. The passionate language used in their love letters to one another gives an insight into the strong feelings that remained between them until their romantic relationship developed back into a friendship towards the end of Woolf's life.

After a series of ongoing mental health issues that had plagued Woolf intermittently throughout her life, Woolf took her on 28th March 1941 at the age of 59 when she waded into the River Ouse and drowned. She was cremated in Brighton. Just South of Lewes you can visit Monks House – now owned by The National Trust – to learn more about Woolf and her family's lives, and both her dark works of fiction and analytical essays continue to be celebrated as literary successes today.

HIGHLIGHTS

Although Brighton is the queer capital of the UK, in recent years there has been a lack of diverse nightlife, causing many Brighton residents to take it upon themselves to create and host their own radical, dynamic events. Two that have managed to encapsulate their own version of queer euphoria are Gal Pals (instagram. com/galpalsclub) and Polyglamorous (instagram.com/ polyglamorousbrighton).

Run by duo Xan and Scarlet, Gal Pals is a queer club night that was brought to Brighton in 2017 after a one-off event at *Dalston Superstore* in London in 2015. Gal Pals is a self-described queer dance party that centres queer women as well as trans and non-binary people. It aims to create a safe space for these groups, meaning ally tickets are available for those attending in support of friends and the space. Gal Pals has a bi-monthly residency at *Komedia* in the heart of Brighton's North Laines, meaning that the events are wheelchair accessible and have gender neutral toilets. On entering this iconic queer club night, expect vivid colours and a real pop party atmosphere, with music exclusively by women, non-binary and trans artists. Whether you want to dance the night away or hang out in the quieter room, Gal Pals will allow you to feel safe and free to do as you please.

Polyglamorous was founded by a group of eight imaginative queers who felt the lack of inclusive nights in Brighton; together they created a monthly party that highlights some of Brighton's best creatives through a combination nightlife, art, fashion, music and dance. Each of their nights has a different colour theme, which you'll find reflected in the decor, lighting and dress code suggestions (although you are free to interpret the theme as liberally or as literally as you see fit). Both local talents and guest acts are invited to attend and perform every month, creating a truly diverse stage presence; you never quite know what you're going to see! Will it be a visual artist, a drag act, or perhaps a pole dancer? Having a space to dress extravagantly and experience these artists' work on stage, all to the backing tracks of the latest pop, disco, house or techno bangers, has proved a vital and joyful addition to Brighton's nightlife scene.

BRIGHTON PIER

THIS WAY TO THE
END OF THE PIER

THE PALACE OF FUN

THIS WAY TO THE
END OF THE PIER

WHERE TICKETS MAKE PRIZES

COME AND TRY OUR
REDEMPTION
MACHINES

BRIGHTON PIER

JEWELLERY GIFTS SHELLS

LISTINGS

STAY

Amsterdam Hotel 1–12 Marine Parade, Kemptown; amsterdamhotelbrighton.com. In the heart of Kemptown and a few minutes' walk from the pier, *Amsterdam Hotel* offers camp entertainment, from drag shows to karaoke and quiz nights.

Artist Residence 33 Regency Square; artistresidencebrighton.co.uk. One of the most original of Brighton's many boutique hotels, this is a Regency townhouse that's been given a quirky modern makeover. It's furnished with upcycled objects such as old crates, junkshop mirrors and vintage beds; tables, shelves and even shower doors are made from recycled timber.

Drakes 43–4 Marine Parade; drakesofbrighton.com. Perfect for a romantic seaside stay, this is an elegant double-fronted townhouse hotel, right on the Kemptown seafront. The styling is smart and contemporary, and the best rooms have high ceilings and huge windows with fabulous sea views.

Grand 97–9 King's Road; grandbrighton.co.uk. Behind the wedding-cake facade of Brighton's landmark hotel is an imposing lobby with a majestic staircase. The rooms, which are luxurious, have tastefully decorated in relaxing shades of soft pink, beige and turquoise.

Happy Brighton 23 Broad St; happybrighton.com. Run by friendly, young, multi-lingual hosts, this great hostel is near the sea and the main attractions – you can choose between regular bunks or sleeping pods in a shared room. There's a common room too, which is a great place to meet people and make friends.

Legends 1–34 Marine Parade, Kemptown; legendsresortbrighton.com. Situated on the seafront, Brighton's most popular LGBTQ+ hotel offers a selection of simple but sparklingly clean rooms. Connected is *Legends Bar and Basement Club*.

Dancing and laughter at Brighton Pride

Grand Brighton Hotel

EAT

64 Degrees 53 Meeting House Lane; 64degrees.co.uk. This strikingly modern eatery has become a favourite among Brighton foodies. Named after the perfect temperature at which to cook an egg, its chefs prepare inventive dishes with scientific precision in the open kitchen. Portions are small; you order a selection to nibble and share.

Arcobaleno 120 St George's Rd, Kemptown; myarcobaleno.com. This café, bar and event space offers delicious Sunday roasts as well as a colourful cocktail menu that caters to everyone. It's also the home of the official Polyglamorous pre-drinks.

The Basketmakers Arms 12 Gloucester Road; basketmakers-brighton.co.uk. Attracting a mix of students, visitors and locals who have been drinking here for decades, this North Laine pub serves some of the best kept real ale in the city. There's a no-nonsense menu of organic fare and a refreshingly traditional atmosphere.

The Breakfast Club 16–17 Market Street; thebreakfastclubcafes.com. Style-conscious Brighton folk have lapped up The Breakfast Club's first foray out of London. Its trademarks are a quirky 70s theme and a huge selection of breakfast specials, many available all day, "because it's always breakfast time somewhere in the world."

The Chilli Pickle 17 Jubilee Street; thechillipickle. com. So popular that it moved from its original home in The Lanes to this bustling spot, *The Chilli Pickle* is an award-winning independent restaurant which offers flavoursome cuisine inspired by Indian street food. As you'd expect, the menu includes some great vegetarian dishes. The owners often jet off to India for fresh inspiration.

The Coal Shed 8 Boyce's Street; coalshed-restaurant. co.uk. Famous for its succulent steak – sold by the cut and the weight, and char-grilled at high temperatures for perfect results – this highly acclaimed little bistro also serves oysters and beautifully presented sharing plates and desserts. There's a great value weekday lunch and pre-theatre menu. If you're vegetarian, check in advance that there's something to suit.

Curry Leaf Café 60 Ship Street; curryleafcafe.com. Run by an Indian chef who used to work at The Chilli Pickle, this little backstreet eatery offers a fresh interpretation of Indian street food, with simpler surroundings and lower prices. Every dish bursts with colourful ingredients and around half the menu is vegetarian.

Food for Friends 17–18 Prince Albert Street; foodforfriends.com. In the heart of the Lanes, this vegetarian eatery has had a few makeovers since it opened in 1981, but it never falls out of favour. These days it's a sophisticated modern restaurant creating light, imaginative dishes inspired by the flavours of the Middle East, North Africa and the Mediterranean. Organic breakfast and brunch served from 9am.

Iydea 17 Kensington Gardens; iydea.co.uk. Awarding-winning no-frills vegetarian restaurant Iydea has a strong ethos when it comes to organic ingredients and environmental packaging. Choose your main course and then add your sides, toppings and sauces. The daily changing menu may include aubergine and goat's cheese stacks or mushroom stroganoff; sides the likes of beetroot, chilli and ginger slaw or sesame roasted vegetables.

Kenny's Rock & Soul Café 1A Kensington Gardens; facebook.com/kennysrockandsoul. With fabulous décor and music, Kenny's offers a diverse menu with plenty of vegan variations. The diner style café features a balcony that looks over Kensington gardens.

Real Patisserie 34 St George's Road; realpatisserie. co.uk. Like a little corner of France transported to Kemptown, this bakery sells delectable fruit tarts, slices of quiche, hot stuffed croissants and sandwiches made from freshly baked bread. They also do takeaway coffee. You could take your hoard down to the beach or just sit at the farmhouse table and scoff the lot.

Redroaster Coffee House 1D St James's Street; redroaster.co.uk. Brighton may be flooded with excellent coffee shops but this long-standing favourite

An aerial view
of Brighton Pier

Seaview bedrooms at *Drakes Hotel*

never goes out of style. Bohemian but not scruffy, it's a spacious and appealing place to relax over a cup of the house roast with a big slice of gateau.

DRINK

The Actors 4 Prince's St, Kemptown; actors.pub. Perfect for cosy date nights, book clubs and coffee date catch ups with old friends. Its warming atmosphere invites welcomes you in to both the pub itself and its upstairs theatre that features live comedy, cabaret and more.

Bar Broadway 10 Steine St, Kemptown; barbroadway. com. Brighton's live cabaret hotspot allows you to let go and sing karaoke all weekend, with drag hosts who will show you how it's done.

The Cricketers 15 Black Lion St; cricketersbrighton. co.uk. This historic pub – Brighton's oldest – was immortalised by Graham Greene in his classic novel *Brighton Rock*, and its cosy, rich-red interior with plenty of hidden nooks has changed little since.

Great Eastern 103 Trafalgar St; facebook.com/ greateasternbrighton. A tiny, 150-year-old traditional pub, serving over 60 American whiskeys and a great selection of real ales. Live music on Thurs and DJs every other Friday or Saturday, as well as traditional roast lunches on Sundays.

The Hope & Ruin 11–12 Queens Rd; hope.pub. This is the perfect place to try Beelzebab's vegan hotdogs. The venue also offers quizzes, small art exhibitions and entertaining DJ sets, as well as a gig venue upstairs. Plus, it's dog-frendly!

Plateau 1 Bartholomews; plateaubrighton.co.uk. Plateau is a relaxed yet buzzy wine bar that values sustainability. It has an unusual list of organic wines made by independent producers, as well as delicious cocktails and sharing plates with a European feel to them; ingredients are sourced from local farms and dishes change seasonally.

The Prince Albert 48 Trafalgar St; princealbertbrighton. co.uk. Stop for a drink, and check out the gigs in its upstairs space every week. The outside wall features Banksy's famous mural, *Kissing Coppers*.

R Bar 5–7 Marine Parade, Kemptown; revenge.co.uk/r-bar. A queer hotspot, *R Bar* features nightly events, including its own "lip-sync for your life" competition, the big queer quiz, and drag bingo.

DANCE

Brighton Coalition 171–181 Kings Rd Arches; drinkinbrighton.co.uk/coalition. Right on the seafront, this club puts on a range of events, from club nights to karaoke. Thursdays hosts District, a night dedicated to alternative rock and indie, with cheap drinks and popular with students.

Concorde 2 286A Madeira Dr; concorde2.co.uk. This grungy music venue has hosted some of the greats, from Jarvis Cocker to local lad, Fatboy Slim.

Green Door Store 2–4 Trafalgar Arches; thegreendoorstore.co.uk. Known for its weekly 80s night, this is the place to listen to your favourite queer anthems whilst dressed up to the nines.

Komedia 44 Gardner St; komedia.co.uk. Achingly cool venue offering everything from cabaret and comedy to rock gigs, club nights and spoken word, and is home of women-centred queer club night Gal Pals. Club nights happen on Fridays and Saturdays from 11pm.

Patterns 10 Marina Parade; patternsbrighton.com. Wildly popular on the club scene, *Pattens* is simply brimming with original ideas and cool cocktails.

Revenge 32–34 Old Steine, Kemptown; revenge.co.uk. Renowned as the South Coast's #1 LGBTQ+ party destination – featuring themed VIP booths, three floors of chaos, and electrifying drag performances – *Revenge* is all about bright lights, big beats and outrageous dressing up.

SHOP

Feminist Bookstore 48 Upper N St; thefeministbookshop.com. This independent bookshop and plant-based café has a radical selection of books, whilst also acting as a community space that hosts book clubs and author signings.

The Queery 46 George St, Kemptown; thequeery.co.uk. A co-op owned and run by its members, this

Pop up sauna on the beach made from a horse box

space features an accessible library, vegan café and bookstore. Its friendly atmosphere welcomes the LGBTQ+ community to its workshops, classes, open mics and other events.

DO

Brighton Fringe Multiple locations; brightonfringe. org. England's largest arts festival takes place across the city annually. With stimulating and entertaining events to suit everyone's taste, it brings together an inspiring collection of creative work, such as the lesbian comedy show, The LOL Word.

Brighton Museum and Art Gallery Royal Pavilion Gardens; brightonmuseums.org.uk. In an ornate building that once housed royal servants, the Brighton Museum and Art Gallery is devoted to fashion, style, furniture, design and performing arts. It also has an illuminating section exploring local history and popular culture through old photos, artefacts and oral accounts; together with two galleries dedicated to ancient Egypt. Resident exhibition *Queer the Pier* highlights and celebrates local LGBTQ+ history.

Brighton Pier The wonderfully tacky half-mile-long pier is an obligatory call; it's a huge amusement arcade, peppered with booths selling fish and chips, candyfloss and the famous Brighton rock; the Brighton Wheel provides sky-high views of the pier from above.

Brighton Pride Preston Rd; brighton-pride.org. Brighton's main queer event takes place annually in August, whilst the sun is glistening on the sea and the queers have taken over town. Its iconic parade ends up in Preston Park, leaving to you dance to pop music all night long.

Ironworks Studio 30 Cheapside; ironworks-studios. co.uk. Emphasising camp cabaret and diverse drag, Ironworks Studios' conference space, dance floor and comedy club work with Brighton Pride to run a variety of events throughout the year. Their diverse timetable is definitely worth checking out!

Piers & Queers Walking Tour Multiple locations; onlyinbrighton.co.uk/piers-queers. This highly reviewed 90-minute tour takes in over 200 years of queer history, featuring some unsung heroes as you walk along the seafront and city centre.

MADRID

Summer

Culturally rich, astonishingly ancient, and of course, unbelievably cool: the city of Madrid has it all and then some. Lively and vibrant, the Spanish capital is an ideal destination for a city break. Whether you're hankering after world-class Michelin-starred cuisine and splendid art galleries or are more partial to street art tours and innovative tapas, there's unequivocally a Madrid for you. There's so much to experience in the Spanish capital that you might not ever want to leave!

Madrid City Hall and Cibeles Fountain celebrating World Pride Week

HISTORY

Madrid's history dates back to the ninth century when it was established as a Muslim defensive outpost on the escarpment above the River Manzanares which later became known as "Mayrit" – the place of many springs. It remained a relatively insignificant backwater until 1561 when Felipe II designated the city his imperial capital by virtue of its position at the heart of the recently unified Spain. The cramped street plan in the city centre provides a clue as to what the city would have been like at this time and the narrow alleys around the Plaza Mayor are still among Madrid's liveliest and most atmospheric. With the Bourbons replacing the Habsburgs at the start of the eighteenth century, a touch of French style, including the sumptuous Palacio Real, was introduced into the capital by Felipe V. It was the "King-Mayor" Carlos III, however, who tried to convert the city into a home worthy of the monarchy after he ascended to

the throne in 1759, ordering the streets to be cleaned, sewers and lighting to be installed and work to begin on the Prado museum complex.

The Spanish capital is one of the most welcoming, safe and accepting cities in Europe. It's always held tolerance and acceptance in high regard and has a strong recent history of LGBTQ+ rights. However, this was not always the case.

The early nineteenth century brought invasion and turmoil to Spain as Napoleon established his brother Joseph (or José to Spaniards) on the throne. Madrid, however, continued to flourish, gaining some very attractive buildings and squares, including the Plaza de Oriente and Plaza de Santa Ana. With the onset of the twentieth century, the capital became the hotbed of the political and intellectual discussions that divided the country; *tertulias* (political/philosophical discussion circles) sprang up in cafés across the city (some of them are still going) as the country entered the turbulent years of the end of the monarchy and the foundation of the Second Republic.

Madrid was a Republican stronghold during the Civil War, with fierce battles raging around the capital as General Francisco Franco's troops laid siege to the city, eventually taking control in 1939. The Civil War, of course, caused untold damage, and led to forty years of isolation. Homosexuality was illegal under Franco's rule; in fact, thousands of members of the LGTBQ+ community were shipped off in disgrace to 'rehabilitation centres' or were sent to prison where many were tortured. The "Social Danger Laws", approved on 4 August 1970, included a list of punishments against gay and transgender people including confinement to asylums and banishment from their hometowns.

The Spanish capital has changed immeasurably, however, in the four decades since Franco's death, initially guided by a poet-mayor, the late Tierno Galván. Thankfully, homosexuality was decriminalised three years after Franco's death in 1978, and subsequently Spain has become one of the most queer-tolerant countries in the world, authorising gay marriage and allowing adoptions by gay couples in 2005.

Galván's efforts – the creation of parks and renovation of public spaces and public life – left an enduring legacy, and were a vital ingredient of the *La Movida Madrileña*, "the happening Madrid" with which the city broke through in the 1980s. It was during this decade that an area called Chueca in central Madrid became known as the ultimate queer neighbourhood. One of the landmark achievements of the queer community in Madrid is how they have transformed Chueca into one of the most liberal and welcoming areas of the city, where LGBTQ+ people and allies could enjoy a true atmosphere of tolerance, freedom, and diversity which would have been unimaginable just a short period prior. The people of the Chueca neighbourhood set a fantastic standard for other cities throughout the world who still look to the city of Madrid for influence.

Aerial view of Plaza Mayor

Madrid has been the location for many iconic films and TV shows, so to talk about Madrid is to talk about film director Pedro Almodóvar. Almodóvar is celebrated as a director with an illustrious history of showcasing multi-dimensional LGBTQ+ characters in his work; not only are his films extraordinarily compelling, they are also progressive and groundbreaking. His work is often marked by elements of dark humour and melodrama interwoven into their their complicated stories, as well as a glossy, bold aesthetic that includes lots of colour.

Almodóvar has never shied away from representations of queerness on the big screen; it has been a staple in his filmography right from the beginning of his career in the 1980s. He endeavoured to show queer people in a positive light through his work, which has helped to create significant legal changes in Madrid and beyond, including the passing of marriage equality laws. From his first film *Pepi, Luci, Bom* (1980), a black comedy about the wild adventures of three friends including an aspiring lesbian punk rock star to *Volver* (2006), a tender film noir about three generations of women, Almodóvar's filmography is always thought-provoking, relevant and inspiring, and makes for an impressive body of work.

Many of his films were set in or filmed on location in the city of Madrid; for example, you can pay a visit to the world-famous cinema *Cine Dore*, featured in his 2002 Oscar-winning film *Hable con Ella* (*Talk to Her*), which is used for Filmoteca Española screenings – one of the most important institutions in Spain for conserving the heritage of filmmaking. You could also wander around one of the city's oldest squares, the Plaza de la Vill, which was a filming location for Almodóvar's *Tie Me Up! Tie Me Down!* (1989), a highly successful dark romantic comedy in which Antonio Banderas stars as a recently released psychiatric patient who kidnaps an actress (Victoria Abril) in order to make her fall in love with him. Dig a little deeper into the rest of his work and you'll find them littered with bars, streets, buildings, and other Madrid landmarks.

Almodóvar is also an activist; he was heavily involved in the Madrid-based cultural renaissance and creative movement called *La Movida Madrileña*, which was one of the most important cultural moments for Spanish artists, film makers, and writers of the last century. The movement helped empower such creators to take advantage of their newfound freedom to feel free and confident and not have to hide their sexuality in the wake of Franco's death.

Almodóvar still lives in the Spanish capital and considers Madrid to be one of the liveliest and most creative cities in Europe.

The Torre de Madrid Building

HIGHLIGHTS

Madrid's annual Pride festival truly is something to behold; a week-long party that culminates in a massive carnival-style parade that brings the city centre to a standstill. Although the majority of activities and events are held in the renowned Chueca neighbourhood, Pride events can be enjoyed across the entire city. Naturally, the most popular and exciting day is the day of the Pride Parade itself; if you are lucky enough to be able to attend, you're guaranteed a fabulous atmosphere as protestors and parade-goers take to the street to celebrate and embrace the values of diversity and acceptance.

Every year on the first Saturday of July, thousands of people gather in Madrid to march from Paseo del Prado, one of the main boulevards in the city, to Colón to demand equal rights for the LGBTIQIA+ community. The official opening ceremony takes place at the Plaza de Pedro Zerolo, with a public LGBTQ+ figure or ally delivering a rousing speech. Throughout the day there are various concerts, performances and live events taking place, including the ever-camp Mr Gay Pride España contest (the final of which is held on the stage in Plaza de España) and wildy popular High-Heels Race. This event is a true spectacle, with glamourous yet hardy competitors taking to the streets in the most epic high heeled shoes to race along Madrid's cobbled streets for enviable prizes – not least of which is the glory of being the winner. Be warned – heels must be at least 15cm high to enter. Ouch! Not surprisingly, this is one of the most eagerly awaited parts of the festival.

Whilst heels are always welcome and admired, non-competitors may wish to opt for more comfortable (if slightly less glam) footwear; you'll be wearing them for a while, as the parade tends to start in the early evening (around 6pm) and goes on until after midnight. It's also a good idea to wear something cool, because even the evenings in Madrid in summer can be very warm. The many drag queens in attendance of course tend to prefer to eschew practicality for sartorial flamboyance; these stunning fashionista queens are instantly recognisable thanks to their long, luscious locks, their impeccable make up and of course, their jealousy-inducing mile-long eye lashes!

Traditional Spanish tapas of green olives, cured ham, and bread with a cocktail

LISTINGS

STAY

Barceló Torre de Madrid Pl. de España, 18; barcelo.com/es-es/barcelo-torre-de-madrid. One of the most LGBTQ-friendly hotels in Madrid, the Barceló is situated in the Tower of Madrid and the interiors, designed by *madrileño* Jaime Hayón, are as striking as the architecture itself. If you love bold colourful hues, quirky sculptures and fancy yourself something of a fashionista, then this is the hotel for you. The best rooms feature far-reaching views of the Gran Vía.

Bless Hotel Madrid C. de Velázquez, 62; blesscollectionhotels.com/es/madrid/bless-hotel-madrid. Experience unrivalled decadence at the five-star Bless Madrid which is situated in the vibrant Salamanca district. The hotel is a short skip and a hop to the city's designer shops and impressive restaurants. This is a design lover's dream, with fantastic pieces of mid-century artwork adorning the walls. Some of the rooms have large balconies that overlook the bustling Calle Velázquez.

Petit Palace Chueca C/ de Hortaleza, 3; petitpalacechueca.com. Upgraded from an old *hostal* several years back, this grand building is now one of the self-styled Petit Palace chain. Its 58 low-key but sleek rooms come complete mini bars and iPads.

Room Mate Óscar Pl. de Pedro Zerolo, 12; room-matehotels.com/en/oscar. The *Room Mate Óscar* is lots of fun and is pretty easy on your purse without compromising on style. There's a rooftop pool, the rooms are airy, bright and modern and it's ideally located on the Gran Vía in the gay-friendly neighbourhood of Chueca.

Only You Boutique Hotel Madrid C. del Barquillo, 21; room-matehotels.com/en/oscar. This beautiful boutique hotel fuses effortless interior design, lots of charm and a great location that nestles between the Chueca and Salesas neighbourhoods. If you're planning to have a late one (and why wouldn't you when in Madrid?!) then one of the main draws of *Only You* is that you can choose to check out later than the standard midday, plus – the best meal of the day, breakfast, is available to order at any time.

EAT

Artemisa C/Ventura de la Vega 4; crestaurantesvegetarianosartemisa.com. There are two branches of this long-standing popular vegetarian restaurant (so popular that you may have to wait for a table), which is good for veggie pizzas and wok dishes and has an imaginative range of salads and soups too. It's reasonably priced, too.

Café Comercial Glorieta de Bilbao 7; cafecomercialmadrid.com. Reopened and spruced up after threatened closure several years back (though they've kept the marble tables), the *Comercial* has retained much of its appeal as a traditional *madrileño* meeting point. Best for breakfasts and afternoon coffee and cakes, though it now also has a very good restaurant too.

La Carmencita C/Libertad 16; tabernalacarmencita. es. A traditional taberna with roots dating back to 1854 and which remains faithful to its origins by serving up classic dishes with carefully sourced ingredients including moutherwatering stews and stuffed peppers.

DiverXO NH Eurobuilding, C. del Padre Damián, 23; diverxo.com/en/home. *DiverXO* is a real gastronomic adventure. Chef David Muñoz uses intense flavours and an avant-garde culinary style in his three-Michelin-star restaurant, located inside the *Eurobuilding* hotel. Expect innovative and surprising dishes that are extraordinary edible works of art.

Dos Cielos Madrid Cuesta Santo Domingo 5. Run under the auspices of Michelin-starred brothers Sergio and Javier Torres and head chef Damián González, Dos Cielos is housed in the elegant surroundings of the Gran Meliá Palacio de los Duques. They offer a taster menu with a selection of delicious bite-size samples of fish, meat and vegetable dishes, and prices are more accessible than many of the other top restaurants; but you can still expect to walk away with your purse noticeably lighter than when you went in!

Los Gatos C. de Jesús, 2; cervecerialosgatos.com. What's new pussycat?! If you live in Madrid and have garnered a reputation for staying out all night, you might well be classed as one of *"los gatos"* ("the

cats"). If that sounds like you, a visit to *Los Gatos* is the best way to begin a night of dancing while lining your stomach in the most delicious way; it positively teems with energy! Try the restaurant's most-loved dish, the alioli shrimps with roquefort and smoked salmon.

Mama Campo Pza. Olavide; instagram.com/mama_campo. You'll find organic food for vegetarians and non-vegetarians alike in this cool and airy restaurant/bar perched on the edge of a popular tree-lined plaza. There are two spaces, one for meals, the other (*La Cantina*) for tapas and snacks. There's always something interesting on offer in the seasonal menu.

Restaurante Cañadio Madrid C. del Conde de Peñalver, 86; restaurantecanadio.com. From fried-squid *rabas* (a quintessential tapas dish) to hake fritters in tempura with alioli, this lively tapas bar is the place to go for an up-beat atmosphere.

Sala de Despiece C. de Ponzano, 11; saladedespiece.com. For anyone looking for creative tapas in the heart of Madrid, *Sala de Despiece* might be small – but boy does it pack a stylistic punch! Think meat hooks,

butcher containers and other quirky touches, and expect flamboyant table-side pyrotechnics (!) and a lively ambience with your dinner.

Vegaviana C/Pelayo 35; instagram.com/restaurantevegaviana. There's a wide range of vegetarian options with an international twist at this small eatery in the heart of Chueca, plus a free-range chicken option for non-veggies, too. Very good value, with big portions, meaning you'll struggle to break the €20 mark.

Yerbabuena C/Bordadores 3; yerbabuena.ws. A cut above most of its competitors, this friendly vegetarian has an extensive and well-presented range of dishes. Spinach crêpes, aubergine burgers, fennel soup and mushroom pie are among the mains.

Zara C/Barbieri 8; restaurantezara.com. There's excellent food at very good prices at this Cuban restaurant; here you'll find *ropa vieja* (strips of beef), fried yucca, minced beef with fried bananas and other specialities. The daiquiris are very good too, and prices are moderate – the perfect combnation.

Madrid Pride Parade

DRINK

La Ardosa C/Colón 13; laardosa.es. One of the city's classic *tabernas*, offering limited but very tasty tapas including great *croquetas*, *salmorejo* (cold tomato soup) and an excellent home-made *tortilla*. Prides itself on its draught beer and Guinness and serves a great pre-lunch *vermút* (vermouth) too.

Casa Camacho C/San Andrés 2 (just off Pza. Dos de Mayo). An irresistible old neighbourhood bodega, with a traditional bar counter, *vermút* (vermouth) on tap and basic tapas. An ideal place to start the evening. Packed out at weekends.

Delic Pza. de la Paja 8; Wdelic.es. Serving home-made cakes, fruit juices and coffee, this is a pleasant café by day, transforming into a crowded and quirky but friendly cocktail bar by night, with tables spilling out onto the leafy plaza.

Fábrica Maravillas C/Valverde 29; fmaravillas. com. Opened over a decade ago in this rejuvenated street running perpendicular to Gran Vía, Fábrica has helped promote the trend for craft beers in Madrid. A tasty selection of ales on offer, including the fruity Malasaña, stout and an excellent IPA.

La Tape C/San Bernardo 88; latape.com. Seven craft beers on tap, most of which are changed on a regular basis. They also have a great selection of bottled beers and some excellent food too. Downstairs is the bar and takeaway section, upstairs the restaurant.

Oldenburg C/Hartzenbusch 12; instagram.com/ cerveceriaoldenburg. This bar has been around for almost 30 years and was one of the first to break the stranglehold of the mass-produced local brews like Mahou. Has featured in the *Guinness Book of Records* for having the highest concentration of different beers per metre squared of any bar in the world.

Vía Lactea C/Velarde 18. Call in here to see where the *movida* began. *Vía Lactea* was a key meeting place for Spain's designers, directors, pop stars and painters in the 1980s, and it retains its original decor from the time, billiard tables included. There's a stage

Statue of Enrique Tierno Galván

downstairs. It attracts a young, studenty clientele and is packed at weekends.

DANCE

Club 33 C/Cabeza 33; club33madrid.es. Formerly women-only, now a mixed club in Lavapiés with a friendly, laidback vibe.

Delirio Dance Club C/Pelayo 59; deliriochueca.com. Fun and friendly atmosphere with drag queens, shows and lightweight singalong pop sounds from Britney Spears to Madonna.

Escape C. de Gravina, 13; facebook.com/escape. chueca. *Escape* is a lesbian nightclub in the Chueca neighbourhood that's open until 6am, and whilst it is predominantly geared towards women in their twenties and thirties, everyone is welcome!

Gris C. de San Marcos, 29; facebook.com/gris.bar.7. One of Madrid's favourite gay bars, *Gris* is a strong alternative to the flamboyant bars playing pop music. It has a fantastic indie vibe, but you can also enjoy the likes of house and electronica here too, plus there's

also some amazing live music on Saturday nights.

La Kama C. de Gravina, 4; grupolakama.com/la-kama-bar. Get your groove on at *La Kama*, with great energy, fabulous vibes and loud music! There's no dedicated dance floor – you can expect people to be dancing and singing along throughout the whole place.

LL Bar C. de Pelayo, 11; llshowbar.com. *LL Bar* is *the* place to see the Madrid's best queens. Whilst the drag queen show is the main attraction, it also makes for a fun place to grab a casual – there's a two-for-one deal on drinks before 11pm!

La Lupe C/Torrecilla del Leal 12; instagram.com/ lalupedehuertas. A mixed gay, lesbian and alternative bar. Good music, cheap drinks and occasional cabaret.

Truco C/Gravina 10; instagram.com/trucochueca. A long-established women's bar with a popular summer terraza that spills out onto Chueca's main plaza.

Tupperware C/Corredera Alta de San Pablo 26; instagram.com/tupperware.bar.madrid. You'll find a refreshingly cosmopolitan musical diet at this legendary Malasaña nightspot which is often packed to the rafters.

MANCHESTER

Summer

And on the sixth day, God created Man... chester. Ask anyone round here. Mancunians are a proud bunch, and with lots of very good reasons. It's a gorgeous hodgepodge of history, architecture, music, nightlife and salt-of-the-earth humour. Birthplace of the Industrial Revolution, the modern computer and the most famous suffragette of them all, Emmeline Pankhurst, Manchester ticks off Roman invasions, socialist uprisings and popular culture phenomena. It's also home to The Village, the LGBTQ+ neighbourhood that became the touchstone for European diversity and inclusivity from the 1990s. Manchester does love like no other city on earth.

Gay Village alongside Canal street

HISTORY

Once upon a time in AD79, a Roman fort was built in what is now the Castlefield area of Manchester. Then, the settlement was called Mamucium and it allowed the Roman heavies to keep an eye on goings-on along the two major roads that ran through it. Now, Castlefield is bursting with bars, restaurants and galleries, as well as quite a lot of the Roman fort.

The juxtaposition of very old and sparkling new is the story of this city and reinvention is key to its success – but there's something about Manchester that means it just does things a little differently. Maybe because it's the birthplace of the modern world, the place where the Industrial Revolution – the same revolution that financed the British Empire's last great hurrah – began, and paid for all those fancy redbrick buildings you'll see all over the place in Manchester, including the glorious Town Hall. Maybe it's because Manchester

is among the world's most musically influential and prolific cities, with natives including (but not limited to) such names as Oasis, the Bee Gees, New Order, The Smiths, Take That, The Stone Roses, Elbow, Lisa Stansfield, Joy Division, Simply Red, 10cc and the Happy Mondays troubling the pop charts since the 1960s. Or maybe it's because Manchester is home to the largest LGBTQ+ population in the UK after London, and has nurtured what has become the blueprint for modern LGBTQ+ neighbourhoods, The Village. It's no coincidence that, in 1964, Manchester is where The Campaign for Homosexual Equality (or CHE as it was known) was born, while, in the 1980s and early '90s, Manchester City Council put its huge weight behind repealing Section 28, Margaret Thatcher's heinous homophobic law that banned "the promotion of homosexuality" in British schools.

ICON

On the one hand, he saved the world, invented the computer, and inspired the Apple logo... on the other, he was forcibly chemically castrated for being gay and tragically took his own life; Alan Turing is arguably one of the most important human beings of the twentieth century. In case being a pivotal figure in cracking the Nazi Enigma code while working at Bletchley Park from 1939 and helping bring an end to World War II wasn't extraordinary enough (Turing's invention, the "Bombe" machine, and the intelligence it procured is estimated to have shortened the war by two to four years), he is also credited with inventing the modern computer, Manchester Mark I, while working at Manchester University between 1948 and 1954.

Sadly, such were his times; homosexuality was illegal in Britain and, in 1952, Turing was convicted of performing homosexual acts. To avoid imprisonment, this saviour of the modern world instead chose chemical castration. The resulting trauma and societal shame became too much for Turing, and he tragically took his own life by eating a poisoned apple at his Wilmslow home in 1954, aged 41. This is the reason that today's tech giant Apple chose their name; their logo is an apple with the bite taken out of it, because founder Steve Jobs and co. were huge fans of Turing and his work.

Now a much-adored LGBTQ+ hero – although Mancunians would probably prefer the word "legend" – Turing was given a rare Royal Pardon in 2013. There's a statue of him holding the poisoned apple in the Gay Village's Sackville Gardens – where, fittingly, the annual Candlelit Village for LGBTQ+ lives lost to HIV/AIDS takes place on the last Sunday of Manchester Pride. The statue makes for a bitter-sweet memorial to a man who dedicated his life to the betterment of mankind and was repaid with ignominy. A plaque beneath the memorial reads, "Father of Computer Science, Mathematician, Logician, Wartime Codebreaker, Victim of Prejudice". Alan Mathison Turing is now the face of the British £50 note.

Sackville Gardens

Hotel Gotham

HIGHLIGHT

THE VILLAGE

All roads lead to The (Gay) Village. Canal Street is its main thoroughfare, named after the Rochdale Canal that trundles beside its well-worn cobbles, part of the network of canals that fed Cottonopolis – Manchester's moniker when it was centre of the newly industrialised world – and the reason for all those swarthy warehouses casting shadows over the glitterballs, sparkling restaurants, sex shops and the concrete carpark that doubles up as a nightclub during Manchester Pride.

On the corner of Canal Street you'll see the *New Union* and its livery of rainbow flags, club flyers and cast-off wigs. Standing since 1865, it became a place for gay men and lesbians to meet up in the 1950s, back when it was illegal for the former to be gay. That's why the *New Union*'s windows were clouded up, so passers-by couldn't see the carryings-on happening inside. Then, in 1991, it changed tack completely; it was called *Manto* and it was an LGBTQ+ bar that had very big glass windows and even an outside balcony.

It was revolutionary. For the first time, Manchester's queer community was being invited to play in public; no more hiding. From here on in, The Village was a hedonistic free-for-all and other cities took notice. Then, another cultural phenomenon took place. In 1999, *Queer As Folk* hit the screens; the TV show, written by Russell T. Davies, followed the lives of three gay men. It was wonderfully celebratory in its depiction of gay urban life in the 1990s and was so explicit that sensibilities across the nation were all a-flutter; the world couldn't get enough. And it was all set in Manchester's very own Gay Village.

Thus, the evolution of The Village was complete; it continues to come up with the goods today; take your pick from over 40 LGBTQ+ venues, get your fill of artisanal treats over at *Kampus*, a boutique garden neighbourhood on the other side of the canal, or start picking out your outfits for Manchester Pride, which takes over the entire Village for four days over the August Bank Holiday weekend. And yes, you guessed it... no-one does Pride like Manchester.

LISTINGS

STAY

The Alan 18 Princess Street, M1 4LG; thealanhotel. com. Welcome to a wonderland of sustainability. Pretty much everything you can see in this six-story Victorian warehouse is gloriously recycled, upcycled, repurposed and put to very good use. Those marble floors you're walking on? Actually made out of Formica found in the building when it was something a lot less lovely. And yes, that is a huge tree right in front of you. You'll find the same situation in the rooms: bare plaster walls, eau-de-nil ceilings, deconstructed open-plan bathrooms, metal beams and pipes and air-con all left exposed. And the story continues downstairs at dinner with local, sustainable ingredients and a dainty, critically-adored menu projected on the wall.

Hotel Gotham 100 King Street, M2 4WU; hotelgotham. co.uk. Manchester does cheeky very, very well. It's in Mancunians' blood. Even in a glitzy five-star that's taken over an architectural masterpiece (Edwin Lutyens' Art Deco 100 King Street, seeing as you ask).

Check-in is met with garrulous humour and a glass of fizz, rooms are decadent-with-a-wink, and up on the roof at *Brass*, the hotel's private members' club, your cocktails come with a side-order of new best friends.

INNSiDE Manchester 1 First Street; melia.com/ en/hotels/united-kingdom/manchester/innside-manchester. In the heart of Manchester, *INNSiDE Manchester* is a cosmopolitan and stylish four-star hotel that still manages to retain friendliness and warmth – not always a given. With staff that will make you feel right at home a free minibar in every room that comes well-stocked with local tipples, this is an accommodation option that's particularly well-suited to couples (or at least very good friends) as the rooms are open plan – meaning that the shower is perfectly visible from everywhere else!

LEVEN 40 Chorlton Street, M1 3HW; liveleven.com. Location, location, location you say? How about *LEVEN*, that rather gorgeous converted warehouse half-way up Canal Street with windows so huge your

Manchester Pride Parade

Vitamin D levels will be jumping for joy, and so close to the action you can feel it, touch it, invite it in for cocktails? This hotel is nothing shy of divine, the rooms are huge with sultry colours and, if you're lucky, come with a roll-top bath right by the window so you can feel/touch/invite the action down below while doing your ablutions. *MAYA* is the restaurant at which you'll be lining your stomach pre-fun, with tasty Manchester-inspired nosh.

Native 51 Ducie Street, M1 2TP; nativeplaces.com. In a city that likes having its game changed, *Native* is a game-changer. A colossal Victorian warehouse is more of self-contained city in itself than aparthotel. Rooms are chic, homely and comfy with yard-thick exposed brick walls; they're huge and almost criminally inexpensive for what they are. Downstairs in the Zeppelin-sized atrium is where it gets very interesting; this they call *Ducie Street Warehouse*, and it's a coming-together of food and drink and pop-ups as well as BLOCK, the coolest gym in town. Not to be missed are their once monthly disco brunches, where you can dine on high-quality brunch specials (pancakes, bagels and avocado on toast feature highly) as well as bottomless cocktails while glittery dancers swirl around you to the likes of Donna Summer.

Treehouse Blackfriars Street, M3 2EQ; treehousehotels.com/manchester. *Treehouse* has taken hospitality – and fun – up to the next level in an extremely literal manner at this eco-centric, towering beauty on the edge of Manchester's Medieval Quarter (*Selfridges* and *Harvey Nichols* are close too, if they're more your vibe). They're not afraid of colour here, with rooms in maximalism-lite to make your pupils pop – or perhaps that's vertigo, judging from those lofty views from *The Nest* up on the roof. The food and drink served here is a minimal-waste fantasia, all down to local names including Mary-Ellen McTague and Justin Crawford.

A historical float at Manchester Pride

EAT

Bondobust 61 Piccadilly, Manchester, M1 2AG; bundobust.com/locations/manchester. Indian food doesn't get more convivial than down at Bondubust, right opposite Manchester's Piccadilly Gardens. This subterranean playground of deliriously wonderful Asian flavours of the street food variety comes in a communal setting, reminiscent of university canteens. It's all washed down by craft beer, and you'll be hard-pushed to find a dish for more than £7, with an abundance of deals always on offer. It's also 100% veggie, and mostly vegan. There really should be a halo above the door of this heavenly place.

Erst 9 Murray Street, Ancoats, M4 6HS; erst-mcr.co.uk. Critics and punters alike have been frothing at the tastebuds for this charmer over in Ancoats, which also happens to be England's first industrial suburb – so you're getting lane after lane of red brick history *en route* to your pan-European nosh and natural wines. In contrast, Erst is all brushed concrete floors and breeze block walls with splashes of brushed wood and clever magazines placed just so, and the menu treads a similar less-is-more path with rarely more than 15 small plates covering savoury and sweet – a godsend for the Virgos among us, as is the food.

The Molly House 26 Richmond Street, M1 3NB; themollyhouse.com. Four hundred ales, beers, spirits and cocktails, anyone? This Gay Village favourite is all about making friends, finding lovers, drinking proper, grown-up drinks (including tea!) and maybe partaking of the pretty decent Spanish tapas menu. *The Molly House* is the first port of call for many a punter round these parts. The music isn't silly-loud – you can actually hear what your fellow diners are saying – and the mural on its wall outside featuring LGBTQ+ icons including Quentin Crisp, Alan Turing and Emmeline Pankhurst just happens to be the largest piece of queer street art in the UK.

Peter Street Kitchen Free Trade Hall, Peter Street, M2 5GP; thekitchensrestaurants.co.uk/peter-street-kitchen. Like many a northern British town, Manchester takes glamour very seriously – and my oh my, is Peter

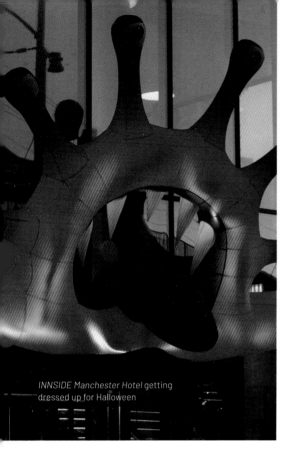

INNSIDE Manchester Hotel getting dressed up for Halloween

spectacle that takes place across the canal.

Tast 20–22 King Street, M2 6AG; tastcatala.com. Exquisite Catalonian tapas brought to you by Barcelona native and Manchester City manager, Pep Guardiola. Manchester does Spanish food brilliantly; *El Gato Negro*, just a few doors down, and *Evuna* in the Northern Quarter are always delicious safe bets too, but Pep's place is next level. Three floors of unique, charcoal-infused flavours and classic, heady cocktails in the chicest of surroundings. Try the vegan tasting menu – it will blow your mind.

DRINK

Richmond Tea Rooms 46 Sackville Street, M1 3WF; richmondtearooms.com. Imagine the house of the most eccentric aunt/drag queen/bunny rabbit you know, then double it; now you might be somewhere close to the off-the-wall-ness of this fun and funny joint, just across the water from the throng of Canal Street. Come for sugar-laden joy and burlesque "tea-se" parties, leave having had to undo the top buttons on your jeans.

Vanilla 39–41 Richmond Street, M1 3WB; instagram. com/vanillagirlsmcr. Let's hear it for the... women! Manchester's longest-running lesbian bar and so-called "lesbian mecca of the North" is proof that good things come in very small packages. The Village's default bar for girls, girls and more girls, *Vanilla* errs on the side of a super-femme, bubble-gum aesthetic but, as a safe space for women, all predilections are welcome – even if quite few are on the fence about its friendliness. Hosting regular events, it's the go-to for girls who want to party until way past bedtime.

Via 28–30 Canal Street, M1 3EZ; viamanchester.co.uk. Sometimes the oldies are the goodies, and *Via* has been doing its thing on Canal Street for three decades. A decadent, cave-like place (is it a pub? Is it a tavern?) with nooks and crannies and plenty an opportunity for banging your head (especially after a few drinks – be careful!), the vibe ranges from cruisy (see said nooks/ crannies) to no-holds-barred dancing when things come over more disco of a weekend. A mixed, friendly LGBTQ+ crowd with no-nonsense frivolity – it's no wonder *Via*'s the grand dame of the Village.

Street Kitchen glamorous. A blingy auditorium just to the right of the bar – perfect for seeing and being seen – is the centre of the action, a cocoon for the chosen ones with expensive hair, and the food is modern Japanese and Mexican (not fusion, Japanese *and* Mexican). But of course, feel free to mix and match; it's all deliriously good. There are also scrumptious vegan options, which are taken very seriously indeed.

Pollen Bakery 8 New Union St; pollenbakery.com. In the canalside district of Ancoats, *Pollen* serves fantastic coffee, though it's the baked goods that steal the show. Cruffins (croissant/muffin hybrids that come adorned with such delicacies as Lucky Charms and dulce de leche) sell out fast, so arrive early in the morning (that is, before 11am) if you want a taste! Otherwise, grab a gigantic ham and cheese croissant and, if the weather allows, grab a table outside. Keep your eyes peeled for the adorable doggy daycare

DANCE

Cruz 101 101 Princess Street, M1 6DD; cruz101.com. Known simply as *Cruz* (Cruise, get it?), this erstwhile shipping warehouse has been on the Gay Village map since 1992... and we don't think they've ever cleaned those carpets – yes, carpets. In a nightclub. Part-owned by drag queen Miss Cara, who introduces the DJs of a weekend, this is a cheap and very cheerful night out attracting everyone from first-time baby-gays to those who've made it their home since it opened. Step downstairs, embrace the cheesy pop-dance tunes, try and make your way to the bar without getting your shoes stuck to said carpet and give yourself up to a true legend of Manchester gay clubbing.

The Eagle 15 Bloom Street, M1 3HZ; eaglemanchester. com. The *Eagle* brand are a global byword for straight-up blokey gay fun and the Manchester 'branch' is no exception. There's a lounge-y bar upstairs but it's down the staircase into the musky abyss where the real fun takes place. There's a bar and a dancefloor, and if you turn back on yourself and hang a right, a sexy back-bar with low-lighting and funky décor. But it's not all testosterone and black leather; sometimes it's testosterone and black rubber. Occassionally they host good ol' cabaret on the mini-stage, because even alphas need their downtime!

G-A-Y 63 Richmond Street, M1 3WB; facebook.com/ GAYManchester; Instagram.com/ gaymanchester. This London import is unashamedly what it is, which is glorious pop fun with no limit of Kylie, Bananarama, and STEPS. There's no such thing as a guilty pleasure over this multi-floor venue-with-balcony, just the pleasure thank you very much! *G-A-Y* stands for Good As You, which is very much emblematic of the attitude here; expect cheap drinks and cheap sounds, but a clientele that is all class. Only kidding! For riotous nights out, step right in.

Kiss Me Again Monthly at Soup Kitchen, 31–31 Spear Street, Stevenson Square, M1 1DF; soupmanchester. com. "Bring the vibes and ditch the prejudice", they command at this alternative every-other-monther in the Northern Quarter. *Kiss Me Again* may be a fairly intimate basement affair but if it's a 'queerdo' scene you're after, this is where you need to head as these nights attract a very recherché selection of DJs bringing a broad spectrum of sounds to the LGBTQ+ in-the-knows of Manchesterford (it's a Victoria Wood thing, another Manc icon, British national treasure, queer icon and one of the world's greatest ever comedians). *Soup Kitchen* also has a whole line-up of other alt-gay events to fill those boots of yours.

New York New York 94–98 Bloom Street, M1 3LY; newyorknewyorkbar.com. A daft, over-the-top knees-up with sticky floors, *New York New York* is legendary. Run by the delightful Tracey for well over 30 years, it's the beating/dancing/singing/caterwauling heart of The Village. Drag queens rule the roost (although Tracey is always the ultimate monarch) and you'll find a Rolodex of DJs, cabaret artists and flamboyant regulars entertaining the up-for-it masses. Come Manchester Pride, be sure to swing by "It's A Gay Knockout", the party palace's outrageous game show that takes all of the above outside and kick-starts the celebrations like no other.

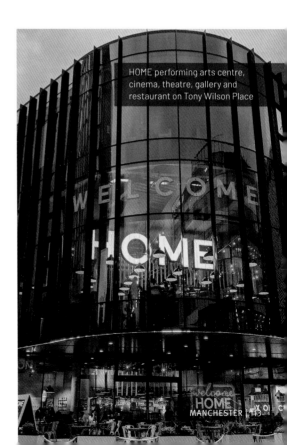

HOME performing arts centre, cinema, theatre, gallery and restaurant on Tony Wilson Place

SHOP

Afflecks 52 Church Street, M4 1PW; afflecks.com. This Northern Quarter icon is a rite of passage. A community of independent retailers bunked up in a rusty, dusty old warehouse – think tiny artisan gems to vintage garms via progressive art prints as well as Manchester's longest running LGBTQ+ bookshop – Afflecks is beloved of pretty much every Mancunian on earth. Teenagers have been skipping school to stock up on Afflecks' crystals and clever t-shirts and hemp-related items for nigh on 40 years.

Cow 61 Church St; wearecow.com. *Cow* is a vintage store with an incredible selection of reworked items and, somewhat unusually for a vintage shop, a fantastic men's section; absolutely ideal for perusing the rails and finding hidden treasures. They always have good tunes on, too.

Family Gorgeous and Friends at the Manchester Museum as part of the Pride festival weekend

Fig + Sparrow 20 Oldham Street, M1 1JA; figandsparrow. online. All cafés should be made like this. Perfect coffee and the outside tables that everyone's vying for on a sunny day – even a rainy one, to be honest. *Fig + Sparrow* also sells the most tip-top perfect selection of very lovely design things, the kinds of things you didn't know you wanted until you laid eyes on them. You'll also find unique and esoteric cards that will make you look very clever indeed when your friends and family receive them, and really delightful wrapping paper.

Fred Aldous 37 Lever Street, M1 1LW; fredaldous. co.uk. Art, glorious art... or at least the stuff you need to create it. A family-run store that has been serving Manchester's creative community since 1886, it's huge, with three floors and 30,000 art, craft, and design products. Upstairs you'll find stationery, gifts, and other gorgeous things, the ground floor is where to go for all your arts and crafts paraphernalia, while down in the basement it's all paper and sketchbooks. If you're after the pencil sharpener of your dreams, come on over. Who isn't?

Manchester Craft and Design Centre 17 Oak Street, M4 5JD; craftanddesign.com. This former Victorian fish market is now alive and kicking with studios belonging to many of the region's most talented artists, designers and makers. Jewellery, ceramics, textiles, prints, homeware, glass and other delightful things are churned out with love, and not only can you see that talent in action here, but you can also buy the fruits of their labour – and delicious they are too. There's also a café on the ground floor and a programme of exhibitions and performances that celebrate even more local and international design talent.

Piccadilly Records 53 Oldham Street, M1 1JR; piccadillyrecords.com. Manchester's not lacking on the record store front but Piccadilly Records will probably be your first port of call if you're looking for the latest in indie, rock, pop, disco, funk, anything that's interesting and new and will look a treat on your turntable. Regularly voted among the world's greatest record shops by people who know about these things, Piccadilly Records has been teasing Manchester's airwaves since 1978, and by the sounds of it they've barely got started.

DO

Factory International Water Street, M3 4JQ; factoryinternational.org. Named after the record label that gave the world New Order, Joy Division and Happy Mondays – and also ran the Haçienda, possibly the most influential night club ever – *Factory International* is a multi-performance and arts venue and crikey, it's a stunner. Designed by Rem Koolhaas's architecture studio *OMA*, it's home to the biennial Manchester International Festival, a year-round programme of theatre, dance, music, visual arts and digital commissions. It also has delightful spots to sit back and relax whilst sipping a gin and tonic and looking very erudite indeed.

HOME 2 Tony Wilson Place, M15 4FN; homemcr.org. A hub of culture and creativity with a heavy bias towards all things LGBTQ+, this sexy little enclave gives you theatres, galleries, creative spaces, one of the loveliest independent cinemas in town, talks and events that let you get up close and personal with the people who create all of the above magic, and of course the requisite restaurants and bars where you can put your feet up and grab a bite to eat after all that culture. They even have their own arts publishing house so you can finally get that gorgeous coffee-table book you've been looking for.

Manchester Museum The University of Manchester, Oxford Road, M13 9PL; museum.manchester.ac.uk. Designed by Alfred Waterhouse, who also worked his genius on Manchester's Town Hall and the Natural History Museum in London, the building alone is a total beauty – but the really good stuff is inside. Archaeology, anthropology and natural history are its focus but, seeing as that's a pretty hefty remit, you'll have no issues finding something in here to tickle your fancy. They've got 4.5million items on display, after all! An ongoing partner of Manchester Pride, its 'Queering Manchester Museum' programme looks at its treasures through an LGBTQ+ lens while delivering year-round events and exhibitions celebrating every colour of that gorgeous rainbow flag of ours.

Masseria Wave

PUGLIA

Summer

For those who prefer their getaway destinations laidback and rugged, Puglia delivers. Long-visited by Italy's LGBTQ+ community, the heel of the Italian boot is turning heads among the community across Europe and beyond, and although the scene is entrenched, it's still off the main gay circuit. With mainland Italy's longest coastline, there are plenty of white beaches to choose from, as well as a globally-recognised food culture and rich history, influenced by the Greeks, Arabs, Spanish and just about every Mediterranean power of the day.

HISTORY

Puglia is Italy's only flat region, and its fertility and strategic location have made it a historically fought-over place. In the eighth century BC, Ancient Spartans colonised and had a profound cultural influence; today there are still towns in Salento where locals speak Griko, a Greek dialect. The Romans ousted the Greeks in 272BC, and made use of Puglia's fecundity to develop it into Italy's breadbasket, a title it still holds; Puglia now produces eighty percent of Europe's pasta, and more olive oil than the rest of Italy put together.

After changing hands between Lombards, Franks, Byzantines, and Muslim Saracens, the Normans conquered and gained popularity in 1087. From 1200, Puglia saw even more rulers – this time to the tune of the Holy Roman Empire, the Angevins, Aragonese, Hapsburgs, Bourbons, and the French – until 1861, when it finally became part of the new, united, Kingdom of Italy.

In 1939, under fascist dictator Benito Mussolini, dozens of gay Italian men were exiled to the Apulian island of San Domino, just off Puglia's northern coast. They lived under harsh conditions, and also became Italy's first openly gay community.

Post-war, Puglia developed in agriculture, domestic tourism and manufacturing. Into the new millennium, Puglia's infrastructure developed with European Union support, and Bari's old town was restored. Celebrities, from Helen Mirren to Meryl Streep to Francis Ford Coppola began to buy up Salentine *masserias* (farmhouses), and a gay tourism scene developed around Gallipoli; in Puglia as a whole, there are no less than five ongoing annual Pride festivals. Puglia elected several left-wing presidents, starting with Nichi Vendola (2005–15) – Italy's first openly LGBTQ+ regional president. In 2006, fellow communist Vladimir Luxuria, from Foggia, was elected to be Europe's first openly transgender member of parliament.

Despite some political wins, Italy remains the only western European country without equal marriage rights for LGBTQ+ people, and Italy elected a far-right government in 2022 that has threatened legal protections of transgender people. As elsewhere in Europe and the world, the fight continues for equality.

Vladimir Luxuria

ICON

Vladimir Luxuria has been an LGBTQ+ tour de force in Italy for the last thirty years. She was born in 1965 in Foggia, Puglia's third largest city, and began her performing career in the city's bars and restaurants, MCing at the *Dirty Dixy Club* and performing drag shows at the medieval *Taverno del Gufo*. After completing her degree in Rome in the 1980s, she became a creative director at the influential *Circolo di cultura omosessuale Mario Mieli* (an association that defends the rights of LGBTQ+ people), hosting famous figures such as Grace Jones and Alexander McQueen.

In 1994 she co-organised Italy's first gay pride festival in the capital, and her activism continued to grow. She joined the Communist Refoundation Party and, despite violent attacks from far-right politicians, was elected to parliament in 2006, becoming Europe's first trans parliamentarian, and the world's second (after New Zealander Georgina Beyer). She successfully submitted a bill protecting transgender rights, but joined a new party for the following 2008 elections which didn't win any seats. Upon leaving parliament, she had greatly increased trans visibility in Italy and had become a household name, including through her entertainment career, a means she has always used to increase visibility.

She has acted in several films since the 1980s, and published five books, including *Chi ha paura della Muccassassina*, which recounts her journey from Foggia to the Chamber of Deputies. She also released her first single in 2019. She is a regular face on Italian television screens, including as presenter on the Italian version of *Survivor*.

After her parliamentary career, she returned to non-partisan activism, playing a central role in establishing pride festivals, especially across the *Mezzogiorno* (Southern Italy), and in campaigning for adoptive, asylum, and matrimonial rights for LGBTQ+ people.

HIGHLIGHTS

GALLIPOLI

Gallipoli in the summer is where the action is at. This beautiful island city has a walled old town (including some wonderful gay bars like *Gogó Food & Drink*) and fantastic beaches. A five-mile cycle south will bring you to Punta Della Suina, a beach of soft sands, calm waters and secluded coves; it is growing in fame as not only one of the best gay beaches in Italy, but one of the best beaches in Europe. Closer to town, Baia Verde is another popular LGBTQ+ beach with shallow waters. In the evening *Pôr do Sol* becomes one of Puglia's most exciting bars, with a vivacious, inclusive vibe.

OSTUNI

With a cosmopolitan vibe, plenty of good eateries and stylish bars, the gorgeous hill-town of Ostuni provides a decent base for visiting the beautiful towns nearby. It is just a 15-minute drive to the closest beach (at Marina Rosa) and 30 minutes from Torre Guaceto.

BEACHES OF SALENTO

Puglia's food and culture are reason enough to visit, but its many white, flat, unspoilt, resort-poor, sandy beaches are what really distinguish it in the European Mediterranean. Such abundance of course means that there are beautiful beaches to suit every crowd and every mood. If you're looking to do the gay beach circuit, Punta della Suina and Spiaggia D'Ayala are the heavyweights. Porto Selvaggio lives by its name if you're looking for a crazy naturist experience (*"Porto Selvaggio"* roughly translates to "wild port"), whereas family-friendly Spiaggia di Pescoluse – known as the "Maldives of Salento" – provides splendid and shallow azure waters, perfect for paddling or a quick dip. Protected Torre Guaceto has different sections to cater for every taste; it does get busy in summer, but its sheer size means that it never really feels crowded. In general, the beaches here have amenities such as parasols for hire, public toilets and a bar or kiosk.

Trulli houses in Alberobello

CYCLING IN THE VALLE D'ITRIA

Hidden away from the crowds of sunbathers in Gargano and Salento, the Valle d'Itria is what many Italians picture when they hear "Puglia". It's a bumpy valley full of olive groves and *trulli*, the Smurf-like, pointy-roofed houses typical of the region. Bring your bike on a train and cycle between towns, eating well along the way to refuel (naturally). Conical Locorotondo, cliff-top Cisternino and *trullo*-rich Alberobello are the main hits on the route. The ancient Apulian Aqueduct has been converted into a cycle way which allows you to ride traffic-free through the groves and above the *trulli*, but if you prefer to get your walking boots on, the valley makes for excellent hiking too.

BAROQUE LECCE

This baroque university city is nicknamed the "Florence of the South", and with good cause. Get lost in its charming limestone streets, dine in world-class restaurants and share bottles of *Primitivo* in its bars.

MASSERIA WAVE

masseriawave.it/en

The most exciting post-pandemic addition to Puglia's cultural calendar, *Masseria Wave* is a project that brings together the *masseria* (a type of eighteenth-century rural Apulian farmhouse), queer culture and world-class electronic music. Founded by Gilberto Genco, an Apulian who bought this masseria in Lequile after returning from a five year stay in London, *Masseria Wave* transposes the wealth of queer culture from around the world into the heart of Salento. The masseria is open as a queer-run hotel throughout the year (*La Restuccia*; larestuccia.it) and *Masseria Wave* is the multidisciplinary array of inclusive projects that takes place from June to September (with some ad hoc events off-season); these include drag performances, DJ sets, live music and many other artistic endeavours that refuse categorisation. 2022 saw collaborations with London's *Dalston Superstore* and Zurich's *Kweer Ball*, as well as Puglia's first ever Kiki ball.

LISTINGS

DRINK

Caffè Letterario Via G. Paladini 46, Lecce; instagram. com/caffeletterariolecce. An arty little bookshop-café with mismatched furniture and board games, perfect for an *aperitivo* or after-dinner drinks. It has cosy outdoor seating along Via Paladini and organises a wealth of events, including DJs, live music and theatre.

La Ciclatera Sotto il Mare Via Venezia 16, Bari; facebook.com/ciclaterasottoilmare. In the heart of Bari's vibrant old city – itself a must for visitors to Puglia – proudly gay-friendly *La Ciclatera* occupies the optimal position for watching the sun set into the Adriatic with an aperitivo.

La Puteau Experience Via R. D'Angiò, Gallipoli. A welcoming bar does really good G&Ts; if you chat to the bar staff, they will make you a cocktail in line with your tastes – ask for the one made with squid ink, if you dare! The cold plates on offer are also really delicious.

DANCE

Lido Pôr do Sol Lungomare Galileo Galilei, Baia Verde; bit.ly/3HGQ1My. In-between in every sense, *Pôr do Sol* is a laidback treat for visitors to Gallipoli that manages to get things very right. It's in-between the LGBTQ+ hotspots Gallipoli and Punta della Suina, where Baia Verde meets the sea. It's in-between lido and bar, and even does decent food. Perhaps because it doesn't fit into one box, it attracts a refreshingly diverse crowd, particularly in age, gender and between tourists and locals. Go on a Sunday night for its LED beach party and for a good time and a relaxed vibe.

Village Picador SP289 Loc. Fontana Gallipoli; facebook.com/picadorvillage. *Village Picador* is an enormous gay club ten minutes outisde of Gallipoli. Expect a giant outdoor space lined with palm trees, raucous entertainment (including drag shows) and hedonistic fun until the small wee hours.

Ostuni

STAY

Anima Bed & Wellness Off Contrada Lamatoccola, 72017, Ostuni; animapuglia.it. For a more Apulian experience, LGBTQ-owned *Anima* offers a peaceful getaway in the Valle d'Itria. Guests stay in self-contained bungalows or *trulli* dotted about the garden which also has a pool, kitchen and sauna.

Arco Vecchio Via Quinto Fabio Balbo 5, Lecce; arcovecchio.it. Spruce, restored palazzo just off the very pleasant Via Paladini, with nine neat, contemporary, minimalist rooms, with flatscreen TVs, satellite. There's also a suite with a fully equipped kitchen and its own terrace, ideal for families.

Borgo Egnazia Strada Comunale Egnazia, Savelletri di Fasano; borgoegnazia.com. The *Borgo* styles itself a "Nowhere Else Place" and there is certainly nowhere else like it in Puglia. It is a high-end resort, dedicated to pure luxury and attracting celebrities (Justin Timberlake married Jessica Biel here) and wealthy European families. Designed on the lines of a Puglian village (though built from scratch) it comprises low-rise, sun-bleached buildings including villas with private pools, and offers every conceivable facility including a Michelin-starred restaurant, a unique spa, and two private beaches.

Casa dei Venti Via Dante 182, Bari. Stylish B&B in the modern town, about a 10min walk from the train station. Five spacious rooms and a suite, with classic furniture and contemporary decor, all with a/c, fridges and TV. Large breakfasts are served in a splendid room wallpapered with Nina Campbell butterflies.

Il Frantoio SS16 km 874, Ostuni; masseriailfrantoio. it/en. A traditional white farmhouse in 72 hectares of olive grove, a 5min drive from Ostuni, with sixteen rooms furnished with family furniture and heirlooms. The estate produces organic olive oil, fruits and vegetables, and they make delicious meals. Rates include access to selected lidos on nearby beaches.

Guesthouse Tipico Trulli Suite Via Monte S. Marco 28, Alberobello. Complete your *trulli* experience by staying in one of the three rooms in this beautifully

The Church of Santa Croce in Lecce

restored set of *trulli* – it's a bit like sleeping in a giant stone igloo. Breakfast is served on a panoramic patio.

La Restuccia Contrada Monte, Lequile; larestuccia.it. A queer-owned, eighteenth-century *masseria* that is home to the annual *Masseria Wave* party, *La Restuccia* is an experience in and of itself; it has 74 rooms, two suites, a huge swimming pool, a restaurant, and spaces dedicated to DJ sets, workshops, concerts, drag shows and art exhibitions. It's not hard to find a place to relax here, or equally to party under the dark, starry sky until the sun comes up. It's like a little queer city unto itself, but if you do feel the need to venture out, it's about a half-hour drive to Gallipoli and Lecce.

Malìa Via Paladini 33, Lecce; beb.it/malialecce/en. Fabulous TV-free boutique B&B designed by owner-architect Laura Aguglia – the huge, elegant sitting room has a star-vaulted ceiling, parquet floor, a vast calico sofa and an ample choice of art and design books and magazines to leaf through. There are only three rooms, but each is gorgeous, different, and imaginatively lit, especially the romantic double with a four-poster bed designed by Laura. Breakfast is served at the nearby *oo Doppiozero Café*.

Masseria Torre Maizza, Contrada Coccaro, between Fasano and Savelletri; masseriatorremaizza. com. Stylish resort hotel with spacious rooms in outbuildings once used to house passing pilgrims. There's an Aveda spa, a chic heated pool, a Moroccan-influenced roof terrace and a restaurant that serves sophisticated Pugliese food. Facilities also include a golf course within the grounds, cooking classes, a beach club 4km away, and the chance to sail on the hotel's 14m yacht.

Paragon 700 Boutique Hotel & Spa Largo Michele Ayroldi Carissimo, 14, Ostuni; paragon700.com. Housed within Ostuni's eighteenth-century *Palazzo Rosso*, *Paragon 700* is a lavish hotel that adeptly combines boutique and rusticity. Its lesbian owners have carefully refurbished the building, topping off the décor with an eclectic mix of objects from their lives around the world. With its Moorish garden, it is a destination unto itself.

EAT

Al Dragone Via Duomo 8, Vieste; aldragone.it. Located in a once-inhabited cave, *Al Dragone* is good for fish dishes, such as the antipasto of marinated grey mullet, and twists on local dishes you won't find anywhere else, such as *orecchiette* with turnip greens, salted anchovies scattered with bottarga and shards of thin crispy bread spiked with capers, parsley, basil, garlic and chilli. There are some unusual desserts too, such as *mostazzuoli* – made with almonds, wine must (the syrup made by boiling down what is left of the grapes after making wine) and egg white.

L'Aratro Via Monte San Michele 25–29, Alberobello; ristorantearatro.it. Inside a *trullo*, this is a stellar option, rigorously sourcing all its ingredients locally, and serving a dizzying number of vegetable and cheese antipasti and local specialities including that Pugliese staple, *purè di fave e cicoria* (puréed broad bean and wild chicory) and *orecchiete con cime di rapa* (pasta – the name means "little ears", which is what they are supposed to look like – with turnip tops and salty anchovies).

Il Bastione Riviera N. Sauro, Gallipoli; ilbastionegallipoli.it. *Il Bastione* is a great place to sample the catch of the day whichever which way you prefer it done – raw, grilled, fried, baked or cooked in salt – on a panoramic seafront terrace.

Corte dei Pandolfi Piazzetta Orsini, Lecce; cortedeipandolfi.com. Intimate place in a charming piazza off Via Paladini, gaining a reputation for creative twists on traditional cuisine, using fresh ingredients, shown off to perfection in several raw fish dishes. Other meals worth trying are the handmade spaghetti with fresh anchovies, capers and tomato.

Martinucci Laboratory Piazza Mercantile, 80, Bari; martinuccilaboratory.it. Come for the *pasticioti*, stay for the gelato. Even if you don't make it to Lecce, home of the *pasticcioto leccese*, a deliciously moreish filled pastry, *Martinucci* has you covered. Chances are they will have a café in your local town, and they take

Colourful rooms at *La Restuccia*

High glamour at *Masseria Wave*

pasticciotti seriously. Have one (or three) with a coffee in your local piazza.

Osteria Piazzetta Cattedrale Largo Arcidiacono, Ostuni; piazzettacattedrale.it. Elegant restaurant opposite the cathedral, which uses locally sourced ingredients to great creative effect – try the stunning *cestino di crepe con crema di cavolfiori, pancetta crocante e vincotto di Primitivo*, a crêpe basket filled with cauliflower purée and crisp bacon and drizzled with sweet wine must – on a constantly evolving seasonal menu.

Pescaria Piazza Aldo Moro 6-8, Polignano a Mare; pescaria.it. Italy is the birthplace of the slow-food movement, but sometimes even Italians need a quick, though no-less delicious, bite to eat. In the heart of beautiful seaside town Polignano, *Pescaria*, with its inexpensive fresh seafood sandwiches, provides exactly that.

Porta Nova Via G. Petrarolo 38, Ostuni; ristoranteportanova.com. Set in a fifteenth-century stone city gate overlooking olive groves and the sea, this is a fine place for fish and shellfish, with

a following for its raw fish (there's a tasting menu for those who want a bite of everything), as well as marvellous dishes such as black *trofie* (a type of short, twisted pasta) served with turnip tops, baby squid, anchovy and toasted breadcrumbs.

Il Rustico Via Quintino Sella 95, Bari. Friendly and hugely popular local trattoria and pizzeria, where heaps of appetisers arrive at your table in waves, followed by the pizza of your choice. Excellent value meal deals, too.

Sagre festivals giraitalia.it/sagre/puglia. Whenever you're visiting, and especially in the autumn, be sure to find out about any *sagre* (food festivals) that may be running. While a nationwide phenomenon, Puglia's *sagre* have particular acclaim. Some, such as Puttignano's *Sagra del Maiale* (Sagra of the Pig) during Europe's oldest carnival, are focused on specific foods; others, such as Noci's *Bacco nelle Gnostre* are focused on a locality's dishes; all have a lively atmosphere, fuelled by vittles and wine to please your belly and soul.

Rainbow flag at the Erasmus University campus

ROTTERDAM

Summer

When you think of the Netherlands, you likely think of serene canals, variegated tulips, and old-fashioned architecture. Rotterdam, however, has little of that. Instead, its centre is filled with soaring skyscrapers, it's home to the largest seaport in Europe, and the architecture is innovative. Still, this often-contrasting city blends the modernity (like the famous Cube Houses designed by Piet Blom near Rotterdam Blaak) with the historic (such as the picturesque Delfshaven) – and it does it well, all while offering a distinctly multicultural vibe. No trip to the Netherlands is complete without a visit to the country's favourite oddball.

HISTORY

You could say that Rotterdam's story began in 1260, when a dam was built right at the Rotte River (hence the name, *Rotte-dam*); today, it's the Hoogstraat, a small shopping street in the centre of town. Less than a hundred years later in 1340, the city received its municipal rights, although just a few thousand people then lived there. Skip ahead roughly 10 years, and Rotterdam landed on its main source of income: the Rotterdamse Schie, a shipping canal. This allowed the city to become a central shipping centre not only within the country, but also with Germany and England.

From the fourteenth cenury onwards the Port of Rotterdam became increasingly influential, further spurred by the success of the Dutch East India and West India Companies. It was one of the major cities of the United Provinces and shared its periods of fortune and decline until the nineteenth century when it was caught unawares; the city was ill prepared for the industrial expansion of the Ruhr, the development of larger ships and the silting up of the Maas, but prosperity did finally return in a big way with the digging of an entirely new ship canal (the "Nieuwe Waterweg") between the city and the North Sea in the 1860s. By the end of the nineteenth century, Rotterdam inaugurated the Witte Huis skyscraper, a 45 metre American/Art Noveau hybrid building that was then the tallest office on the continent.

Rotterdam has been a major seaport ever since, though it has faced trials and tribulations, especially during World War II. Nazi Germany launched an invasion on the Netherlands in May 1940 as the war began, expecting a quick victory; in the face of surprising resistance, Germany decided to force the Dutch army to surrender by heavily bombing the city from 10th to 14th May, killing around 1,000 people and displacing no less than 85,000. The city centre was almost completely destroyed, and much of the harbour was destroyed four years later on their retreat, with Allied bombing doing much damage in between.

The postwar period saw the rapid reconstruction of the docks and, when huge container ships and oil tankers made the existing port facilities obsolete, Rotterdammers promptly built an entirely new deep-sea port, the Europoort, through which pass more than half of all goods heading into Europe.

The same spirit of enterprise was reflected in the council's plans to rebuild the devastated city centre. There was to be no return to the crowded terrace houses of yesteryear; instead the centre was to be a modern extravaganza of concrete and glass, high-rise and pedestrianised areas. Decades in the making, parts of the plan worked – and works – very well indeed, marking Rotterdam as a truly resilient city. Or, as the former Queen Wilhelmina said: "*Sterker door strijd*" ("Stronger through effort").

Today, the city is home to nearly 200 nationalities and an impressive collection of avant-garde architecture, with its elegant Erasmus bridge, playful Blaak cube houses and the vast Tetris-block "De Rotterdam". There's also plenty to keep visitors entertained, including a great museum park, the bohemian Witte de Wittstraat artistic quarter and, last but not least, the welcoming and independent-spirited Rotterdammers themselves.

ICON

Piet Gamekoorn may not be a famous name the world over, but he is certainly a person that queer visitors to Rotterdam should know about.

Gamekoorn (pronounced *HA-muh-corn*) was born in the Bloemhof District in 1944 and for the most part had a happy childhood; by the time he was a teenager, however, he had begun to struggle with his sexuality.

Sex education was virtually non-existent, which meant it took years for him to fully realise what it meant to be a gay man. The queer community of the era was mostly underground – men would go cruising in secret, and anybody who went to the few secluded gay bars was seen as something of a pariah. Tensions and worries were high within the gay community itself, as HIV/AIDS

The Erasmus Bridge

ran rampant. In a world where Piet needed to pass as straight when working as a carpenter in the shipyard, he felt as though he were living a double life. Coming out proved to be tumultuous: when he told his parents about his sexuality, his mother said, "Either he leaves, or I do."

Things began to change, however, when Gamekoorn discovered the *Cosmo Bar*, the oldest gay bar in Rotterdam and then a quintessential household name. Though his family would often joke about the clientele, Piet knew it was a place where he would belong – and he was right. In his own words, "I had a place where I could be myself, like a fish in the water!" The gay nightlife that had opened up to him represented a world of possibility, where anything and everything was possible.

Gamekoorn became a staple on the Rotterdam LGBTQ+ scene, working with volunteers to give out free condoms or provide support for closeted men. Eventually, he became a co-owner of *Gay Palace*, but also worked in several other queer-friendly establishments around town. He spent decades in the industry, collecting thousands of memories and stories – so much so that in 2022, he self-published his own memoir, entitled *Pietje, een Rotterdamse jongen* (*Pietje, A Boy from Rotterdam*).

Today, *Cosmo Bar* and *Gay Palace* have both sadly closed, but fortunately many say that the raw, gritty feel of the Gamekoorn's childhood and teenage years has vanished to make way for an increasingly modern, progressive city. Despite the closures of his old stomping grounds, however, Piet remains busy, even though he is now almost 80. When you're in Rotterdam, chances are high you'll find him at his very own aptly-named queer adult entertainment shop, *GayToys*. Stop by and have him tell you a story of the olden days, and don't forget to ask about upcoming queer and community events in Rotterdam; he's a wealth of information and very friendly. You won't regret it!

HIGHLIGHT

The city of Rotterdam's Pride celebrations have been steadily growing in recent years, making an excellent reason to travel to the city in June.

Rotterdam Pride is not restricted to just one day, but rather is celebrated over as many as 10 days, meaning there's something for all ages, genders and personal preferences. You can attend dance workshops, living libraries, queer cinema nights, workshops, lectures, brunches, and more – many for free!

The best day is *Roze Zaterdag* (Pink Saturday), which is the day when the Pride March takes place. Start your day with a big breakfast, and head out into the city before 11am if you want to join the march, which usually starts by the Willemsplein. It's an eclectic crowd – expats, students, families, tourists, locals – but overwhelmingly a welcoming one. The walk itself takes around two hours as you work your way through the city centre, ending at the City Hall by the Coolsingel, but the festivities are only just beginning.

After the march, Pink Saturday soon becomes an open-air festival, with pop-up stores, bars, and information centres scattered around the main streets, offering plenty of amusement before the performances start. In recent years, Rotterdam Pride has begun to attract ever-bigger names to perform; celebrities such as 2019 Eurovision winner Duncan Laurence have performed here. Join the crowds and dance or find a spot to relax in the shade; there's a full programme until 10pm, so pace yourself.

As it gets dark, Pride morphs into an even bigger party. Venues like *Ferry*, *Perron*, or *Tech Noir* are the places to be for the (after)party, providing a good time until early into the morning.

Whether your idea of celebrating Pride involves hitting the club until late at night or watching queer arthouse cinema, you can be certain of one thing: there's a place for you in Rotterdam Pride – and you won't forget it any time soon.

Blaak cube houses

LISTINGS

STAY

citizenM Rotterdam Gelderseplein 50; citizenm.com/hotels/europe/rotterdam/rotterdam-hotel. Modern hotel with stylish and snug rooms that come with comfortable beds. You'll find one of the better hotel breakfasts in town here.

Hotel Not Hotel Rotterdam Schaatsbaan 83; hotelnothotelrotterdam.com. Unique hotel offering art exhibition-style hotel room experiences, like a vertical swimming pool or a gingerbread house – this one has to be seen to be believed. Some rooms are hidden behind bookshelves and mirrors. Conveniently located a stone's throw from the main train station, you can be downtown in minutes.

King Kong Hostel Witte de Withstraat 74; kingkonghostel.com. Located on the hippest street in town, this designer hostel offers stylish rooms (both private and shared) with lots of natural light, plus a spacious bar/café.

Mainport Hotel Leuvehaven 77; mainporthotel.com. This 5-star wellness hotel is right on the banks of the River Mass, providing breathtaking views of the Rotterdam skyline. This is a solid choice for visitors who want to go all out.

New York Koninginnenhoofd 1; hotelnewyork.com. This distinctive, four-star hotel occupies the grand and sympathetically modernised early twentieth-century former head office of a shipping line. All the rooms are well appointed and many have smashing river views. It's situated across from the city centre on the south bank of the Nieuwe Maas – a 10min walk from Wilhelminaplein metro station.

nHow Rotterdam Wilhelminakade 137; nh-hotels.nl/hotel/nhow-rotterdam. Located in a new building complex, this state-of-the-art hotel boasts one of the best views of the Maas River and Erasmus Bridge from its lovely outdoor terrace.

Stayokay Hostel Rotterdam Overblaak 85–87; stayokay.com/en/hostel/rotterdam. For a once-in-a-lifetime experience, stay in one of Rotterdam's iconic cube houses-turned-hostel. Unforgettable views to be found here!

Lilith Coffee

EAT

Alfredo's Taqueria Goudsesingel 204; alfredostaqueria.nl. This is one of the few taco places in town worth making a stop for. In addition to a respectable menu, you'll find several tequilas and mezcals to pair with dinner.

Hamburg Witte de Withstraat 94B; restauranthamburg. nl. For arguably the best burgers in town, visit this tiny yet bustling restaurant. Almost all burgers can be made with a meat replacement for veggies and vegans.

Koekela Nieuwe Binnenweg 79A; koekela.nl. You'll be hard-pressed to find a Rotterdammer that doesn't know Koekela. Perhaps the most popular local bakery in town, it serves up American-style sweets, with gluten-free and vegan options as well.

Lilith Nieuwe Binnenweg 125H; lilithcoffee.nl. Perhaps the original Rotterdam brunch location, this no-reservation veggie spot has the fluffiest pancakes in town. On Tuesdays, you can have a bottomless brunch for a modest sum.

Restaurant Fitzgerald Gelderseplein 49; restaurantfitzgerald.com. This Michelin-star restaurant is known for having an extensive collection of wine collection and creative flavour pairings. Try the pigeon, their signature dish.

San Frou Frou Proveniersstraat 29A; sansfroufrou. nl. Authentic, tiny French bistro just to the north of Central Station serving "no bullsh*t" food. The owners serve up surprising flavour combinations paired with delicious wines while ensuring an intimate dining experience.

Viva Afrika Nieuwe Binnenweg 153A/B; vivaafrika. nl. Homey, colourful East African spot focused on Ethiopian and Eritrean cuisine. This is the place to try more adventurous dishes like crocodile or ostrich.

Williams Canteen William Boothlaan 5A; williams-canteen.com. Tucked away in the city centre you'll find this modern kitchen that serves wholesome brunches, and natural, organic wines all with gorgeous and artful presentation.

DRINK

#Wunderbar Boomgaardsstraat 71; worm.org/spaces/wunderbar. *#Wunderbar* is an alternative, underground-style bar serving organic drinks and a 100% vegan menu. Keep an eye on the agenda of the main space, *Worm* – curious, interesting events often take place in this experimental cultural centre.

Ballroom Witte de Withstraat 88b; ballroomrotterdam.nl. With over 160 gins to be matched with a dozen tonics, this is the largest gin collection in Europe. If you can, try to bag a table in the gorgeous garden oasis in the back.

Bar Loge 90 Schiedamsedijk 4; loge90.nl. This kitschy LGBTQ+ dive bar is extremely popular amongst locals for after-work drinks, as it is with an ever-changing roster of tourists. All are treated with the same friendly welcome by the ever-lovely staff.

By Jarmusch Goudsesingel 64; byjarmusch.nl. Though it's technically an upscale American-style diner, fans of unlimited filter coffee or anyone in need of a caffeine boost should stop here for a cup (or five) of java.

Hopper Coffee Rotterdam Two locations; hoppercoffee.nl. Large, open concrete space that serves exceptionally good coffee. Almost all of the baked goods are made in-house, and it's an ideal spot to get some afternoon work done.

Kaapse Maria Mauritsweg 52; kaapsebrouwers.nl. *Kaapse Brouwers* is a well-known local microbrewery in town; their little sister serves up small plates paired along with their beers. *Kaapse Maria* is a great spot for lovers of sour beer in particular.

Spikizi Bar Zwarte Paardenstraat 91a; spikizibar.com. A trendy cocktail bar just off the Witte de Withstraat, offering playful and sexy cocktails. The staff are extremely knowledgeable without being stuffy about it. No reservations, so just walk on in.

Wijnbaar Janssen en van Dijk Westewagenstraat 58; wijnbarjanssenenvandijk.nl. No-nonsense wine bar serving traditional Dutch snacks and sandwiches. Excellent spot to people watch on a sultry summer day.

Hotel New York

DANCE

Bonaparte Nieuwe Binnenweg 117A; cafe-bonaparte. business.site. This LGBTQ+ bar is a great place to frequent drag shows or kick off a legendary night out.

Café Strano Van Oldenbarneveldstraat 154; facebook. com/strano010. Recognised by Rotterdammers because of its bright red leather couches, this trendy LGBTQ+ bar has long been a staple in the Rotterdam queer scene. Party as late as 6am at the weekend.

Ferry Westblaak 127; ferryrotterdam.com. One of the main hotspots for the LGBTQ+ community, here you'll find karaoke, drag and more. Also open during the day.

Now&Wow Club Maashaven Zuidzijde 1; maassilo. com/now-and-wow-club. This expansive club is located in an old industrial building; these eccentric parties are the place to see and be seen.

PERRON Schiestraat 42; perron.nl. "Lots of smoke, little light" – that's *Perron*'s slogan. The underground techno nightclub has preserved some of Rotterdam's earlier grit, while providing excellent acoustics.

SHOP

Afrikaanderplein Market Afrikaanderplein; marktenmarkten.nl/markt/markt-afrikaanderplein-in-zuid/44. Open Wednesdays and Saturdays, this Rotterdam South market is a veritable melting pot of all nationalities, where you can find fruits, vegetables, and other goods from across the globe.

De Bijenkorf Coolsingel 105; debijenkorf.nl/rotterdam. For all your luxury needs, a visit to the Bijenkorf store is in order; it's home to international brands like Prada, Gucci, and Louis Vitton. If that sounds way out of your budget, the nearby shopping district of Lijnbaan has more affordable international chains.

Demonfuzz Records Nieuwe Binnenweg 86; demonfuzz.com. Excellent record store in the city centre boasting a large collection of vinyls. Extremely helpful staff can guide you through your purchases, especially if you're looking for a gift.

KKEC Beurtraverse 186; kkec.nl. This sprawling gift shop is the perfect place to find unique cards, prints,

Delfshaven

Fenix Food Factory

and other unexpected gifts, like date night coupons or lucky golden cats.

ReShare Store Korte Hoogstraat 11–1; resharestore. nl/winkels/reshare-store-rotterdam. Look fashionable while being sustainable by shopping at this second-hand clothing store, part of the Salvation Army. Large selection of clothes, all for very reasonable prices.

Zwaanshals Although it's not right in the city centre, this quaint shopping street has a plethora of stylish vintage and design stores to browse through. End your shopping escapade at the Zaagmolenkade and soak in the waterfront views.

DO

De Doelen Schouwburgplein 50; dedoelen.nl. While it's often visited for its classical or jazz concerts (roughly 600 a year!), this multipurpose venue offers music jams, art expositions, and many other exciting and quirky cultural events.

Delfshaven en.rotterdam.info/locations/historic-delfshaven-en-2. Famous for being one of the only parts of the old city that wasn't destroyed during the World War II bombing, this canal-lined district is home to many gorgeous shops and cafés. Have a beer and a bite to eat at *Stadsbrouwerij De Pelgrim*, right next to where the Pilgrims set sail for America.

Fenix Food Factory Nico Koomanskade 1025; fenixfoodfactory.nl. A sunny Rotterdam day calls for a leisurely stroll along the river with this location as your destination. Here you'll find several hip stores serving craft beers, natural wine, and artisanal baked goods. Sitting outside will reward you with the stunning views of the Rotterdam skyline and Erasmus Bridge.

Vroesenpark Stadhoudersweg 181; en.rotterdam. info/locations/vroesenpark-en. No summer trip to Rotterdam is complete without a visit to this city park in Rotterdam North. It's a gorgeously landscaped outdoor space, a perfect place for a laid-back picnic or barbeque with pals. There are often festivals held here in summer.

STOCKHOLM

Summer

Anyone with even a sporadic knowledge of LGBTQ+ rights in Europe would put Sweden pretty high on the list when it comes to inclusivity. It is unsurprising therefore that Stockholm lives up to its proud claim of being "the world's most open city". One of the first countries to decriminalise homosexuality in 1944, and to legalise fully equal marriage in 2010, Stockholm continuously proves itself to be one of the most welcoming destinations for LGBTQ+ people. On top of its inclusion and celebration of the LGBTQ+ community, Stockholm simultaneously manages to tick culture, history, nature, cuisine and nightlife boxes, all wrapped up in one well-connected package.

HISTORY

Officially founded in 1252, the history of Stockholm is a twisting narrative of the kind of repeated overthrowing and recapturing that you would expect from a political and royal residence made up of fourteen islands. From the seventeenth century onwards, increasing revenue from trade and industrialism funded a boom in building which led to some of the beautiful historic architecture we see in Stockholm today. During this time the central government departments were officially located here, and the city became an independent administrative unit. The old city walls were torn down, and new districts grew up north and south of the "city between the bridges".

When fires destroyed large parts of the city, in the eighteenth century, stone buildings were constructed to replace the old wooden houses. With new architectural opportunities, a significant amount of the city was designed specifically to allow its residents access to light, fresh air and nature, which has also remained a feature to this day. By the 1800s, Stockholm had become the cultural centre of Sweden; many of its literary societies and scientific academies date from this time.

Stockholm has also been the backdrop to many of the legal and social LGBTQ+ historical milestones which make it such a friendly city (and indeed, make Sweden such a friendly country) to visit. In 1944 same-sex activity and relationships were legalised in Sweden, 23 years before the same happened in the UK and 59 years before the US. Sweden was also one of the first countries to legalise gay marriage in 2009; you can visit the Swedish parliament buildings in Stockholm to see the place where the marriage bill made history by passing uncontested and supported unanimously by the Swedish church.

Today, Stockholm has the air of a grand European capital yet on a small, Scandinavian scale. It's a vibrant and instantly likeable city, where water and green space dominate the landscape. However, there are still plenty of distinctly urban attractions that provide delightful diversions for any visitor to the city, from elegant museums and royal palaces to achingly cool bars and clubs.

The ABBA Museum

ICON

Ascending to the Swedish throne in 1632 aged just six, Queen Christina of Sweden is an almost mythical figure of royal history that scholars have been arguing over for centuries; depictions range from a headstrong troublemaker to a feminist 400 years ahead of her time. She was likely to have been both.

Christina abdicated the throne at the age of 27, citing her refusal to convert from Catholicism to the Lutheran church, a sense of revulsion towards the idea of marriage and an aversion to the pressures of her role as reasons. She spent the next part of her life plotting (unsuccessfully) to steal the crowns of no less than three different kingdoms. Stories of her behaviour during this time are rousing and chaotic, including having a French Marquis beheaded for betraying her plot to become the Queen of Naples.

Christina also raised eyebrows with her gender expression and sexuality. She reportedly "walked like a man, sat and rode like a man, and could eat and swear like the roughest soldiers", routinely shocking the courts she visited.

Christina's self-described "bed-fellow" Countess Ebba Sparre, with whom she shared "a long-time intimate companionship", was also a source of repeated controversy. A lack of language to describe LGBTQ+ relationships until relatively modern times means that there are many historical relationships that we would now categorise as LGBTQ+ portrayed contemporaneously as "close friendships". For this reason, we can never know for sure if Christina was a member of the LGBTQ+ community, but what we do know is that she held the same defiant attitude and refusal to be anything but herself which the modern LGBTQ+ community also embraces. Take a tour of the Royal Palaces during your trip to learn more about her and Stockholm's tumultuous royal history.

HIGHLIGHTS

Stockholm presents an incredibly varied experience for any traveller, including an unexpected descent into nature just 20 minutes away from Stockholm itself Leaving behind the city, the Stockholm Archipeligo is a breathtaking collection of 30,000 islands covering 650 square miles. This area of outstanding natural beauty is best viewed (and in most places only accessible) by boat, with options ranging from efficient ferry systems to private tours. As you cruise through the islands, keep an eye out for jealousy-inducing summer houses, as well as the occasional Viking-style ship sailing through on tours throughout the summer.

The islands themselves are home to everything from working ports and traditional hotels to private houses, abandoned military fortifications and eco-glamping pods. The latter at Island Lodge is the epitome of environmentally friendly lodgings with a luxury twist; private cabins, a woodfired jacuzzi and foraged catering courtesy of the hosts.

On the other end of the scale, Stockholm's annual LGBTQ+ Pride celebrations in August are unmissable. Stockholm Pride has been officially running since 1998, with over half a million spectators and 40,000 participants in the parade, the largest Pride celebration in Scandinavia. Combining the spirit of protest with celebration, the parade features community and political organisations more than corporations. With typical Swedish understatedness, barriers are minimal and onlookers are welcome to join the parade at any point. Culminating in Pride Park, paying guests will be treated to an all-day (and most of the night) party, with the best Swedish performers headlining

Options for celebrating Pride in Stockholm are endless, with the whole city hanging out its rainbow flags; as well as the parade and afterparty in the park, you can choose between brunch, all-day happy hours, and boat trips. With family-friendly options too, Stockholm in August is a must for any LGBTQ+ traveller.

Djurgården Island

LISTINGS

STAY

Af Chapman Flaggmansvägen 8. This smart square-rigged 1888 ship – a landmark in its own right – has views over Gamla Stan that are unsurpassed at the price. One of the quirkiest places to stay in Stockholm, though advance reservations are a must. Make sure you get a room aboard the boat, rather than one on dry land.

Anno 1647 Mariagränd 3; anno1647.se;. Located in a seventeenth-century building, with pine floors and period furniture, this hotel is an oasis of elegance and Gustavian charm and has perfect views of the colourful roofs and buildings of Gamla Stan.

Diplomat Strandvägen; diplomathotel.com. One of the city's most famous hotels, this Art Nouveau town house offers individually decorated rooms with elegant furnishings, lovely high ceilings and wonderful views over Stockholm's inner harbour, though the rooms and suites don't come cheap.

Hotel Hasselbacken Hazeliusbacken 20, hasselbacken.com. Recently renovated and with 113 hotel rooms, a restaurant, a bar and a relaxation area, the *Hasselbacken* has a rich queer history and is now owned by Björn Ulvaeus's company, the of ABBA fame. A refined hotel with fabulous marble bathrooms – not to mention that the restaurant was where the delicious Hasselback potato dish was first cooked up. Well-located with excellent food and a historic setting.

Hotel Rival Mariatorget 3, SE-118 91; rival.se. Owned by ABBA legend Benny Andersson, the Rival is a beautiful boutique hotel overlooking a picturesque Stockholm square. With a glamorous art-deco bar and spacious yet cosy rooms, the Rival is perfect for Stockholm stays all year round. Some rooms have balconies overlooking the square, and the building includes a bistro and a bakery.

Hotel Skeppsholmen Gröna gången 1, 111 49; hotelskeppsholmen.se. On a peaceful and lush island in the middle of the bustling city lies a 300+-year-old historic house dating back to 1699, today home to the award-winning, LGBTQ-run *Hotel Skeppsholmen*, a

modern and eco-friendly hotspot situated right on the waterfront.

Island Lodge Bergholmen, 185 99 Vaxholm; islandlodge.se. Inspired by your visit to the Stockholm archipelago? Take your trip one step further with a stay on one of the islands itself. *Island Lodge* is a fully eco-friendly luxury glamping experience, complete with bathrooms and an on-site kitchen.

Jumbo Stay Jumbovägen 4, Arlanda Airport; jumbostay.com. Flying visit? Consider treating yourself to a night at a working hotel and hostel built into the shell of an old Boeing 747. Up front in the flight deck, with two adjustable beds and a flat-screen TV, the Cockpit Suite is the reserve of first-class travellers. Thankfully there's cheaper accommodation further back in the fuselage.

Lord Nelson Västerlånggatan 22; lordnelsonhotel. se. This is one of the narrowest hotels in Sweden at just 5m wide. It's stuffed full of naval antiques and curiosities including an original letter from Nelson to Lady Hamilton. Rooms are small with ship's teak floorboards and lots of mahogany and brass.

M/S Monika Kungsholms Strand 133. One of Stockholm's more intimate "floatels", this charming wooden boat from 1908 bobs around just off Kungsholmen's north shore. There are just three quirky but compact rooms; the whole boat can be rented out on request.

Sven Vintappare Sven Vintappares Gränd 3; hotelsvenvintappare.se. Housed in a charming building from 1607, with just seven rooms, all decorated in Swedish Gustavian style. The bathrooms are to die for, their granite floors and marble walls completing the sense of royal elegance.

Tre Små Rum Högbergsgatan 81; tresmarum.se. A clean, comfy option in the heart of Södermalm; the seven simple basement rooms with shared bathrooms are very popular, so book in advance. A help-yourself breakfast from the kitchen fridge is available.

Villa Dagmar Nybrogatan 25-27, 114 39; hotelvilladagmar.com. Part of Stockholm's luxury hotel scene in chic Östermalm, *Villa Dagmar* is an intimate, LGBTQ-owned boutique luxury hotel with 70 individually designed suites as well as a range of

Stadion metro station is a "cave station" with walls painted with rainbows

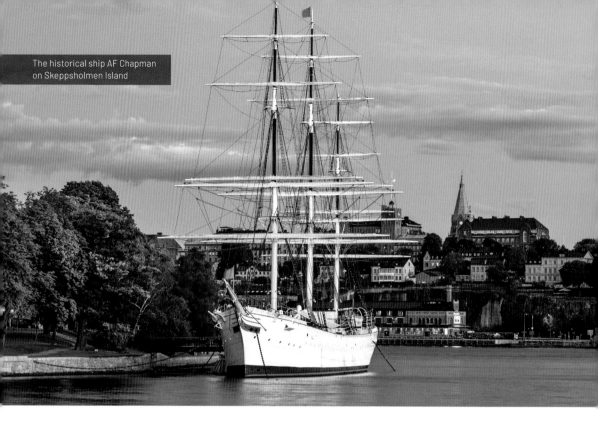

The historical ship AF Chapman on Skeppsholmen Island

dining experiences, right next to Stockholm's iconic Östermalms Saluhall.

EAT

B.A.R. Blasieholmsgatan 4A; restaurangbar.se/en. *The* place to eat fish in Stockholm. Go up to the fish counter and choose the piece you'd like to eat. There are also meat dishes on offer, including a steak tartare.

Barobao Hornsgatan 66; barobao.se. Decorated with hanging plants, this small, Asian-inspired restaurant serves beautifully soft steamed buns loaded with everything from pork belly to slow-cooked beef with green apple chutney. Veggie options are available too.

Blå Porten Djurgårdsvägen 64; blaporten.com. Glorious café set in a glass-walled building overlooking a courtyard with outdoor seating around an old fountain. The open sandwiches and lunches here are Provençal-influenced and include a wide choice of quiches, pies, salads and soups, including vegetarian options.

Cirkus Djurgårdsslätten 43-45, 115 21; cirkus.se. Located in the Royal Djurgården district of Stockholm, *Cirkus* was inaugurated in 1892 to house the many prominent circus companies of the time. Over the years, it became an arena for all types of activities, including concerts, congresses, TV productions, and above all for theatre, musicals and shows. The restaurant serves Michelin-star quality vegetarian and vegan food, paired with cocktails and a fantastic wine list; not one to be missed.

Crêperie Fyra Knop Svartensgatan 4. Excellent, affordable galettes and crêpes, served in this tiny French-owned and -run restaurant which consists of one intimate little room with rough maroon walls, battered wooden chairs and tables and an ancient Stella Artois advertisement.

The Hills Götgatan 29, 116 21; thehillsstockholm.se. This LGBTQ-owned brasserie and trendy Stockholm hotspot marks the highest point in the lively neighbourhood of Götgatsbacken, Södermalm. Serving mainly French food with Scandinavian influences, *The Hills* has a great wine list with many organic wines from all over the world, served in a restaurant with interior design by famous Swedish designer Jonas Bohlin.

Kalf & Hansen Mariatorget 2; kalfochhansen.se. This tiny, casual place, overseen by a celebrity chef, specialises in organic fast food with a Nordic twist. Choose between fresh meat, fish and veggie options, served up with seasonal vegetables and bread.

K25 Kungsgatan 25; k25.nu/en;. Bustling modern food court stuffed to bursting with cheap and delicious food, from dumplings and burgers to steaming bowls of Vietnamese *pho*.

Mälarpaviljongen Norr Mälarstrand 64, 112 35; ny.malarpaviljongen.se. On the banks of Lake Mälaren, you will find *Mälarpaviljongen*: an idyllic, green oasis, where the rainbow flag is a strong symbol but where everyone is welcome. You can relax in the sun, take a swim in the blue waters of Mälaren or just enjoy a coffee or a refreshing drink – they offer a large selection of beers and wines as well as serving lunch

and dinner. Open from the beginning of April until the end of September, *Mälarpaviljongen* is LGBTQ owned and donates a proportion of its profits to global LGBTQ first-response causes around the world such as in Chechnya and Uganda. It also sponsors LGBTQ refugees to work at the venue to help them integrate into Swedish society.

Mamas & Tapas Scheelegatan 3; tapas.nu. Consistently one of Stockholm's best tapas restaurants and the place to come for authentic and reasonably priced Spanish cuisine. Here you'll find tasty tapas, delicious paella and a good-value mixed meat platter including pork, steak, chorizo and vegetables.

Pelikan Blekingegatan 40; pelikan.se. Atmospheric beer hall (turn right from the entrance hall) with excellent traditional food, including *pytt i panna* and meatballs "as big as golf balls". Left of the entrance hall is a smarter restaurant, though still based on wholesome home cooking.

Urban Deli Nytorget 4. Attached to an impressively well-stocked deli, this chic bistro is always busy;

Seafood dishes at *B.A.R.*

there's a handful of tables, plus stools at a long bar. Try the weekend brunch, which includes everything from fresh oysters to a classic Swedish fish stew.

DRINK AND DANCE

Backdoor Johanneshov, Arenavägen 75, 121 77; facebook.com/clubbackdoorstockholm. Scandinavia's biggest gay bar; and that's enough said!

Hellstens Glashus Wollmar Yxkullsgatan 13, 118 50; hellstensglashus.se. A member of the *Hellsten Hotels* family, *Hellstens Glashaus* is situated in the heart of what is today the most interesting, hip and popular area of Stockholm. Behind the 7-metre glass facade you'll also find a restaurant whose floor showcases exposed bedrock from thousands of years ago.

Moxy Hökstigen 114, 182 70; klubbmoxy.se. Sweden's largest lesbian club, *Moxy* is a huge part of the LGBTQ+ nightlife scene and has been around for over 10 years running dinners, cruises and theme nights.

Secret Garden Kornhamnstorg 59, 111 2; secretgardensthlm.se. Twice awarded "Gay Place of The Year" by QX Magazine, *Secret Garden* welcomes all of the LGBTQ+ community with friendly staff and a cosy, warmly-lit, colourful bar.

Sidetrack Wollmar Yxkullsgatan 7, 118 50; sidetrack. nu. Central gay bar and restaurant of the Stockholm gay scene with a male-leaning clientele.

SHOP

BRUNO Götgatan 36, 118 26; brunogallerian.se. A small shopping centre with a big heart, even though *Bruno* is located at the vibrant Götgatan, it feels like a hidden gem. Locals, tourists, fashion lovers and cocktail connoisseurs have found their special place here. Explore Swedish brands like Hope and Aplace, or enjoy the warm atmosphere with a department store vibe. The rooftop bar is also a great spot for a summer drink.

Södermalm Södermalm; visitstockholm.com/see-do/ attractions/see-the-sights-of-sodermalm. Sprawling Södermalm island has a relaxed, creative vibe, with artsy shops, eclectic cafés and the stylish Fotografiska, a contemporary photo gallery in a former industrial building by the water. Head there for Swedish fashion, vintage and homewares.

DO

ABBA The Museum Djurgårdsvägen 68, 115 21; abbathemuseum.com. ABBA is one of the world's most

The Royal Palace

Skansen open air museum
on Djurgården Island

successful pop groups with more than 380 million albums sold and of course an intrinsic part of queer culture. At this museum dedicated to their legacy, you can get up on stage with ABBA, sing karaoke in the Polar Studios and dance in an ABBA music video. You'll also find ABBA's spectacular costumes, gold records and original items for a fully immersive experience.

Nationalmuseum Södra Blasieholmshamnen 2; nationalmuseum.se/en. The striking waterfront Nationalmuseum contains an impressive collection of Swedish and European arts from the late medieval period to the present day, contained on three floors.

Royal Djurgården 115 21; royaldjurgarden.se. Located in the heart of Stockholm, Royal Djurgården is the Stockholmer's escape from an often-hectic life. Once upon a time a royal hunting ground, the Djurgården of today offers Scandinavia's biggest attractions. It has

welcomed visitors from every part of the world for over 400 years.

The Royal Palace Kungliga slottet, 107 70; theroyalpalace.se. His Majesty The King's official residence, the palace has over 600 rooms, and the well-preserved interior provides historical insight from the 1700s. The Royal Apartments also include the Hall of State with Queen Christina's silver throne and the Apartments of the Orders of Chivalry, which houses a permanent collection of the regal orders.

Skansen Djurgårdsslätten 49-51, 115 21; skansen. se/en. Explore the world's oldest open-air museum, showcasing the whole of Swedish culture with traditional houses, farmsteads and beautiful gardens from all over the country. Skansen is home to wild Nordic animals and several Swedish rare breeds that are also included in conservation projects.

Flying the rainbow flag
across from the Acropolis

ATHENS
Autumn

Sprawling, vibrant and surprisingly edgy, Athens is so much more than its postcard image of ancient monuments and learned philosophers. Of course, these ancient buildings are unmissable, but if history isn't your bag, there's still so much to see and do in Greece's capital. A trip to Athens will see your schedule crammed tighter than the crowds at the Parthenon; think historic landmarks, culinary gems and underrated neighbourhoods chock-full of world-class street art, eccentric cafés and stellar speakeasies that have become an unofficial Athens institution.

HISTORY

Athens has been inhabited continuously for over seven thousand years, and is the epitome of acceptance and diversity. Whilst there's always progress to be made, the Greeks have done a pretty stellar job when it comes to all things queer. In fact, it's well documented that in ancient Athens, homosexuality was not just tolerated – it was a way of life. Even the ancient philosophical texts spoke openly of homosexuality; for example, Plato's *Symposium* referenced "men who take pleasure in having sex with men and uniting with them." These attitudes can still be seen today in statues, sculptures, literature and plays of the time, all of which are testament to progressive attitudes in ancient Athens.

Wander through the streets of Athens today and you will be hard-pressed not to find hallmarks of this free-thinking landscape of the past, from Athens's archeological sites and impressive museums to neighbourhoods like Gazi, which is home to a fantastic selection of LGBTQ+ friendly cafés and bars. It can also be found in other cultural offerings, including the city's Pride festival, the first of which took place officially in 2005.

Of course, it's not always been plain sailing and sadly prejudice and homophobic attitudes do still exist, despite Athens being widely recognised as a welcoming city. One sad instance of this abhorrent behaviour was the unthinkable murder of LGBTQ+ rights activist and drag performer Zak Kostopoulos in September 2018, which sparked a wider conversation on LGBTQ+ rights.

In 2022, two separate organisations – Athens Pride and Athens Queer Collective – joined forces to form a dedicated organization called the Athens Pride and Queer Collective. Not only does it now organise the world-renowned Pride festival, but it also helps to raise awareness and affect change for members of the queer communities in the greater Athens area.

ICON

In 2021, Nicholas Yatromanolakis became the first openly gay person to serve as a Greek government minister. The Athens native was appointed as the new deputy minister of culture after previously serving as the culture ministry's general secretary.

Yatromanolakis studied Political Science and International Relations at Panteion University in Athens before going on to study for a master's degree in Public Policy at Harvard University in America. His appointment as a prominent political figure was widely lauded as a historic moment for the LGBTQ+ community in terms of political representation in Greece, and indeed the world over. Speaking on his choice to be an openly gay politician, Yatromanolakis says, "Everyone claims they want honest politicians. Being open about my identity is part of being honest. Visibility matters, especially in traditionally conservative environments like politics that have the power to affect the lives of many people."

Yatromanolakis has been a strong advocate for the queer community and their rights throughout his political career, as well as striving to support the Greek creative sector. He campaigns to develop educational initiatives that will help artists and creatives with their work which includes dance, film, literature and art.

Yatromanolakis loves the city in which he has lived for several years and is proud to call his home. He says, "Athens is a friendly, safe, exciting, and very diverse city where there's always something for everyone, any time of the year, any time of the day. It has a lively night scene, fantastic restaurants, eclectic stores, unique landmarks, and a vibrant art scene." When asked what one unusual thing visitors to Athens shouldn't miss, Yatromanolakis says, "In the summertime one should definitely experience the magic of the Athenian open-air cinemas. Tucked between residential buildings, often filled with bougainvillaea and sprawling green, it's a unique treat!"

The Acropolis

Graffiti in the streets of Athens

HIGHLIGHTS

As well as being a great gay-friendly destination, Athens is also one of the coolest cities in the world. From stellar speakeasies to spectacular street art, the Greek capital is certainly a force to be reckoned with.

One particular highlight is the street art scene, which is as colourful as the remarkable city itself; evocative and vibrant, the artists have showcased visual storytelling techniques to express themselves, thereby providing the perfect juxtaposition of gorgeous colours against the gritty backdrop of industrial buildings, as well as ancient citadels and monuments.

A walking tour is a fantastic way to get to know Athens as well as getting the chance to see lots of works of art and find out about the history of the pieces and the artists who created them. Alternative Athens (alternativeathens.com) offers lots of small-group themed walking tours, and is particularly strong on street art.

Thematically, you can expect references to the city's ancient past in some of the artwork, and none more so than the owl mural that sits in a nondescript side street in the Metaxourgeio neighbourhood. Entitled *Knowledge Speaks, Wisdom Listens*, this mesmerising piece of art is one of the most iconic in the whole city and features a grey owl with huge amber eyes that seem to glow. The owl is the symbol of the ancient Greek goddess Athena from whom the Greek capital takes its name, and is also known as a symbol of wisdom – a characteristic for which Athens and its people are also well-known. The work is by the artist known as Wild Drawing or simply WD, a painter and muralist from Bali who has made his home in Athens. The Owl is not WD's only piece of artwork in the city; he has created several other pieces that are markedly political in their tone. You can find more of this work throughout on Instagram (instagram.com/wd_wilddrawing).

Athens has attracted many street artists from not just Greece, but all over the world. One fine example is the artist Simple G (instagram.com/simpleg1) who creates expansive pieces of work that can be spotted in locations all over the city. Most of Simple G's artworks are large, towering over the viewer as they stretch from the ground to the very tops of buildings. One standout is the piece entitled *So Many Books, So Little Time* in the Metaxourgeio district; the piece takes up the entire side of a building and shows a woman utterly captivated by a book, with another selection of books behind her. This is a nod to Athens's literary scene, both past and present, which is held in high regard all over the world.

In fact, Athens is a city that is fit-to-bursting with alternative art, and in recent years establishments have been popping up that help cement the city's hip art scene. One such establishment is The Queer Archive (Papadiamantopoulou 83; thequeerarchive. com), a dedicated art gallery and production house that is working to create a community of emerging and established artists. It acts as a unique platform that showcases engaging and progressive contemporary art of all kinds that reflects modern queer culture – what's more, it often hosts events including lectures and Q&As with artists, as well as immersive parties and gigs. There's also a fantastic online shop where you can buy various products with different pieces of art emblazoned on them.

Since 2021, the owners of the gallery have also produced The Queer Archive Festival which takes place annually in May with the support of Stegi-Onassis Foundation. The Queer Archive Festival is quickly growing into a cultural meeting point and creative hub for like-minded individuals to come together and collaborate. Taking place over almost two weeks, the festival incorporates a real plethora of events including club nights, workshops, exhibition openings, performances, film screenings, talks, dinners and parties.

LISTINGS

STAY

A is for Athens Miaouli 2; aforathens.com. Centrally located above scenic and vibrant Monastiraki Square, *A is for Athens* is a stellar choice for travellers and a favourite among locals for drinks at its rooftop bar where you can enjoy staggering views of the city. Don't forget to try their standout cocktail, the intriguingly-named *Wear Sunscreen* which contains coconut and edible sunscreen. Yep, you read that right!

Altar Suites Astiggos 11; altarsuites.com. Discover classic charm and elegance at the boutique getaway that is *Altar Suites* in the neighbourhood of the Twelve Gods. Intimate and luxurious, this elegant hotel has the most breathtaking views of the Acropolis and is a relaxing retreat with an achingly-cool minimalistic modern style.

Dave Red Athens Veranzerou 25 & M. Kotopouli; brownhotels.com/Athens/Davered. Funky design hotel in this otherwise neglected neighbourhood (although it's a short walk to the metro which will take you into more happening parts of town). Housed in the Communist Party's former headquarters, it pays homage to this in its (red) decoration. There is a fabulous rooftop bar and jacuzzi which are great for mingling.

Fresh Hotel Sofokléous 26; freshhotel.gr. LGBTQ+-friendly, glossy, designer hotel in the heart of the market area, with lavish use of colour, elegant furnishings and great lighting and bathrooms – though some rooms are tiny. Facilities include bike hire and an elegant rooftop pool, bar and restaurant.

innAthens G Souri 3; innathens.com. Shaped like a triangle around a gorgeous courtyard with a lemon tree at its centre, this boutique hotel has 22 suites with quirky furnishings such as off-cuts of marble for tables and sink backsplashes. Although in a relatively

A view of Acropolis from a rooftop coffee shop in Monastiraki Square

People dining outside in the Plaka district

busy neighbourhood, it's a quiet oasis after a day's sightseeing.

Moon & Stars Platia Agion Asomaton; moonandstarsathens.com. In an enviable location in Thissío overlooking the Acropolis and by the Beit Shalom Synagogue lies this lovely family boutique hotel, which offers five suites in a stunning renovated former toy maker's workshop and residence. The roof terrace is a great place to relax and watch the world go by, as is the internal courtyard.

Shila Mantzarou 10; shila-athens.com. In the heart of Kolonkai, surrounded by boutique shops and restaurants, Shila is housed in an old mansion and offers six uniquely designed shabby chic suites; it also often hosts fashion shoots and evening events. Local Greek designers showcase their clothes in the rooms and are for sale. Breakfast, which is made using locally sourced products, is served on their relaxing roof terrace with a plethora of plant life.

St George Lycabettus Lifestyle Hotel Kleomenous 2; sgl.gr. Offering panoramic views over Athens to the Acropolis and beyond, this luxury boutique hotel sits at the foot of Lycabettus Hill in the heart of the city. From the impressive views at the rooftop bar to enjoying a relaxing film at its very own 30-seat mini-cinema, you won't be short of things to do even if you never leave the building.

Sweet Home Athens Patroou 5; sweethomehotel. gr. A small boutique hotel in a lovingly restored Neoclassical building, with six rooms (including doubles and triples) over three floors. The interesting and lovely touches like geranium-clad balconies, the wooden staircase, gorgeous artwork and various antiquities make up for the rather small room sizes in this traditional old home.

Vasi Vlachava 5; vasihotels.com. Intimate minimalism greets you at this family run boutique hotel – originally an old tissue factory situated in a side street off the main Athinais Street, not far from the Central Market. With 18 rooms over eight floors, choose one at the back that offers Acropolis views or spoil yourself and book their jacuzzi room.

EAT

Acropolis Museum Restaurant Acropolis Museum, Dhionysíou Areopayítou; theacropolismuseum.gr. Café serving light meals such as octopus with pasta, as well as salads and cakes – the quality is superb. Don't go to the ground-floor café; instead, grab a free pass to the second floor where the menu is the same but with views of the Acropolis.

Avocado Níkis 30; avocadoathens.com. Vegetarian and vegan café in the heart of Athens offering a range of dishes such as homemade guacamole, which goes deliciously with their sweet potato chips. Pastas such as penne avocado come with gluten-free cream, and their chickpea burgers are huge – all for reasonable prices. Be sure to try one of their many juices, too.

Café Avissinia Kynétou 7. With two floors and a delicious, modern take on traditional Greek cooking (wild boar meatballs, for example, or mussel *pilaf*),

Café Avissinia is always busy, with a local alternative crowd. There's live music most weekday evenings and weekend lunchtimes.

Ellyz Café Agiou Fillipou 11; ellyz.gr. It's time to think pink! From delicate macarons to pastel-hued lattes, it's hard not to fall in love with the blooming marvellous decor at *Ellyz Café*. An unequivocal floral wonderland, this is a fabulous fairytale spot to enjoy brunch, lunch, or an afternoon drink.

Karamanlidika Sokrátous & Evripidou 1. In the heart of the Bazaar area, *Karamanlidika* is an excellent deli and mezédhes restaurant that makes your mouth water from the minute you set foot inside. On display are meats sourced from regions around Greece plus aged cheeses, while the *mezédhes* include spicy sausage and *pastirma* pie with filo pastry served with eggs.

Katsourbos Amínta 2, Pangráti; katsourbos.gr. Cretan food is fashionable in Athens, and this modern-looking

The *Acropolis Museum Restaurant*

place serves tasty food created from ingredients sourced from the island – try the baked Cretan Cheese with honey. Relatively expensive, but so worth it.

Kimolia Iperidou 5; instagram.com/kimoliaartcafe. This neoclassical 1920S building houses a gem of a café. Enjoy your coffee, a selection of teas and homemade cake or, later on, a cocktail in this family-run business in eclectic surroundings with vintage furniture and surrounded by local art. A great place for meeting friends and co-working.

Nice 'n' Easy Skoufá 60; niceneasy.gr. Very popular with locals and tourists alike, this organic restaurant has a film-star-themed contemporary Mediterranean menu. It breeds its own water buffalo on an organic farm in Northern Greece for dishes such as the gluten-free "Marvin Gay" burger or "Bruce Lee" spring rolls.

Nudie Foodie Eschilou 42; facebook.com/nudiefoodie psiri. Vegans and coeliacs rejoice! The *Nudie Foodie* is a quaint little café housed down a bustling lane in the Psiri neighbourhood. It's both vegan and gluten-free, as well as being ideal for those wanting to enjoy a healthy breakfast. The gluten-free heart-shaped waffles adorned with hundreds and thousands are simply to die for!

Oikonomou Kidantidon 32. Wonderful, traditional taverna where home-cooked food is served to packed pavement tables in summer. There's no menu, just a dozen or so inexpensive daily specials such as *pastitsio* (like lasagne, but with tubed pasta): check out what others are eating as the waiters may not know the names of some of the dishes in English.

Phita Ntourm 1; instagram.com/phitathens. Centred around seafood, Phita in the Neos Kosmos neighbourhood serves traditional Greek fare with a creative modern twist. Meticulously executed, choose from tasty taramasalata, succulent seafood such as grilled sardines and eel or pumpkin soup, amongst other delectable dishes. It is one of the best value-for-money restaurants in Athens and offers great service and a buzzing atmosphere.

Scholarhio Tripódhon 14; scholarhio.gr. Attractive, split-level *ouzerí* operating since 1935 with a summer terrace. It has a great selection of mezédhes brought out on trays so that you can point to the ones you fancy. Especially good are the flaming sausages, *bouréki* (thin pastry filled with ham and cheese) and grilled aubergine. The house red wine is good too.

DRINK

Rooster Pl. Agias Irinis 4; roostercafe.gr. Rooster is a gay-friendly, all-day café situated in the buzzing Agias Irinis square. From a delightful boozy brunch to nighttime drinks, *Rooster* is a great addition to the bar scene in Athens.

Shamone Club Konstantinoupoleos Ave. 46; shamone.gr. Beautifully decorated, this glitzy gay and lesbian bar transforms into a decadent nightclub after midnight. They host fabulous drag shows and throw themed parties, and not only are the drinks delicious, but it's a great place to dance all night long too!

DANCE

BeQueer Keleou 10; facebook.com/bequeerathens. *BeQueer* offers an inclusive and alternative clubbing experience which aims to unite the LGBTQ+ community. It also has a superb range of alternative drag shows and has one of the best vibes throughout the entire club scene in the city.

Koukles Club Drag Queen Show Zan Moreas 32; facebook.com/Kouklesclubathens. Run by trans women, *Koukles* is famous for its live drag shows, cabaret, and nightly shows of vibrant performances and comedy. This club plays a huge part of the local queer culture in the city, and no queer club-goers trip to Athens would be complete without a visit.

Noiz Konstantinoupóleos 78; instagram.com/noizclub_ath. Friendly lesbian bar and club with good international sounds and a welcoming atmosphere.

Sodade2 Triptolemou 10; instagram.com/sodade2. *Sodade2* is the most legendary nightclub for the LGBTQ+ community in Athens, offering a truly electric atmosphere. Favouring pop, trance and house music, this club deserves every accolade afforded it. It's worth noting that the popularity of this club means that you may have to queue on weekends, but it's worth it!

The ruins of ancient Hadrian's Library

Theatre of Dionysus

DO

Ancient sites The obvious thing to do in Athens is to visit some of the awe-inspiring ancient sites; if you are visiting several, the combined ticket is excellent value and covers the Acropolis, the Theatre of Dionysus, the Ancient Agora and the Roman Forum, as well as other minor sites such as the Lykeion, and Hadrian's Library.

Alexander Sauna Meg. Alexandrou 134; alexandersauna.com. The Gazi neighbourhood is synonymous with entertainment and nightlife, thanks to its medley of nightclubs, restaurants, shops and gay bars. It's also home to the Alexander Sauna which is the premium cruising spa in Athens.

Big Olive Walks: 'Tales of Same Sex Love' facebook. com/bigolivewalks. Immerse yourself in Big Olive's narratives about the queer history of Athens through a walking tour that takes you all around the city.

Catch a film Athens is a great place to catch a movie. In summer, dozens of outdoor screens spring up in every neighbourhood; they make for a quintessentially Greek film-going experience. Outdoor screens tend to concentrate on art-house and alternative offerings, classics and themed festival seasons. There are also plenty of regular indoor cinemas including a number in the centre, though many of these, with no air conditioning, close from mid-May to October. Films are almost always shown in the original language with Greek subtitles, though you may never hear the soundtrack above the din of locals cracking passatémpo (pumpkin seeds), drinking and chatting (sit near a speaker if you want to hear). Some good options to try include Cine Paris (Kydhathinéon 22, cineparis.gr), an outdoor screen in a rooftop setting with side view of the Acropolis, right in the heart of town, with first-run mainstream movies and the odd classic; Thission (Apostólou Pávlou 7; cine-thisio. gr), an old-fashioned outdoor summer theatre, with an Acropolis view; shows mainly arty new releases; and Zéphyros (Tróön 36), a smarter than most, trendy cinema showing arthouse and foreign-language movies as well as mainstream classics that is a particular favourite of Athenian thirtysomethings.

A couple at the Bologna Gay Pride Parade

BOLOGNA

Autumn

Bologna is known as *"la Dotta, la Grassa, la Rossa"* – "the learned, the fat, the red." Life in the city is centred around Bologna's ancient university, fuelled by the rich cuisine, and distinguished by the warm hues of the medieval houses and terracotta roofs as well as its left-wing politics. Arguably the most open and tolerant city in Italy and historically supportive of the LGBTQ+ community, Bologna also boasts leaning towers, world-class museums and fantastic food under its miles of covered walkways or *portici*. And, as you would expect in a city dominated by a university, there is also a vibrant nightlife scene, with many pubs, wine and cocktail bars.

HISTORY

Bologna is known for its medieval architecture, but underneath the cellars of many of its buildings are its Roman foundations, dating back to the second century BC. Bologna University, established in 1088, is thought to be the oldest in the Western world, and counts the poet Petrarch, the writer Umberto Eco and the astronomer Nicolaus Copernicus among its alumni. From the fifteenth century, Bologna developed a flourishing silk industry and refined its distinctive and delicious cuisine; a fmous dish you'll certainly have heard of is *spaghetti alla bolognese*, a version of which finds its roots in eighteenth-century Imola (some 20 miles or 33 kilometres outside of Bolgona) and which has taken on the city's name. The city also became renowned for its figurative art in the fourteenth and seventeenth centuries.

At the end of the nineteenth century, Italy decriminalised same-sex sexual activity. For decades afterwards, Italy became a refuge for homosexuals from other parts of Europe. However, the rise of fascism during the first half of the twentieth century meant that gay people were persecuted once more, both under Mussolini (who was prime minister between 1922 and 1943) and in the Italian social republic of 1943–45; a monument to the gay victims of the Nazi regime has stood in Bologna's Giardini di Villa Cassarini since 1990. Thousands of Bologna's citizens who died fighting the fascists in World War II are also commemorated at the city's Piazza del Nettuno.

In the post-war decades, Bologna became a communist stronghold in Italy's so-called "red belt"; it was during this period that "Red Bologna" became the Italian Left's stronghold and spiritual home, having evolved out of the resistance movement to German occupation. Consequently, Bologna's train station was singled out by Fascist groups in 1980 for a bomb attack

A morning view over Bologna

in Italy's worst postwar terrorist atrocity – a glassed-in jagged gash in the station wall commemorates the tragedy in which 84 people died. In subsequent decades, the city's political leanings have been less predictable, alt-hough its "leftist" reputation continues to stick.

Bologna's queer scene began to take shape in the 1970s alongside student uprisings, with the emergence of Italy's first ever gay club, the *Kinki* nightclub in Via Zamboni, as well as one of Italy's first gay collectives, called *Collettivo Frocialist Bolognese*. In 1982, Bologna became the first city in Italy to allow a municipal building to be used as an LGBTQ+ centre. The centre, known as *Il Cassero* is still in operation today in Via Don Giovanni Minzoni. It is home to the national headquarters of Arcigay, Italy's largest LGBTQ+ nonprofit organisation, which continues to promote and fight for LGBTQ+ rights. In 2021, Arcigay led widespread protests after the Italian Senate refused to pass a law which would have classified homophobic and transphobic attacks as hate crimes.

Today, Bologna is a thriving city whose light-engineering and high-tech industries have brought conspicuous wealth to the old brick palaces and atmospheric porticoed streets. It's well known for its food – which many would argue is the richest in the country – and for its aforementioned politics, and is certainly one of Italy's best-looking cities. Its centre is startlingly medieval in plan, a jumble of red brick, tiled roofs and balconies radiating out from the great central square of Piazza Maggiore. There are enough monuments and curi-osities for several days' leisured exploration, including plenty of small, quirky museums, some tremendously grand Gothic and Renaissance architecture and, most conspicuously, the Due Torri, the city's own "leaning towers". Thanks to the university, there's always something happening – be it theatre, music or just the café and bar scene, which is among northern Italy's most convivial – and that's really saying something.

ICON

Pier Paolo Pasolini was an openly gay Italian film director, poet, writer, journalist, playwright, novelist, translator and intellectual who was born in 1922 in Bologna's Via Borgonuovo; he would come to be known as one of the foremost intellectuals of twentieth-century Italy. He went to school at the Liceo Galvani in Via Castiglione and studied literature and philosophy at Bologna University, where his artistic vision was influenced by his art history professor, Roberto Longhi.

One of Italy's most important artists, Pasolini was an influential figure who had both strongly Catholic beliefs and Marxist beliefs, possibly influenced by the politics of his birthplace; he was known for his provocative and often controversial views on religion, sexuality, and politics, and his work was often censored or banned by the Italian government and the Vatican. His films addressed themes of social injustice, sexual liberation, and religious faith, with his last work, *Salò, or the 120 Days of Sodom*, featuring graphic sex scenes and violence.

In his writings and art, Pasolini took aim at global consumerism, mass media and Italian politics. He predicted the Italian Christian Democratic party would be brought down by its links to the mafia decades before the scandal actually unfolded, and at the time of his death in 1975 was working on a novel about the corporate world, the mafia, and the government.

Although Pasolini lived in Rome for much of his life, he once described Bologna as the most beautiful city in Italy after Venice. Some of his most famous films include scenes set in Bologna, including *Edipo re*, which features scenes under the Portico di Servi and in Piazza Maggiore, and the aforementioned *Salò, or the 120 Days of Sodom*, where exterior shots were filmed in the square in front of Villa Aldini.

In 1975, Pasolini was murdered in Rome under mysterious circumstances. It has been speculated his death was a homophobic attack, a mafia-style assassination, politically motivated, or a combination of all three. He is remembered in Bologna at the Cinema Lumière, home to the city's Pier Paolo Pasolini archive, where a square is named after him.

HIGHLIGHTS

At the heart of Bologna, you will find the symbol of the city: the leaning Asinelli and Garisenda towers. Used in the early twelfth century for military and strategic purposes, the towers also gave prestige to the noble families who constructed and named them. Both towers stand at the central crossroads of the ancient roads leading to the historic gates of the city. In medieval times, Bologna would have played host to 80–100 towers, but just 20 now remain. The Garisenda Tower also appears in Dante Alighieri's masterpiece, *Inferno*. It's possible to walk up to the top of the Asinelli Tower to take in views over the city, although it does mean climbing 498 steps. Be warned: local legend has it that students who make it to the top may never get to graduate! If you want to take your chances, make sure to book a timeslot in advance at the Bologna Welcome Centre in Piazza Maggiore.

You may be hungry after all that climbing. There are several delis nearby, such as *Tamburini, Salumeria Simoni* or *Ceccarelli*, which showcase Bologna's unique cuisine. Buy some exquisite thinly sliced *mortadella*, pick up some bread from the nearby *Paolo Atti & Figli Panificio* bakery and make your way to the incredibly atmospheric fifteenth-century *Osteria del Sole* where you can bring your own food to eat while sampling glasses of local wine. To try some of Bologna's famous tortellini (stuffed pasta famously shaped to look like the navel of Venus) with Bolognese ragu, head to *Le Sfogline* in Via Belvedere for homemade pasta by sisters Monica and Daniela Venturi. Nearby is the city's *Mercato delle Erbe*, the best food market in Bologna.

Finally, a trip to the Anatomical Theatre of the Archiginnasio is highly recommended. The eighteenth century building, originally used for anatomy lectures for medical students at the University of Bologna, was painstakingly reconstructed following World War II, with the original wooden sculptures of famous physicians. Hippocrates and Galenus can be seen alongside Bologna-born plastic surgery pioneer Gaspare Tagliacozzi, who is holding a nose in a nod to his profession. The *Spellati* (skinned) statues show off tendons and muscles while supporting a canopy on either side of the teacher's chair.

LISTINGS

STAY

Corona d'Oro Via Oberdan 12; hco.it. Graced with a lovely wooden portico, the city's oldest on its northern side, this hotel offers four-star opulence with parquet flooring throughout – the deluxe suite has a beautiful painted panel ceiling. The televisions are out of sight behind cupboard doors, which is a nice touch.

Grand Hotel Majestic già Baglioni Via dell'Indipendenza, 8; grandhotelmajestic. duetorrihotels.com. This high-class hotel features frescoes, antiques and fine art. Located right in the heart of the city, it's a favourite with visiting celebrities – so keep your eyes peeled.

Hotel Touring Via De' Mattuiani, 1/2; hoteltouring.it. Boasting a rooftop jacuzzi, a super central location within walking distance of all the main attractions and bright, comfortable rooms, *Hotel Touring* is an extremely romantic choice for visitors to Bologna.

EAT

Al Sangiovese Vicolo del Falcone 2. Tucked away on an unprepossessing backstreet by the Porta San Mamolo, this traditional trattoria serves excellent pasta dishes such as *strozzapreti* with porcini mushrooms, peas and ham, as well as meaty mains, washed down with a fine Sangiovese red from the family vineyard.

Aroma Caffe Via Porta Nova, 12b; ilpiaceredelcaffe.it. You can sample a range of exotic and interesting coffee varieties under the expert eye of top barista Alessandro Galtieri at Aroma Caffe or even buy some beans to take away. Expect to find drip coffee, cold brews and plant milk options alongside the usual espressos and cappuccinos. The coffees with added *zabaione, fior di latte* or chocolate also get rave reviews.

Banco 32 Mercato delle Erbe, Via Ugo Bassi 25. Spilling out of the old market hall on to a terrace, *Banco 32* is an exciting venture run by an Italian, French and

Basilica di Santo Stefano

Madonna di San Luca

English trio. Its tapas-style menu changes daily, with tasty standards such as *cartoccio di alici*, a little bag/cone of fried anchovies with fried vegetables, plus unusual dishes like the aromatic tuna salad with spiced yoghurt. No booking – you'll have to queue most evenings, but it's worth it.

Cantina Bentivoglio Via Mascarella, 4/b; cantinabentivoglio.it. Situated in buzzy Via Mascarella, *Bentivoglio* is one of the most atmospheric and friendly venues in the area to drink local wines, eat good food, and listen to jazz and live music. Known for its tolerant and friendly atmosphere, this live jazz venue has been in operation for 30 years, and also features a variety of wines, with over 500 to choose from in its cellar. It's a great place to sample or buy local wines or try regional food, with an emphasis on handmade pasta and locally sourced ingredients.

I Conoscenti Via Manzoni, 6/d; iconoscenti.com. Visitors swoon over the fabulous cocktails at this hip bar and restaurant. Chef Salvatore Amato cooks up dishes such as beef *carpaccio* with almonds, raisins and capers or pigeon with madeira sauce paired with cocktails including wine negronis and New York sours.

Il Gelatauro Via S. Vitale 98/B. A 10min walk east of the centre, the charming Giovanni and his team serve up organic pastries, speciality wines, delicious hot chocolate and fantastic ice cream, in flavours that include pumpkin and cinnamon and the "*Principe di Calabria*", with bergamot, jasmine and sponge cake.

Sfoglia Rina Via Castiglione, 5/b; sfogliarina.it. Come here to try freshly made tortellini, gnocchi or lasagna, prepared with free range eggs and flour from local wheat varieties. Prepare to queue at busy times, but it's worth it for some seriously good pasta. There is a choice of a traditional or seasonal menu.

Tamburini Via Caprarie 1. A.F. Tamburini's fabulous delicatessen is a gourmet's delight, its ceiling thick with hanging hams and its counters bulging with giant cheeses. It's also got a popular café selling roasted meats and plates of filled pasta.

DRINK

Altotasso Piazza S. Francesco, 6d; altotasso.com. Located in buzzing Via Del Pratello, this *enoteca* (wine bar) specialises in organic and biodynamic wines, craft beers on tap and a menu with zero food miles, all ingredients sourced directly from vineyards and farmers. It has many wines on tap, as well as cocktail offerings. There's also live jazz and rock in the large back room on Wednesdays.

Bar Senza Nome Via Del Belvedere 11b. A popular bar situated close to Bologna's Mercato Del Erbe is *Senza Nome*, which means "without a name". The bar was founded in 2012 by Sara Longhi and Alfonso Marrazzo, who are both deaf, as are all the staff working in the bar. To order, visitors must either use Italian sign language, try the servers' lip-reading skills or use the "*Angolo del cocciuto*" (stubborn corner) which is a bulletin board with the various names of dishes and drinks written down on small pieces of paper. There are also pictorial guides to how to sign for these items. Both can be taken off the wall and used to order at the counter. As well as offering a good selection of local wines, draft beers, cocktails and snacks, the venue also hosts workshops and art exhibitions with the cultural association *Farm*.

Camera con Vista Bistrot Via Santo Stefano 14/2a; cameraconvista.it. Ideally placed in the most beautiful square in Bologna, *Camera con Vista Bistrot* is a lovely place to sit outside and enjoy a cocktail from a huge selection created by state-of-the-art mixologists. Sit back with a Negroni Hotel cocktail and enjoy people watching as the shadows lengthen over the ancient Church of Santa Stefano. The interior of the bar is equally stunning, with chandeliers, mirrors and frescos left over from its former incarnation as an eighteenth century palazzo. If you get hungry and don't want to move, there is also the possibility to order food.

Cantina Bentivoglio Via Mascarella 4/B. This place has live jazz from around 10pm in the cellars of a sixteenth-century palazzo, and the food (snacks to full meals) and wines are excellent.

Cassero LGBTI+ Centre Via Don Giovanni Minzoni, 18; cassero.it. A Bologna LGBTQ+ institution, when *Il Cassero* first opened in 1982, it was the first time

Fountain of Neptune on Piazza Maggiore

a municipal building had been used as an LGBTQ+ centre in Italy. Housed in a former salt warehouse overlooking a canal, it hosts art exhibitions, as well as dance and theatre performances. It's also a popular night spot, hosting DJ club nights which carry on into the small hours. To enter, you need to first buy annual membership for €13.

Enoteca des Arts Via San Felice 9. This tiny, dark bar is a proper *enoteca* – all warm wood and dusty bottles – serving cheap local wine and preparing simple snacks (panini, cold meat platters) on request. Organises regular tastings.

Macondo Via Pratello 22. There's music most evenings in the small back room at this popular venue, mainly jazz, blues and rock. There's a good spread of *aperitivi* to keep you going till the music starts, as well as a great cocktail menu and deliciously messy burgers.

Osteria del Sole Vicolo Ranocchi 1/D. There's been an osteria on this spot since 1465, and it retains a charmingly old-fashioned atmosphere. Turning the usual concept of BYO on its head, here you pick up a bite to eat in the nearby market and buy a glass of wine or two to wash it down with.

Il Punto Via San Rocco 1G. Laidback queer-friendly bar where the modern industrial feel is tempered by sofas and wooden fittings. They have one hundred bottled beers plus eight on tap, mainly Italian craft beers, and hold regular beer tastings and food pairings. The hamburgers and cheese and meat platters are delicious.

Red Bar Via del Tipografo, 2; redbologna.it. A popular gay bar with three dancefloors, Red regularly organises big LGBTQ+ parties, especially on weekends. There is even a pool to make the most of in summer. It's a little way out of the city centre but can be reached by bus and is well worth the journey.

Le Stanze Via del Borgo di San Pietro 1/A. Elegant place to unwind and sip wine and cocktails in the airy splendour of a former Bentivoglio chapel; there's a good aperitivo buffet, but the bistro also serves pasta dishes and mains. The sixteenth-century frescoed ceilings, romantic candles and occasional art exhibitions produce an evocative atmosphere.

Grand Hotel Majestic's chic entrance

Cheese and wine at *Cantina Bentivoglio*

DO

Basilica di Santo Stefano santostefanobologna.it. It's worth setting aside some time to wander through the warren of buildings hidden inside this beautiful basilica; it contains seven historic churches built at different times between the fourth and the fourteenth centuries.

Cinéma Lumière Piazzetta P. P. Pasolini 2/b; programmazione.cinetecadibologna.it. This historic cinema shows a variety of classic films in their original languages, making it one of the best places to watch English-language films in Bologna. It also hosts the Cinema Ritrovata festival in Bologna in the summer months – a fabulous chance to watch classic films outside in Bologna's squares and public places.

Giardini di Margherita Viale Giovanni Gozzadini; giardinimargherita.com. A popular hangout for the Bolognese since it opened in 1879, this beautiful park, the largest in Bologna, is a queer-friendly space. The park's restored municipal greenhouses in

Via Castiglione 134 are also well worth a visit; they have been restored in the last decade and provide a place to see free films and concerts between May and September. The greenhouses are also open throughout the year for seasonal and sustainable food, drinking, co-working and art projects.

Museo Nazionale del Bargello Via del Proconsolo 4; bargellomusei.beniculturali.it. This art gallery offers world class art without the queues. Here you can see artwork from the Renaissance to the Baroque by the likes of Raphael, Perugino, Tintoretto, Titian, the Carraccis, Guercino and Reni.

Sanctuary of the Madonna di San Luca Via di San Luca 36; santuariodisanluca.it. Hike up to this gorgeous viewpoint from the centre of Bologna along *Portico di San Luca*, the world's longest *portico* or covered walkway; it racks up a total of 666 arches and 489 stairs across its 3,796-metres length. There's also a tourist train that runs from Piazza Maggiore, called the San Luca Express.

Face paint at the Belgian Gay Pride Parade in Brussels

BRUSSELS

Autumn

Brussels has much to offer; it's easy to see traces of the city's rich history in its cobbled streets, Art Nouveau architecture, and sweeping town square with gold-licked buildings dating back to the fifteenth century. Inside the city's many cosy café-bars is where you'll first encounter Brussels' excellent cuisine: think Belgian waffles, fries, chocolate and beer. It's best to arrive here on an empty stomach! What's more, Belgium consistently ranks at the top of Rainbow Europe's Country Ranking for LGBTQ+ rights and, in recent times, the city's queer community have worked hard to put Brussels' LGBTQ+ history on the map.

HISTORY

Brussels is the capital of Belgium, a Western European nation sharing borders with the Netherlands, Germany, France and Luxembourg. Its modern name "Brussels" holds etymology that roughly translates to "settlement in the marsh", which gives an idea of the area's pre-settlement topography.

Throughout its expansive history, Belgium was ruled by a number of different nations including the Romans, French, Dutch and Spanish – the latter were responsible for bringing cocoa to the country (hello, Belgian chocolate). Brussels itself was founded in the tenth century before growing to become an important economic, political and cultural hub.

On 4th October 1830, following the Belgian Revolution, the country gained independence from the Northern Netherlands, signalling the beginning of the Belgian state as we know it today. Following World War I, The Treaty of Brussels was signed here in 1948. This established the Western European Union which later became the European Union.

Today, Belgium is split into three distinct regions: the Flemish-speaking (Dutch) Flanders region to the north, the French-speaking Wallonia region to the south, and the tiny Brussels-Capital Region which embraces both cultural heritages and languages.

Contemporary Brussels is famous for many things

Rue des Bouchers is famous for its many restaurants

– its excellent cuisine, active art scene, museums and architecture. Its history as "the comic strip capital" (Tintin and the Smurfs both hail from here) and its bizarre but oddly endearing "pissing" statues – the petit Mannekin Pis, Jeanneke Pis and Het Zinneker – tempt tourists from across the world. The latter statue, a bronze sculpture of a mongrel dog nicknamed "Zinneker Pis", has become a symbol of the city's multicultural heart; today the expression "zinneke" refers to Brussels's culturally-diverse inhabitants.

Same-sex marriage has been legal here since 2003, adoption since 2006 and the right to change legal gender (surgery not required) since 2018 but what makes Brussels a unique destination for LGBTQ+ travellers is its multi-generational queer artists and activists. Queer women and non-binary folk in particular should check out magazine *Girls Like Us*, the brilliant interactive online map and archive *BAD (Brussels Almanac Dyke)*, and Marian Lens who organises tours of the city aimed at exploring lesbian, feminist history; there are many up-and-coming, queer collectives to boot. Equally, one of the city centre's best-known quarters, the bustling *Les Marolles*, is where many of Brussels's more mainstream gay bars can be found.

A note on travelling as a feminine-presenting person: though in general Brussels is a very safe and welcoming city, it's worth noting that sexual harassment can be an issue. Take care when walking alone, particularly at night.

A Belgian street decorated with a rainbow flag

ICON

Our Brussels icon is a former Belgian cycling champion named Willy De Bruyn. Ring any bells? Thankfully, Willy's story is a fair amount more impressive than our cycling puns...

Unless you're a history buff from Brussels, it's unlikely that you'll have heard their story. In fact, much of it remains a mystery, even to this day – and it's for precisely this reason that we've chosen to shine a light on what we do know of their life. Note that De Bruyn is sometimes referred to as trans and sometimes intersex; as is common with historical matters of gender, it's unclear precisely how they chose to refer to themselves while they were living; it's possible that they used both male and female pronouns interchangibly, perhaps perferring one over the other

at different times in their life. This may have been of choice or perhaps because of a historical lack of non-binary linguistic options – it's impossible to say with any certainty. This being the case, neutral pronouns have been used here.

Born in the Flanders region of Belgium in at the beginning of the First World War in 1914, Willy De Bruyn was raised as female and christened Elvira, nicknamed "Elvire" (a name they continued to refer to in their later life). They grew up in Erembodegem which is just outside of Brussels. After finishing school they worked for a while at a cigarette company and then at their parents' café, before discovering a talent for cycling in 1932. De Bruyn saw a stratospheric rise to fame through the sport, winning the Women's European

Championship in 1933; by 1934, they were the World Champion, securing the title at an event in Brussels in front of some 100,000 spectators. They earned the title once again in 1936 and, along with it, secured their place as a Belgian cycling star.

As a young adult, De Bruyn became more and more interested in their identity, eventually stating that they "felt like a man, never like a woman". They continued cycling to earn money but became more and more uncomfortable competing in women's races, often delibertaely coming in second or third place. By 1937, they were living as Willy De Bruyn (full name Willem Maurits De Bruyn); they were possibly the first Belgian to legally change their gender. They appeared before a court in Oudenaarde and their gender was officially changed to "male" on their birth certificate.

They married fellow cyclist Clementine Juchters in 1938 and together the pair ran the (apparently quite raucous) *Denderleeuw Caf*é pub in the north of Brussels for many years. De Bruyn continued to cycle, but no longer professionally or competitively.

While at *Denderleeuw*, Willy took on the public moniker "Willy ex Elvira De Bruyn" and "Elvira de Bruyn, world champion cycling for women, became a man in 1937". In later life, it appears that Willy spent time in the US, including reportedly selling *smoutballen* (a traditional Belgian beignet) at the landmark 1964 New York World's Fair.

Willy died in Belgium in 1989 and, despite their former fame, was sadly largely forgotten. That is until 2019, when, due to the construction of new buildings on the road, a new section of the canalside street Allée Verte in the north of Brussels was named Rue Willy De Bruyn in their honour.

HIGHLIGHT

One highlight any LGBTQ+ visitor would do well to factor into their trip is the longstanding film festival, Pink Screens (pinkscreens.org/en). Hosted at the much-loved punk cinema space *Cinema Nova* (Rue d'Arenberg 3, 1000; nova-cinema.org), Pink Screens is a 10-day film festival celebrating all things queer onscreen. Created in 2001 by the volunteer-led *Genres d'à Côté* with the goal of "promoting alternative sexuality and gender", the aim of Pink Screens is to "assault and deconstruct binary normality". And what better way to shimmy beyond the gender binary than with a carton of warm popcorn in hand?

Throughout the festival, you'll be invited to discover feature films, documentaries, shorts and experimental cinema from Brussels, Belgium and internationally, many of which are in English or subtitled. What's more, Pink Screens's closing night party, Pink Night, is a now-legendary local affair with a welcoming crowd of all shapes, sizes and sexualities.

You can also expect accompanying exhibitions at venues throughout the city, audience-led debate and discussion and the opportunity to mingle with an international LGBTQ+ crowd. And if you can't make it to Pink Screens – worry not, film buff! Every month throughout the year, Cinéclub hosts a range of LGBTQ+ films at *Aventure Cinema* (Rue des Fripiers 15, 1000).

It's worth noting that, as well as Pink Screens, there are many other LGBTQ+ focused events taking place during Brussels's most golden-hued months. There's the event-packed Belgium Bearpride Brussels in September which celebrates all things bear culture (including the Mister Bear Belgium contest) as well as Bru-X-elles Festival, Tel Quels Festival, and Homografia, all of which are festivals that celebrate and explore different aspects of queer culture during the late summer and autumn months. If you fancy finding out more, it's worth popping into the *RainbowHouse* or checking out the online calendar *What's up Brussels?*.

The Hoxton Brussels

Careful pouring at the *Cantillon Brewery*

LISTINGS

STAY

The Dominican rue Léopold 9; thedominican.be. This deluxe four-star boasts a prime location close to the Grand-Place, and a claim to fame as the place where the painter Jacques-Louis David drew his last breath in 1825 – hence the plaque on the facade. The spacious foyer sets the funky, stylish tone, as do the generous banquettes in the courtyard-style breakfast area behind. Beyond, all 150 rooms are stylishly kitted out with wooden floors and earthy tones.

The Hoxton Square Victoria Régina 1; thehoxton.com/brussels. Close to the Botanical Gardens and housed in a Brutalist-style tower building, ever-trendy hotel chain The Hoxton's Brussels branch serves up sleek 1970s vibes. Complete with rooftop terrace.

JAM Hotel 132 Chaussée de Charleroi; jamhotel.be. A former art school, this trendy hotel manages to combine a youthful, urban feel with that of a traditional Japanese *ryokan* (there's even an Atsukan 'swim bar'). One for the novelty-seeker.

La Légende rue du Lombard 35; hotellalegende.com. This old mansion set around a small courtyard is very centrally located but enjoys a pleasant, tucked-away feel. All of the 26 rooms have en-suite facilities and TV, and the decor is crisp and modern.

Maison Flagey 39, Avenue General de Gaulle; maisonflagey.com. Located in the chic Louise neighbourhood, this homely hotel is in a great location for those looking for boutiques, gourmet cuisine and pretty streets straight out of the *Belle Epoque*.

Meininger quai du Hainaut 33; meininger-hotels.com. Brilliant hotel/hostel inside a former red-brick brewery. Carbon neutral and with loft-style rooms, there's lots of art, exposed brick walls and a trendy bar. Family rooms are available too, and pets are welcome.

EAT

Le 203 Chau. de Waterloo 203; le203.com. Intimate, inviting and with a frequently-changing menu, owners Richard and Matilda specialise in warm welcomes and the use of seasonal produce to create new and interesting dishes inspired by a multitude of cuisines.

Bij den Boer quai aux Briques 60; bijdenboer.com. This atmospheric, bistro-style place with tiled floors and old posters on the walls is the best of the fish and seafood restaurants that line the Quais. Their four-course menus are excellent value.

Café Congo Rue de la Petite Île 1A; cafecongo.tumblr.com. Belgian-Congolese journalist Gia Abrassart runs this hodgepodge café-cum-arts space. The food is cheap and cheerful, but what's even more interesting is their expansive library dedicated to art, decolonisation, feminism *et plus*.

L'eau Chaude 25 Rue Des Renards; leauchaude.be. *L'eau Chaude* is a co-operative that's all about hearty and homemade meals made with ingredients largely sourced from organic and local farms. Meals are vegetarian and heavily inspired by the seasons.

The Judgy Vegan Rue des Capucins 55; thejudgyvegan.com/notre-cafe-bar. With a laid-back atmosphere, this not-so-judgy café serves sweet and savoury vegan dishes aplenty. Plus, board games and plenty of beers.

Le Perroquet Rue Watteeu 31. Spacious and lively Art Nouveau café on the corner serving up good-value pittas and salads – vegan options and milk subsitutes are available. A good place to relax, with outside tables and pretty stained glass windows.

Super Fourchette Rue des hirondelles 3; superfourchette.be. Owned by couple Marie-Eve and Charlotte, café and record store *Super Fourchette* mixes wholesome, veggie-based meals with indie music. Once you're done with lunch, thumb through cassettes and vinyl or stay for a live music performance.

Viva M'Boma Rue de Flandre 17; vivamboma.be. The name means "long live grandma" in the Brussels dialect, and this – a former tripe shop – is one of the best stops in the city for tasting local cuisine, especially offal, prepared in the traditional manner. The food is great, and as refined or as rustic as you like, with lots of traditional Belgian dishes.

DRINK

Cantillon Brewery Rue Gheude 56; cantillon.be. Brussels's oldest active brewery with a history stretching back over 100 years, Cantillon is famous for their lambic-style beers and 'spontaneous fermentation' process involving a local (good) bacteria called *Brettanomyces Bruxellensis* (yes, really).

La Cave à vin Rue du Lombard 4; lacave-a-vin.business.site. Perfect for an aperitif, *La Cave à vin* is a French-style wine bar and another favourite with *Bruxelles* locals. Serving excellent wine *avec charcuterie et fromage* to boot; the owner will advise you if you're not sure what you'd like. Right by the Mannekin Pis.

The Crazy Circle Rue du Prince Royal 11; thecrazycircle.com. Located in the southeastern suburb of Ixelles, this unassuming white-panelled building hosts everything from DJ sets and comedy to drag shows and karaoke. A favourite with queer women and non-binary folk.

La Fleur en Papier Doré Rue des Alexiens 53; goudblommekeinpapier.be. A cosy bar recently reopened by a group of enthusiasts keen to preserve this slice of Brussels heritage, *La Fleur* was one of the preferred watering holes of René Magritte, while novelist Hugo Claus apparently held his wedding reception here. Idiosyncratic antique decor and a good choice of beers, excellent house wine and classic Belgian food.

COMMUNITY

Fatsabbats instagram.com/fatsabbats. Crucial organisation by and for LGBTQIA+ PoC and allies in Brussels. Covering arts, culture, safe spaces, family, love and self-care, *Fatsabbats* is working to make Brussels safer and more inclusive for all.

Naast Monique 230 Quai de l'industrie; naastmonique.pink. "A focal point and a friendly meeting place", Naast Monique is a bricks-and-mortar space run for and by queer, non-binary, and trans people, with a café, bike shop and hairdressers.

RainbowHouse Rue du Marché au Charbon 42; rainbowhouse.be/en. As well as being an essential resource, well-established LGBIQ+ hub *RainbowHouse* runs a café and organises several diverse festivals and events throughout the year. Chat to staff over coffee to learn more.

DANCE

The Agenda Plattesteen 18/20; theagendabxl. business.site. This inclusive bar hosts all manner of LGBTQ+ events; think techno, DJs, drag and bingo! This is where the queer kids go to get their groove on.

Le Belgica Rue Marché au Charbon 32; lebelgica.be. Arguably the capital's most popular gay bar. It's a tad run-down, but has a lively, friendly atmosphere. Come at the weekend when the place is heaving to slam back a few of the lemon-vodka "Belgica" shots.

Cabaret Mademoiselle Rue du Marché au Charbon 53; cabaretmademoiselle.be. A lively and centrally located multidisciplinary space hosting drag shows, comedy, burlesque, circus acts and more, all with a distinct 1930s-esque vibe.

What's up Brussels? gettingshitdone.eu/managing/ whats-up-bxl. Many nighttime LGBTQ+ events are collective-run pop-ups hosted at changing venues. To find out what's on when, try *What's up Brussels?* created by Lyne Brenac, a truly excellent free resource.

SHOP

Feeelings Chau. de Haecht 6; feeelingsfeeelings.club. An artist-run boutique selling locally made wares, games, books and other objects. With friendship and tenderness at its heart, this "anti-business" seeks to lift up Brussels's artists first and foremost.

Jeu de Balle Flea Market Place Jeu de Balle 79; tinyurl.com/visitbrusselsfleamarket. Held in bustling Les Marolles, this popular daily market is the perfect place to potter about looking for trinkets and quirky souvenirs. There are plenty of eateries nearby.

Ko Store Rue du Rem des Moines 19; instagram.com/ kostorebe. This small boutique is all about ethically and sustainably sourced jewellery, handbags, accessories and gifts; well worth a visit.

Moirés Rue du Marché au Charbon Kolenmarkt 81; instagram.com/moires.brussels. A veritable rainbow of all things print-based, from delightful cards and gifts to screen-printed posters and artworks, all manner of stationary and beautiful bric-a-brac.

The Royal Museum of Fine Arts

The façade of the Old England Building

DO

Comics The Belgians love their comics, and the *Brüsel* comic shop (blvd Anspach 100; brusel.com) has the best range in the city, stocking more than eight thousand new issues. You'll also find the complete works of Belgian comic-book artist Schuiten, most popularly known for his controversial comic *Brüsel*, which depicts the architectural destruction of a city (guess which one) in the 1960s. Other good comic book shops to have a nosey around include *La Boutique Tintin* (rue de la Colline 13; boutique.tintin.com) and *Slumberland* (rue des Sables 20).

Kanal 11-12 Sainctelette Square; kanal.brussels/en. By Centre Pompidou, *Kanal* is a unique cultural space housed within the sprawling buildings of a former Citroën garage. Inside, brightly-coloured lines adorn its concrete floors, guiding you towards its ever-changing exhibitions.

Musée Royaux des Beaux-Arts Pl. Royal; fine-arts-museum.be/en. Climb the Mont des Arts towards Place Royale and find the Musée Royaux des Beaux-Arts comprising three interconnecting museums: the Musée d'Art Ancien, the Musée Fin-de-Siècle and the Musée Magritte. Keep your eyes peeled for the Old England Building as you climb the Mont des Arts – it's one of the best examples of Art Nouveau in the city.

Parc Duden Avenue Victor Rousseau. South of Saint-Gilles and perfect for stretching out your city legs. Pick up a coffee from the many nearby cafés (*Jackie's*, *Kami*, and *Mayabro* all serve good stuff) and embrace your inner *flâneur*.

that's what x said Rue Blaes 142; thatswhatxsaid.com/en A socio-political gallery space, well known in LGBTQ+ crowds. Founded by Elisa Huberty and Rébecca Prosper, much of its work pushes for systemic change for queer and other marginalised groups in society. Prints and stickers abound.

36

CAFE AND BAR
Chalk
RABAT · MALTA

milkshake

The
Coffee
Break
HERE
FOR YOU

Segafredo
ZANETTI

WE SELL
Coca Cola
PART OF EVERY DAY
Served ice cold

Coffee

FLICO
cheese local
#fresh
#salads
#ftira
#platters
#cakes

MOR
SEATIN
Upstair

LOVE

MALTA
Autumn

Picture the scene: the hot sun bounces off the limestone rocks, Baroque domes catch the late afternoon light, the azure sea shimmers beyond. As Europe's most southerly country, Malta is perfectly situated for an autumnal visit – and, as the continent's most queer-friendly island, its lure is even more irresistible; it holds first place on the ILGA-Europe Rainbow Index, which ranks countries on LGBTQ+ equality. Up in the hilly capital of Valletta, don't be surprised to pass same-sex couples holding hands as they wander the atmospheric backstreets, or watch the sun set from the lofty vantage point of Upper Barrakka Gardens, with its panoramic views over the harbour.

HISTORY

First, a fanfare: Malta is one of the few countries in the world to have made LGBTQ+ rights equal at a constitutional level – but rewind to the misty past and its many conquerors had some pretty different ideas. For example, during the rule of the Order of St John in the seventeenth century, while sodomy was commonplace it was nonetheless punishable by death. Then as a British colony from 1800–1964, Malta adopted the penal code of Great Britain, which criminalised same-sex relations between men.

Sexual politics aside for a moment, the reason the country has changed hands so often is due to its prime location: at the heart of the Mediterranean, it's been eyed up by everyone from the Romans to the Arabs, as well as a short-lived seizure by Napoleon (although the French emperor only managed to hang on to it for two short years).

Fast forward to the 1960s and, once the country achieved independence and became a republic, thankfully things took a turn for the better for LGBTQ+ people. Same-sex activity was legalised in 1973, with an age of consent equal to that of heterosexual people. But it's the twenty-first century that has seen the most progress; in 2001 the Malta Gay Rights Movement (since renamed Malta LGBTQ+ Rights Movement) was set up, the country's first ever lobbying group, with the inaugural Pride March – and an important national gay helpline – coming shortly afterwards in 2004.

Since then, progress has been steady: Malta was the first country in the European Union to ban conversion therapy in 2016, the same year that the same-sex marriage bill was passed, while it also become the first European state to add gender identity to its constitution as a protected category. With its annual Pride festival every September becoming increasingly well-attended, in 2023 Valletta will host EuroPride, the largest celebration of diversity the islands have ever seen, with around 50,000 attendees.

ICON

Though still not a name that is widely known outside Malta, Katya Saunders was a trans pioneer from a time when the islands were utterly conservative. Born in 1957, she was one of the first transgender women to fight for social change and so naturally faced almost insurmountable difficulties and prejudices from those around her. At the time, trans people could not legally change their name or gender, nor could they enjoy any kind of formal partnership, as was the case for all LGBTQ+ people.

In recent years Malta LGBTQ+ Rights Movement (MGRM) have been working on Katya's legacy to ensure she remains known to future generations. The first fruit of the project is a biography named *Katya: Easy on the Tonic* – a nod to her favourite boozy catchphrase. The book takes an in-depth look at what was a truly unique life. Written by Ramona Depares, it celebrates both Katya's Hollywood-style elegance – think oversized hats and high sartorial chic – and avant-garde sensibility. According to Depares, she was featured in *Vogue* magazine alongside Karl Lagerfeld, modelled for photographers in London and New York in the 1970s and 80s, and was even rumoured to be friends with David Bowie. Back in Malta, she was a muse for local designers Charles & Ron, who still have a store in Valletta.

However, it's her work as an LGBTQ+ mentor for which she most deserves the term "icon". Katya helped those struggling with their gender or sexual orientation, many of whom had no other support at all, by taking them in and simply talking to them and providing an understanding listening ear. She made it her goal to help people get back on their feet, despite her own limited financial means and personal battles with mental health and addiction.

Katya sadly passed away in Malta in 2019 at the age of 61. As part of MGRM's project, the publication of her biography has been accompanied by exhibitions

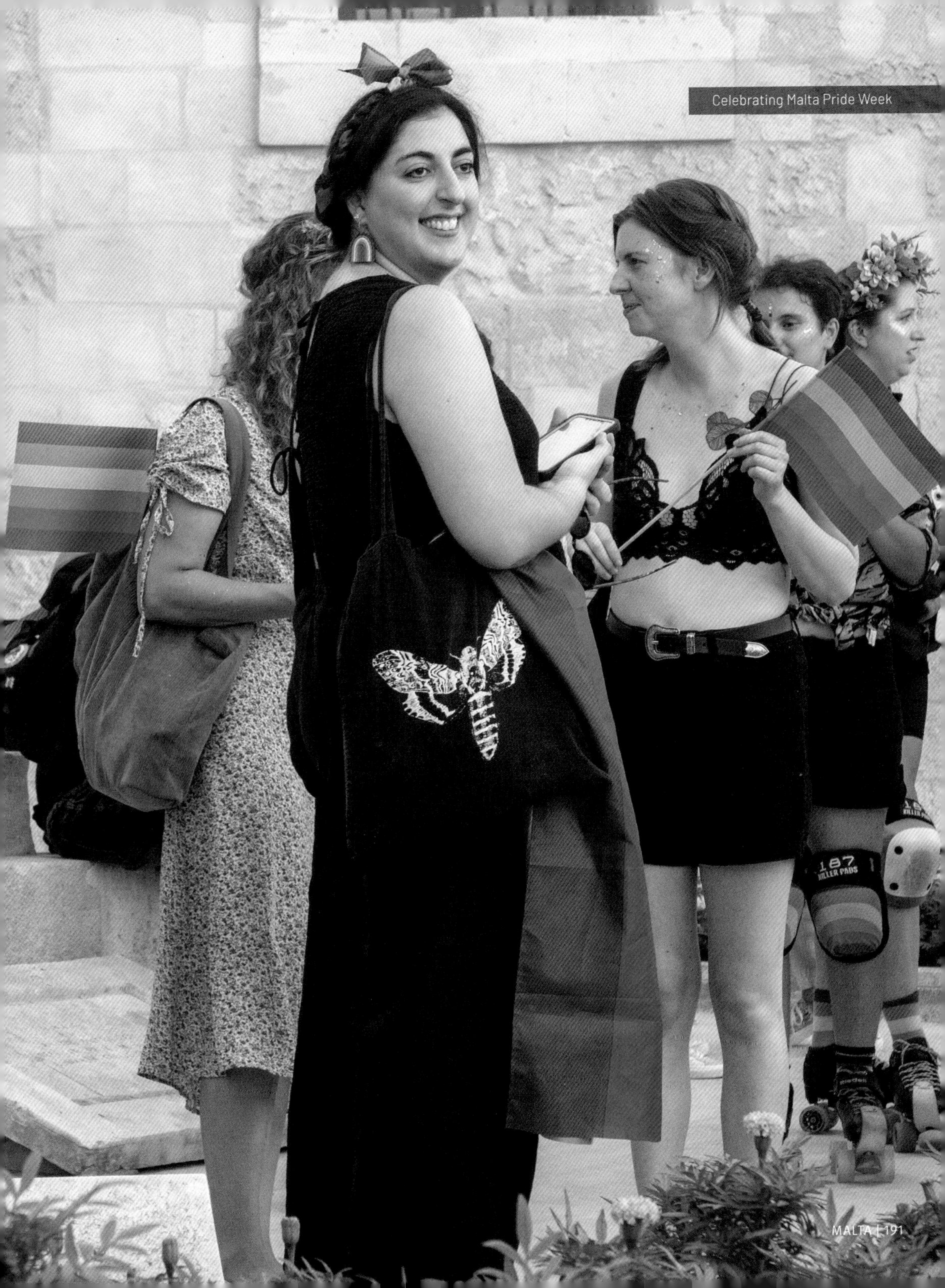

Celebrating Malta Pride Week

featuring her clothes, portraits and accessories staged at various galleries in Valletta. Find out more on Katya at www.katya.mt and on MGRM's website, www.maltagayrights.org.

HIGHLIGHTS

MDINA, MALTA'S WALLED CAPITAL

With views of most of the country from atop its golden ring of fortifications, tiny, achingly beautiful Mdina is one of Malta's major highlights. One of the island's earliest urban settlements, it also served as the capital until Valletta took over in 1571. First established by the Phoenicians and later taken over by the Romans, ancient Mdina used to be up to three times its current size. Few remains survive from the Roman period, with the most significant at Domus Romana.

Today, Mdina is a majestic pedestrianised village still enclosed by early medieval fortifications, and autumn is the perfect time to stroll through without the throng of summer visitors. It's best to forget street names and let your feet and eyes guide you through the series of small piazzas and winding alleys; the village is so small it's impossible to remain lost for long. Don't overlook the lovely coats of arms and elaborate bronze door-knockers adorning many facades.

To get a feel for St Paul's Square and the sandstone cathedral, it's best to visit in the late afternoon when the crowds are thinning, and its twisting alleyways and crepuscular side streets may already be emptying; it's also attractively lamp-lit in the evening. There are epic views at one end and much-photographed Pjazza Mesquita at the other, where the key brothel scene in

Game of Thrones's first season was filmed in 2011. In fact, film buffs should take note: the island has served as a backdrop for dozens of Hollywood blockbusters, from *Popeye* (1980) and *Gladiator* (2000) to *Troy* (2004) and *Murder on The Orient Express* (2017).

MEDIEVAL BIRGU IN THE THREE CITIES

A high point of any stay is crossing the water from Valletta to Birgu on a *dghajsa*, a gondola-style traditional wooden motorboat. Upon arrival, the port at Birgu is photogenically packed with yachts, and its centre, Collachio, untouched by modernity. Entering through the Three Gates, it's a blissful stroll through the narrow streets, where you can explore the preserved medieval Norman House and tucked-away galleries. The views from the Gardjola gardens in neighbouring Senglea back over Valletta are breathtaking, while a final meander along the

waterfront as the sun is dipping makes for a romantic end to the day. If you are visiting during the first week of October, make sure to stop by during Birgufest, an annual celebration of Birgu's beauty, history and culture. The festival sees the village lit by hundreds of thousands of candles.

ANCIENT GOZO

The smaller island of Gozo, easily accessible by fast ferry from Valletta, has more of a laidback atmosphere than its larger neighbour, as well as dramatic coastlines and a plethora of ancient monuments. Most notable are the Ggantija Temples, the oldest man-made giant structures in the world, erected in 3600 BC and predating both Stonehenge and the Pyramids of Egypt. Restored with money from the EU, the Cittadella in capital Victoria (*Rabat* in Maltese) with its bulwark castle makes for a peaceful afternoon jaunt. Another

The city of Mdina

essential spot on the island is in Dwerja, where a 20-metre-high natural arch called the Azure Window once stood, before it collapsed into the sea during a storm in 2017. It's an energetic scramble over crater-like topography, while behind is the scenic Inland Sea, a landlocked body of water popular with bathers.

LISTINGS

STAY

Barrakka Suites Battery Street, Il-Belt Valletta; barrakkasuites.com. Chic apartments with stone walls, tiled floors and contemporary furnishings located opposite Upper Barrakka Gardens. If you can, try to book the room with the sea view.

Boho Hostel Villa Cycas, Dun G. Xerri St, St Julian's; bohohostel.com. *Boho Hostel* lives up to its name, with eclectic style and rainbow-coloured rooms. Its standout feature is the lively garden, with multiple outdoor dining areas, barbecue and hammocks. Shared facilities include a lounge/TV area and kitchen.

Casa Ellul 81 Old Theatre St, Valletta; casaellul.com. Malta's most exclusive boutique hotel, located in a Victorian palazzo opposite the Carmelite Church, with eight suites designed by Maltese architect Chris Briffa. Rooms have luxurious touches; expect two-storey ceilings, walk-in showers, espresso machines, Maltese balconies, breathtaking bathtubs and one-of-a-kind antiques. Two suites facing the church's impressive dome boast private terraces with jacuzzis.

Fauzia 8, Triq il-Ferrovija, Hamrun; fauziabnbmalta. com. Situated in the town of Hamrun just 2.5km from Valletta, this elegant LGBTQ+-owned bed-and-breakfast has the advantage of the owners being on hand to provide recommendations.

Number 11 Triq Schreiber San Giljan; number11.com. Located in Paceville, *Number 11* is a smart adults-only hotel with complimentary breakfast buffet, rooftop pool, and spa and wellness centre in nearby sister hotel *The George Urban Boutique Hotel*.

Senglea Suites 10-12 triq San Frangisk, ISL 1457 Senglea; instagram.com/sengleasuites. LGBTQ+-owned boutique hotel with six bedrooms handy for Birgu, and a short ferry ride to Valletta. Five minutes' walk from the beach.

Xara Palace Relais & Chataux Misraħ Il-Kunsill Mdina; xarapalace.com.mt. Set in a seventeenth-century palace, this impossibly romantic hotel is one of Malta's best (and a favourite of Hollywood celebrities). An elegant lobby is arranged around a central courtyard, with creeping ivy and a glass roof.

EAT

Harbour Club 5 Barriera Wharf; theharbourclubmalta. com. *Harbour Club*'s breathtaking views and small but superb menu makes it a popular choice among locals for long, leisurely meals. The kitchen offers consistently outstanding local fish and handmade pasta, while the pork served three ways is a lovely contemporary homage to the Maltese *majjalata* (pig roast) tradition.

Is-Suq tal-Belt Triq il-Merkanti, Valletta; issuqtalbelt. com. The buzzy Food Market, a once-derelict nineteenth century Victorian structure, is now a must for international streetfood, as well as traditional Maltese dishes like *timpana* (baked pasta in pastry).

Kingsway 57 Republic St, Valletta; kingswayvalletta. com. This café in the middle of Valletta serves brunch, wraps, and *pinsa* (hand-pressed pizza), as well as an evening sharing menu; join lingering after-work locals with an Aperol spritz.

Noni 211 Republic Street, Valletta; noni.com.mt. In the basement of a former confectioners, Michelin-starred Noni's set menu showcases traditional dishes with ultra-contemporary techniques, from cured sea bass to cuttlefish risotto.

Le Regatta Triq Ir-Rampa Ta' L-Isla, Senglea; leregatta. com. Set on a stunning stretch of waterfront, this French-owned restaurant in the Three Cities is *the* destination for mouthwatering dishes such as *chermoula* sardines or octopus and polenta.

Terrone 1 Triq il-Wilga, Marsaxlokk; terrone.com. mt. Located across from Marsasxlokk's seafront promenade, the menu at *Terrone* changes almost daily according to what's fresh. Dishes include smoky chargrilled calamari, *strozzapreti* pasta with fresh

yellowfin tuna and pine nuts, and dreamy pistachio and honey cake with pistachio gelato – all sure bets.

Zest 25 Triq San Ġorġ, St Julian's; zestflavours.com. Michelin-starred *Zest* introduced the Asian fusion concept to Malta in 2002 and has been a favourite amongst locals since. House specialities include Indonesian beef *rendang* and top-notch sushi. During the summer, tables on the restaurant's small terrace offer lovely sunset views.

DRINK

222 City Lounge 222 Great Siege Road, Valletta; facebook.com/MichelangeloCafeLounge. Formerly *MonaLiza Lounge*, LGBTQ+-friendly bar *222* has vaulted ceilings, an outside terrace, and stunning views, a chilled sister to the island's only LGBTQ+ club, *Michaelangelo*.

Charles Grech 10 Republic St; charlesgrech.com. *Charles Grech*, which can trace its roots back to 1881, is an upmarket and classically styled café bar. Try to snag a table outside for some superb people-watching.

City Bar Triq il-Kbira, Mosta. A popular, quirky pub located just off Mosta's main square, this fifty-year-old institution offers reliably cheap drinks, always served with free snacks. Owing to its massive popularity with locals of all ages, the pub frequently hosts special events from live music to poetry readings.

il-Gabbana Triq it-Torri, Sliema; ilgabbana.com. Essentially an upscale kiosk, *il-Gabbana* offers lovely sea views and a large outdoor terrace. The *focaccia semplice* makes for a perfect light bite.

Hole In the Wall 31 High Street; holeinthewall.com. mt. This cool corner spot is reputedly the oldest in Sliema (dating back 100 years), and as good a choice for an artisan coffee as a craft beer. Plus, there's also an independent cinema, as well as occasional live music and art shows.

Maori Maori Triq il-lanca, Valletta; facebook.com/HMSMaori. A relaxed bar on the coast with murals and ocean views. Regular queer events are organised here by maltagay.com in the summer.

The Pub 136 Archbishop St. Movie fans should make a beeline for *The Pub*, Valletta's boozer with a backstory: this is the watering hole where legendary actor Oliver

Celeriac steak at the *Harbour Club*

Reed died when he was in town filming *Gladiator*. It's now a shrine to the star.

Yard 32 Strait St; yard32.com. Strait Street is an exquisitely named stretch of the old red-light district, and an appropriate location for this gin bar: there are 200 varieties, as well as a chalked-up board of negronis to sip outside on the cobbles.

DANCE

Café del Mar Triq it-Trunciera St Paul's Bay, Qawra; facebook.com/CafeDelMarMalta. *Café del Mar* opened its doors for the first time in 2013 and has been pleasing punters with cocktails and sunsets ever since. It's splendid and glamorous beach club complex with an infinity pool overlooking the sea, an on-site restaurant offering excellent salads and pizzas, and a fully stocked bar with sunbed service. Entry will set you back €15–30 per person depending on the quality of sunbed you opt for, but drink and food prices are surprisingly affordable once you're inside.

Club Havana 86 Triq San Ġorġ, Paċeville; instagram. com/havanaclubmalta. This club is very popular and is usually full (and sweaty) at weekends with a young crowd. The ground floor specialises in hip-hop, while the upper level leans more towards R'n'B and soul.

Hugo's Terrace St. George's Bay, Paċeville; hugosterrace.com. A comfortable lounge popular with a more mature crowd of locals and expats that offers a dance floor (with DJs mixing lounge and house music) within sight of St. George's Bay Beach.

Lollipop various venues; instagram.com/ lollipopmalta. Billing itself as "Malta's favourite queer night out", *Lollipop*'s regular disco, tech and house events take place fortnightly throughout the warmer months and once a month during autumn and winter. There are themed events and a fun, inclusive vibe.

Maltagay.com. This website was founded in 2015 to round up the many one-off events at the various clubs across the island. It's an essential resource to discover both LGBTQ+ nights and the many local queer-owned businesses.

Michelangelo St Rita steps Paceville, St Julians; michelangelomaltacom.wordpress.com. The state-of-the-art club is set over two floors with private rooms and chill out lounge. At weekends it attracts party-goers of all ages, but with a predominantly younger gay male crowd. Believe it or not, it's the island's only LGBTQ+ club.

SHOP

Barber's Arch Republic Square, Il-Belt Valletta; barbersarch.com. This LGBTQ+-friendly high-end men's grooming and styling station, with two locations on the island, gives a choice of pronouns when booking online.

Ċekċik 15 Melita St; cekcik.com.mt. A quirky independent shop with a unique collection of vintage items, ceramics, locally designed clothing, original artwork and beautiful postcards.

Charles & Ron 58 Republic St; charlesandron.com. A celeb favourite, this long-running contemporary lifestyle brand sells clothing and bags. Maltese culture plays a key part in its design aesthetic.

Christine X Art Gallery 17 Triq Tigne, Sliema; christinexart.com. A small but excellent art gallery exclusively stocking local work.

Malta Chocolate Factory 179 Triq Sant' Antnin Street, Bugibba; maltachocolatefactory.com. Based in the north of the island, sweet-toothed visitors should swing by this chocolate shop and café. A viewing window allows customers to watch the chefs tempering, moulding and shaping the goods.

Meli Book Shop 185 Old Bakery St. A tiny independent bookshop that looks to have come straight out of the 1960s, with an excellent stock of new fiction titles and a vast selection of books about Malta and Maltese-language literature.

Souvenirs That Don't Suck 108 Triq Manwel Dimech Tas-Sliema and 8, St John's Square, Valletta; souvenirsthatdontsuck.mt. This witty brand has two high-quality stores on the island and stocks womenswear, menswear and more. There's a Pride collection in collaboration with the people behind the Malta Gay website.

Ta' Dbieġi Crafts Village Triq Franġisk Portelli, San Lawrenz; gozoartisans.com. A cluster of artisan workshops producing and selling good-quality and relatively inexpensive local crafts such as ceramics, leather goods, Maltese lace, wool sweaters and filigree jewellery.

The Renzo Piano project brings together Malta's modern Parliament building and the historic fortification walls in Valletta

Casa Rocca Piccola in Valletta

DO

Casa Rocca Piccola 74 Republic St, Valletta; casaroccapiccola.com. Tours of this private sixteenth-century palazzo, complete with bomb shelter, are run by charismatic owner Baron Nicholas De Piro or his wife Frances; they're a noble family descended from the Knights who have been in Malta for over 400 years.

City Gate, Valletta Don't miss this stunning 2013-built gate which, along with the Parliament building, was designed by the architect Renzo Piano who also designed London's The Shard. Nearby the Royal Opera House, bombed in WWII, was redesigned in 2013 as an outdoor performance venue called Pjazza Teatru Rjal.

Gozo's Citadel. Offering panoramic views and home to no less than four museums, a cathedral, and a superb interpretation centre, the compact, honey-coloured Citadel punches far above its weight.

Rainbow Library 32, Triq il-Parrocca Mosta; maltagayrights.org/rainbow-library. The first LGBTQ+ library in Malta contains around 300 books, including biographies, history, trans/non-binary works, poetry, queer classics, fiction and zines. Contact MGRM via the website before you visit to check opening times.

Rolling Geeks Xatt ir-Riżq, Birgu; rolling-geeks.com. Take a self-driving electric car – complete with pre-programmed GPS – out on a fun tour that takes in the famous Malta Film Studios, imposing forts and ridiculously picturesque alleyways.

Spazju Kreattiv Pjazza Kastilja Pope Pius V Street Il-Belt Valletta; kreattivita.org. This sixteenth-century fort combines arthouse cinema, exhibition spaces and a cultural programme of music, comedy and drama. It hosted the island's first Katya Saunders exhibition.

Valletta Contemporary 15, 16, 17 East Street, Valletta; vallettacontemporary.com. An independent exhibition space, this gallery is housed in a 400-year-old former warehouse a few metres from Lower Barrakka Gardens.

MILAN

Autumn

Milan is a stylish and open-minded city in one of Europe's more conservative countries. Owing to its role as one of Europe's fashion capitals, its physical distance from the Vatican and its longtime status as a centre of artistic excellence, it makes sense that a vibrant gay scene has sprung up in this Northern powerhouse. Although there's no central gay district, there are streets packed with nightlife options which means you won't have to walk far to find atmospheric bars and exciting events.

HISTORY

Milan was Italy's first city to register civil unions between same-sex couples in 2012, and its legacy shows. Mayor Gieseppe Sala has recently described Milan as experiencing a 'wind of change' and has promised that it would "always be more free and contemporary [than other cities in Italy]". This feels especially vital in a county where the new Italian prime minister, elected in 2022, has drawn attention for her deeply-held Conservative values. The city had been declared the capital of the Kingdom of Italy by Napoleon in the late eighteenth century, but it wasn't until Italy was unified in 1876 and all its different states came together to become a country, that Milan really pulled away as the industrialised, wealthy city it remains today.

Until the last decade or so, owing to the influence of Catholicism across the country, Milan's gay scene was a more private affair than it is today. Parties and events took place behind closed doors, and you'd have to know a friend of a friend to gain access. Knocking on doors to be let into a semi-underground scene was the experience shared by many Milanese throughout the twentieth century. Today, the scene is much more open, especially during the biannual fashion shows.

Milan's centre can feel quite small when compared to those of some of Europe's bigger cities, and walking around the city late at night and seeing rainbow flags draped across bar windows can generate a real sense of queer solidarity and safety. Porta Venezia metro station has even been painted rainbow colours to celebrate the neighbourhood's LGBTQ+ inhabitants.

ICON

Little is known about Da Vinci's sex and love life. There has been little mention of him having sexual or romantic relationships with either men or women, although historians tend to agree that it is an 'open secret' that he was gay.

When Da Vinci was completing his apprenticeship at artist Verrocchio's workshop, an anonymous note was handed in to the town hall accusing four men of 'sodomising' a male sex worker – artist's model and goldsmith Salterelli. The accusation read that Salterelli had been "party to many wretched affairs and consents to please those persons who request such wickedness of him." Da Vinci was one of the four men accused. Charges were eventually dropped because another of the accused had friends in high places.

Da Vinci also lived with a young man called Salai for several decades, who some historians believe could be the real face of the *Mona Lisa*. Da Vinci's erotic sketch *Angelo Incarnato* ('Angel Incarnate') shows Salai as a nude angel.

Although he was born in Tuscany, Da Vinci lived in Milan for much of his life because his patron was the Duke of Milan, Ludovico Sforza. He was given a house to live in by his patron so he could focus on producing great work, and when he died, Da Vinci gifted Salai half of his garden in his will. Visitors can check out La Vigna di Leonardo, his private garden and vineyard just a few steps away from *The Last Supper*; it's easy to imagine him relaxing there, perhaps with the young Salai, as the church bells of Milan tolled.

Milan Pride Parade

HIGHLIGHT

Most nights out start in Porta Venezia, a cool and eclectic neighbourhood where student bars nudge up against Korean diners and queer venues. Walking tours celebrating Milan's queer scene tend to start here and stretch up into Corso Buenos Aires. It's a pulsing, lively place; Porta Venezia is a place where all subsections of the city come to rub shoulders, with lots of bars and venues to stop off at. The city's oldest bars are here too – *Leccomilano* and *Mono*. They were the first bars to open on the city's main streets rather than its back alleys, and they're worth a visit mainly because they're fantastic bars in and of themselves, but also because they showcase the city's original LGBTQ+ vibe.

This is a neighbourhood that thrums with energy behind closed doors; you can often find fashionistas spilling out of private events holding drinks on late summer nights, and small galleries often host private viewings. It's always a good idea to ask at local bars what's happening during your stay and if they have any recommendations – most places are very friendly and will be happy to advise. Another good tip it to keep an eye on local galleries' social media, as that's where you will catch wind of any new exhibitions. Galleria Pisacane Arte (pisacanearte.it) and Gli Eroica Fuori (eroica.cc/it/eroica-cc/eventi) are two contemporary spaces that are well worth a visit in Porta Venezia, while the grander and bigger Museum of Modern Art highlights mostly Italian and European art from the nineth and twentieth centuries and is perfect to drift in and out of before the next round of coffee and pastries.

The neighbourhood isn't just for LGBTQ+ drinkers either – biblio- and cinephiles will find much to amuse them here too. *Antigone* (libreriantigone.com), just a couple of hundred metres past Porta Venezia metro station, is packed with excellent queer books. It runs talks and book launches, and even sells sex toys. Porta Venezia hosts Milan's annual gay pride in June, and MiX (filmitalia.org/en/festival/26940), one of Europe's most prominent and well-established queer film festivals, tends to follow or precede it by a week.

Pinacoteca di Brera

LISTINGS

STAY

Armani Hotel Milan Via Alessandro Manzoni 31, locations.armani.com/armani-hotels/italy/armani-hotel-milano. Come for luxury and risk never leaving. This is an LGBTQ+ friendly, high-fashion hotel just paces away from the city's fashion centre.

BioCity Hotel Via Edolo 18; biocityhotel.it. An excellent budget choice with immaculate, tastefully furnished rooms 750m north of Stazione Centrale. The hotel prides itself on being ecofriendly – complimentary beauty products are organic and biodegradable, bathrooms feature recycled toilet paper, and breakfast includes home-made cakes, organic jams and eggs.

Hotel Straf Via S. Raffaele 3; straf.it. A deeply sexy and stylish design hotel, this LGBTQ+ friendly accommodation option is slap-bang in the city centre. Expect soft beds and cosy throws, with a beautiful bar thrown in.

LaFavia Milano Via Carlo Farini 4; lafaviamilano.com. A charming B&B in a nineteenth-century building with warm and welcoming rooms decorated in different styles, featuring retro armchairs and lamps, hand-woven carpets and designer wallpaper. Breakfast is served on the leafy roof terrace garden. The owners also manage a number of attractive apartments in the area.

Senato Hotel Via Senato 22; senatohotelmilano.it;. A stylish boutique hotel a short walk from the Fashion District with attractive black, white and golden interiors. Set around a sleek interior courtyard, the airy rooms have oak wood flooring, brass lamps and black armchairs, while light dishes can be ordered throughout the day at the pleasant *Senato Caffé*.

The Yard Piazza XXIV Maggio 8; theyardmilano.com. This fashionable boutique hotel bursts with character, with interiors packed with curios and sporting memorabilia that the owner has collected over the years. Themed rooms are mainly sports-related although you'll also find British style interiors in some, with plenty of tweed, hunting prints and wooden furniture. The cool bar serves up great cocktails, while the restaurant attracts a hip crowd.

EAT

Bello e Buono Viale Sabotino 14; belloebuonogastronomia.it. This tiny laidback place offers exceptional home cooking at incredible prices. Expect traditional Mediterranean recipes that have been passed down from generation to generation – the *melanzane parmigiana* is to die for.

Chocolat Via Boccaccio 9; chocolatmilano.it. A sleek, stylish café and gelateria offering 26 delicious flavours, in-cluding seven chocolate options such as orange chocolate, rum chocolate and ginger chocolate. Their ice cream is blended with unusual ingredients such as chilli, aniseed and vinegar. The café also offers delicious cakes that can be enjoyed at the tables on the ground floor or on the mezzanine.

La Dogana del Buongusto Via Molino delle Armi 48; ladoganadel-buongusto.it. Warm and welcoming family-run restaurant serving exceptional cuisine in a rustic interior with cavernous exposed brick walls, wooden ceilings and old-world knick-knacks. The hearty cold cut platters include wild boar and deer ham, and the menu includes some excellent Milanese dishes. The 30cm meat *brochette* served with baked potato and herb flavoured butter is a must.

Drogheria Milanese Via Conca del Naviglio 7; drogheriamilanese.it. This fashionable bistro-style restaurant has a welcoming interior with low-hanging light bulbs and a long communal table. The menu features Mediterranean and international dishes, including pasta, burgers and fish.

Gastronomia Yamamoto Via Amedei 5. This friendly family-run deli and restaurant serves authentic Japanese fare in two attractive dining areas that take inspiration from traditional 1960s and 1970s Japanese interiors. Tuck into meat and vegetable curry, stewed *hijiki* (cooked seaweed) or *unadon* (steamed rice topped with grilled eel).

Romoletto Corso di Porta Ticinese 14; romolettostreetfood.com. This is a great little spot to refuel on delicious Roman street food as you explore town. The pizza slices are divine, thinner and crunchier than Neapolitan pizza, and there are a dozen types to choose from. You'll also find *supplì*, fried rice balls traditionally made with meat and tomatoes and stuffed with melted mozzarella.

The Leonardo Da Vinci monument in Piazza della Scala

DRINK

Blue Note Via Borsieri 37; bluenotemilano.com. Top-name jazz club located in the alternative neighbour-hood of Isola, just north of Stazione Garibaldi. Quality bookings and a relaxed atmosphere make this place an excellent venue. There's a small restaurant too, as well as the bar.

The Doping Club The Yard Hotel, Piazza XXIV Maggio 8; thedopingclub.com. Located in the lounge of *The Yard Hotel*, this fashionable bar serves creative cocktails prepared by award-winning mixologists in a cool and wacky setting. Expect plenty of comfy velvet couches and interiors jam-packed with all manner of curios, from sporting memorabilia to hatboxes. If you manage to get your hands on the password, you may be able to sneak into the speakeasy at the back.

Eppol Via Malpighi 7; eppolmilano.com. Bistrot, cocktail bar, and brunch spot, *Eppol* serves up food and cocktails in a space that's as grungy as it is great. It's queer-friendly and inclusive – families often swing by for the weekend brunch menu, although during evenings the clientele becomes strictly more queer. Come for a perfectly-made negroni, complete with bitter orange rind twist.

Just Cavalli Torre Branca, Via Luigi Camoens; justcavallimilano.com. A chic, glamorous club that is *the* place to go if you want to be surrounded by beautiful people. Offering comfortable cushioned seating, the candle-lit outdoor garden is a great spot for an *aperitivo* and mingling.

Lacerba Via Orti 4; lacerba.it. A popular *aperitivo* spot attracting a young alternative crowd for its laidback atmosphere; seating is on colourful stools and worn sofas, while shelves are decorated with knick-knacks from toy trains to umbrellas.

Leccomilano Via Lecco 5; leccomilano.it. A cosy bar for lesbians and gay men, *Leccomilano* transforms into a pumping dancefloor on weekends. As well as club nights with local and international DJs, the venue hosts thought-provoking exhibitions, pop ups, debates and book readings. There are plenty of rooms, great *aperitivi,* and an animated crowd that often spills out onto the pavement.

The entrance to the *Armani Hotel*

ARMANI HOTEL

Gourmet octopus dish at *Just Cavall*

Mag Cafè Ripa di Porta Ticinese 43; instagram.com/ magcafe. This cosy little place has plenty of character and atmosphere, with quirky paintings, antique cabinets and mismatched armchairs dotted about. A café during the day, in the evenings it morphs into a popular bar serving great cocktails.

Memà Largo Bellintani 2; instagram.com/ memamilano. Giving onto a lovely little square, this Sicilian bar serves a great *aperitivo* buffet with all manner of Sicilian specialities including *pane cunzato* (bread topped with cheese, tomatoes and anchovies). It's a great spot to mingle.

Mono Via Lecco 6; instagram.com/monobarmilano. This LGBTQ-friendly, vintage cocktail bar has 1960s decor and a happy hour. The musical flavour is indie, rock and electro with DJ sets at the end of the week and over the weekend.

NoLoSo Via Luigi Varanini, 5; nolosomilano.it. A vibrant bar in the NoLo district of the city ('*Non lo so*' means 'I don't know', which is precisely where your night could take you if you start here). Come for the jazzy bright pink and green walls, but stay for the perfect terrace, expertly made cocktails, and delicious pizza.

Nottingham Forest Viale Piave 1; nottingham-forest. com. Arguably one of Milan's best cocktail bars, shaking up all manner of creatively presented drinks, each served in different funky glasses and containers (there's even a cocktail served in a first aid kit) in an intimate environment.

Rita Via Angelo Fumagalli 1. This discreet little bar just off Porta Ticinese shakes up creative cocktails using the freshest in-gredients around. *Aperitivo* includes delicious finger food as well as tapas-sized portions of Mediterranean dishes that change daily.

ToscaNino Via Melzo angolo Via Lambro; toscanino. com. The counter of this Tuscan deli-restaurant groans with Tuscan produce, from cold cuts to cheeses. Perfect for a relaxed dinner or an *aperitivo*.

DANCE

Note that many of Milan's clubs need an Arco Card to enter. An Arco Card will allow you to enter gay and queer clubs across Italy just by showing your app or your ID, and helps to provide safety for club-goers. You can register for a card using the app (arco.lgbt/en/arco-cards); three-month passes are available for tourists. Membership also includes some STI/HIV testing.

Afterline Via Giovanni Battista Sammartini 25; afterline.it. Themed nights, scantily clad dancers, and disco-classics, Afterline is a fun place to flirt, dance the night away with friends, and pump along to all those classic club anthems you haven't heard in years. Centrally located and a guaranteed fun night.

Bangalov Via Calabria 5; bangalov.com. A cruise/fetish club for men and trans men: nights which include naked, leather, and no-face-night, with a more of a 'heavy-duty' nature. It's clean, modern, and welcoming. Check the website for the dress code of the night before showing up, or be prepared to be refused entry.

Company Club Via Benadir 14; companyclub.org/en/il-club. Far from the Porta Venezia district, Company hosts more 'masculine' nights (in its own words), with bears and leather-lovers well-catered for. It's been running since 1994; expect an older and more mixed crowd, but a very welcoming one nonetheless.

Dude Club Via Boncompagni 44; instagram.com/dudeclubmilano. Electronica and techno music are the flavours at this club, which hosts regular international DJ sets – check Instagram for details of who's playing.

One Way Club Via Felice Cavallotti, 204; instagram.com/onewaydiscoclubmilano. Open since 1980, this is a fun and established club, with lots of fun tracks and no pretensions. Expect an older crowd, disco parties and lots of pop tunes. There's a lovely patio and small cruising area. Keep an eye on their website to find out more about the party nights.

Toilet Club Viale Umbria 118; toiboy.it/toiletclub. A non-conformist club with no door policy. It's friendly, inclusive and plays a variety of music, from R'n'B to techno, and welcomes all genders.

Da Vinci's masterpiece, The Last Supper

Milan's Duomo

DO

Fenix Via Oropa 3; fenixsauna.it. If you've come to Milan to embrace all things style and fashion, then Fenix feels is a great option. Split over several floors with a small outdoor pool, it's open almost 24-hours and is kept spotlessly clean.

The Last Supper Piazza di Santa Maria delle Grazie; cenacolovinciano.net. Leonardo Da Vinci's *The Last Supper* is a mural in the church of Santa Maria delle Grazie. It took him three years to paint, and is one of the world's most well-known artworks – it depicts Jesus and his disciples on the night before he was crucified. Da Vinci painted the work 19 years after he was put on trial for sodomy in 1476.

Metro Club Sauna Via Giovanni Schiaparelli 1; metroclubmilano.it. A central sauna with a mixed clientele, ranging across three floors with whirlpool, sauna and a dark room. Closes early, around 1.30am.

Milan's Duomo Piazza del Duomo; duomomilano. it/en. Wander around the world's largest Gothic cathedral, begun in 1386 and not completed until almost five centuries later. The roof has the best views of the city and the mountains beyond.

Pinacoteca di Brera Via Brera 28; pinacotecabrera. org/en. Milan's most prestigious gallery, the awe-inspiring Pinacoteca di Brera was opened in 1809 by Napoleon who filled it with works looted from the churches and aristocratic collections of French-occupied Italy.

Shopping Steel yourself for the ultimate shopping trip in the fashion and design capital of the world. Milan is synonymous with shopping. If your pockets are not deep enough to tackle the big-name designer boutiques, you could always rummage through last season's leftovers at the many factory outlets around town, or check out the city's wide range of medium- and budget-range clothes shops. Milan also excels in furniture and design, with showrooms from the world's top companies, plus a handful of shops offering a selection of brands and labels under one roof.

Schwester
Theresia
-Priorese-
Die Schwestern der
Perpetuellen Indulgenz
Abtei „Bavaria"

PRAGUE

Autumn

Baroque, Gothic, Renaissance; the city of a hundred spires is a breathtaking place, home to a dizzying array of stunning architecture, with delicious food, refreshing beer, and endless culture to accompany it. Steeped in history, the former capital of the Kingdom of Bohemia has become one of the most visited cities in Europe, receiving millions of visitors each year. With famed attractions such as the iconic Charles Bridge, the imposing Vyšehrad, and the remarkable Dancing House, it's easy to see why tourists from around the world flock to this Central European city in droves.

HISTORY

Prague Castle, perhaps the city's most famous landmark, was built in the 800s by Prince Borivoj, with the historic fort Vyšehrad built less than a century later. Eventually, the Prague region was used as a seat for dukes and Bohemian kings, with Vratislaus II becoming the first Czech king in 1085. However it wasn't until the fourteenth century that the city truly entered its golden age, which included the construction of landmarks such as Charles University (the oldest Central European university) and the *Nové Město* (New Town).

The city also underwent a great deal of turmoil during this time. In Easter 1389, roughly 3,000 Jews were murdered in a two-day pogrom. Then the Hussite Revolution in the fifteenth century (a conflict between the Roman Catholic church and members of the Protestant Christian movement known as Hussites) led to much damage and the destruction of historical relics around town, including the castle. The Battle of Prague, a great fire, and plagues also decimated much of the population.

By the eighteenth century, the city's population began to increase, and the cultural movement known as the National Revival, led by Josef Dobrovský and Josef Jungmann, helped the local identity flourish. The Industrial Revolution also further helped Prague become a cosmopolitan and powerful European City. Czechoslovakia was officially formed in 1918 and Prague was designated the capital.

Physically, the Prague we see today may have weathered the twentieth century very well but it suffered in other ways. The city that produced the music of Dvořák and Smetana, the literature of Čapek and Kafka and modernist architecture to rival Bauhaus, was forced to endure a brutal Nazi occupation during World War II. Prague had always been a multiethnic city, with a large Jewish and German-speaking population – in the aftermath of the war, only the Czechs were left.

Then for forty years, during the Communist period, the city lay hidden behind the Iron Curtain, seldom visited by Westerners. Once the Velvet Revolution started in 1989, communism came to an end and the first democratic elections took place a year later. In 1993, after the Velvet Divorce, Czechoslovakia became two independent countries: Slovakia and the Czech Republic. Prague was designated the Czech capital.

Throughout the decade that followed, Prague began to once again achieve some of its lost glory and Prague became a European cultural hotspot. With several noteworthy museums, theatres, cinemas, galleries, and other cultural destinations, visitors began visiting in earnest to experience the city's rich history for themselves. Though just 1.3 million people live in Prague, the city sees over 8 million tourists a year, making it one of the most popular European city break destinations with a highly developed tourist industry to match. It also has a large expat population who, if nothing else, help to boost the city's nightlife.

ICON

Ladislav Fuks was a Czech author born in Prague in 1923. The resounding theme throughout his (often autobiographical) psychological prose is fear and anxiety; a closer look at his life reveals why.

Fuks didn't have an easy life growing up; his father was a cold, distant man, and his mother wanted her son to fully fit into society. By the time he was a teenager, Europe was on the cusp of World War II and Fuks realised that he was gay. It was a terrifying burden to bear as he was forced to witness first-hand the Nazi persecution and deportation of his Jewish classmates and Romani people. This oppressive burden eventually led to his alienation directly impacted his later work.

He left school and went on to study philosophy, psychology and art history at Chares University, eventually receiving a doctorate in 1949; it wasn't until the 1960s that he began seriously dabbling in writing. Much of his early work was centred around the Jewish diaspora, which later received some attention from literary critics who noted that, for someone who wasn't Jewish, his work showed an almost preternatural amount of empathy.

Prague Lookout Tower on Petrin hill

His debut novel, *Mr. Theodore Mundstock*, told the story of a Jew in 1942 Prague during the German occupation of the country. A deeply psychological novel, it was universally well-received. His 1964 short story collection *Mí černovlasí bratři (My Dark-haired Brothers)* is a direct reference to his close bond with his persecuted Jewish friends.

Fuks published novels in the 1960s, many of them secretly autobiographical, with the main character usually a young, highly sensitive boy. His work in the 70s and 80s was more varied and included detective novels and historical tales – but none had quite the same raw emotion of his earlier work.

Throughout his life, Fuks kept much hidden. He married a rich Italian woman called Giulia Limiti, although he fled from the wedding reception after allegedly seducing a waiter. Somewhat predictably after such a rocky start, their marriage didn't last very long; after just a few days of marriage he left her and returned to Prague. He also kept his religious and political beliefs a secret and seemed to suffer from schizophrenic behaviours throughout his life.

It seems Ladislav Fuks was destined to be the prototype of the tortured artist. Though his work was influential and brought a rare perspective into the landscape of Czech and international literature, he spent the last years of his life alone, isolated and without friends. On August 19 1994, he died in his hometown – finally free of the anxiety that had haunted him throughout his life.

HIGHLIGHT

Perhaps the best-known attraction of Prague is *Pražský hrad* – the Prague Castle. A sprawling complex spread out over nearly 70,000 square metres, the UNESCO World Heritage site is one of the most-visited attractions in the city, featuring palaces and buildings from various architectural eras. No trip to Prague is complete without a visit to the official office of the Czech president.

If you want full access to the Prague Castle complex, adult tickets are 250CZK (around €10). However, there's plenty you can see for free if you're on a budget, since almost all the castle grounds are open to the public.

Start by taking in the views from *Černá věž* (The Black Tower) to orient yourself and get a fantastic view of Prague from above. Then walk to *Zlatá ulička* (The Golden Lane); the street is filled with quaint, colourful houses where the Prague Castle guards used to live, and it feels almost as if you've stepped into a fairy tale as you stroll down the street.

Spend the next few hours visiting some of the smaller churches and palaces like the Old Royal Palace or St. George's Basilica. The true showstopper here is St. Vitus Cathedral, perhaps the most imposing Gothic church in all of Europe. It's the largest church in the Czech Republic, soaring 102 metres above visitors' heads, and is truly a remarkable feat of architecture.

After you've had your fill of museums and royal buildings, it's time to head to your next destination: the *Petřínská rozhledna* (Petřín Lookout Tower). Head onto Loretánská street and take the steep stairs onto Úvoz street, turning right and following the road onto Vlašská. The walk usually takes less than an hour, although be warned – the last 20 minutes are uphill. If you're not up for the climb, never fear; you can take the funicular up instead for 60CZK.

The Lookout Tower was built in 1891 and looks a bit like the Eiffel Tower's little cousin, reaching nearly 60 metres tall. You can climb the nearly 300 steps to the top (an adult ticket is 150CZK) or take the elevator. Once you've made it to the top, you'll be rewarded with a phenomenal view of not just Prague, but much of old Bohemia if the weather is clear.

Once you've descended, you can escape the hustle and bustle in the nearby gardens and enjoy the view on one of the grassy knolls. Alternatively, reward yourself with a beer from one of the cafés on the square. You've earned it!

While Prague is beautiful in any season, high season is summer; during these months, temperatures often soar to over 30°C and the queues for attractions can be daunting. Instead, try visiting in autumn or even early winter. The weather is still generally sunny, and the walking will keep you warm even if it's a bit chilly.

LISTINGS

STAY

While food and beer are quite affordable in Prague (especially compared with western European countries) hotels and hostels can be on the pricier side, particularly in summer. Prague is increasingly popular year-round, so book early; note that it can be a good deal to book an Airbnb or similar homestay, as prices can be cheaper than hotels for more space.

Czech Inn Francouzská 240/76; czech-inn.com. Though it's not the most central, this hostel will get you the best bang for your buck. It's stylish and trendy, offering all-you-can-eat brekkies, generous happy hours, and regular events in the sprawling cellar bar.

Dancing House Hotel Jiráskovo náměstí 6; dancinghousehotel.com. Few can fail to be impressed by what former Czech footballer Vladimír Šmicer has done with the building to turn it into one of Prague's more interesting twenty first-century hotels. The Fred Royal and Ginger Royal suites in the building's towers, with truly awesome views of Prague Castle, are two of the most desirable rooms in the capital.

Hotel Josef Rybná 20; hoteljosef.com. This modern hotel is right amidst the commotion of the city centre, and offers a unique twist on the traditional Czech experience. They serve up excellent breakfasts, and a visit to their artisanal on-site French bakery is a must.

Mandarin Oriental Nebovidská 459/1; mandarinoriental.com/en/prague/mala-strana. The all-out option for those who are after a treat. This 5-star hotel offers sweeping views of Prague Castle from the timeless Malá Strana district. Serenity, luxury, and pure bliss await you.

Pension Dientzenhofer Nosticova 465/2; dientzenhofer.cz/en. This rustic pension is a few minutes away from the Charles Bridge. Most important to note is that it's one of the few accommodation options with excellent wheelchair access.

Residence Řetězová Řetězová 225/9; hotelsprague. cz/retezova_e.php. These spacious studios and apartments (up to 115 square metres) are located in the Old Town, making it the perfect location for an extended stay in the city.

Designer hotel suite in *Hotel Josef Prague*

A volunteer putting up rainbow decorations for Prague's Pride celebration

EAT

Kantýna Politických vězňů 1511/5; kantyna.ambi.cz/en/kantyna. A unique blend of canteen and butcher, you can either order food and drink to eat on-site or take it home to cook later. They don't take reservations, so it may take some time to find a seat.

Lehká hlava Boršov 2; lehkahlava.cz. *Lehká hlava* translates to 'clear head', and it's with a clear head and a clean conscience that you'll find yourself in this exotic, cave-like veggie restaurant just off Karoliny světlé. Tapas, soups, salads and Mediterranean dishes are all on offer, and all delicious.

Lokál Various locations; lokal-dlouha.ambi.cz/en. Chain of traditional Czech beer halls serving good, honest food. Loud, feisty, and good fun for all. The *pivo* (beer) comes straight from tanks, and food options are traditional and hearty.

Maitrea restaurace Týnská ulička 1064/6; restaurace-maitrea.cz/en. One of the few excellent veggie (and vegan) restaurants in town. *Maitrea restaurace* offers clever veggie alternatives to traditional Czech dishes in a smart, contemporary setting.

Naše maso Dlouhá 727/39; nasemaso.cz/en. Another butcher/restaurant that's a must-visit. There's often a long queue of locals waiting to get meat for dinner, despite prices that aren't the lowest. There's only a handful of tables, so expect to grab and go. Good options include the pastrami, meatloaf, or pulled beef.

Oh Deer Bakery Bělehradská 606/87; ohdeerbakery.cz. For a quick pick-me-up, try grabbing one of the many delicious cronuts (a croissant-donut hybrid) with a coffee from this colourful bakery.

Pho Vietnam Anglická 15, Anglická 529; pho-vietnam.cz. Prague is home to a large Vietnamese community, and accordingly there are plenty of great Vietnamese options to choose from. Try the noodles, which are exquisite; the *pho* is another very popular choice.

Salabka Troja, K Bohnicím 57/2; salabka.cz. Although it's a bit out of town, this fine dining restaurant is well-worth it. Serving up modern dishes in a cosy winery, head chef Petr Kunch is sure to wow you with his inventive culinary taste.

Sweet & Pepper DAYS Anglická 390/19; sweetandpepperdays.cz. Located in the green and leafy Vinohrady neighbourhood, this bistro serves all-organic breakfast and brunch dishes from various world cuisines (think Turkish eggs or pumpkin chocolate pancakes). The perfect spot for a lazy weekend morning.

DRINK

Biergarten Letna-Schlösschen Letenské sady 341; letenskyzamecek.cz/en. You can find good *pivo* anywhere, but this is hands down the best view you can get while sipping a cold beer, and you can wander through the park before or after. Cash only.

Piano Bar Milešovská 1986/10; piano-bar.cz. Quirky LGBTQ+ bar with regular drag shows and bingo nights. Popular with both locals and tourists and a great place to begin an unforgettable night out on the town.

Q Café Opatovická 166; q-cafe.cz. A quiet, unassuming LGBTQ+ bar serving a respectable assortment of alcoholic and non-alcoholic drinks. Not a spot for a rowdy night out, but a great place to sit quietly with a book or even get some work done. If you're in luck, you'll spot a friendly dog...

VELTLIN Křižíkova 488/115; veltlin.cz/en. A natural wine bar located in the hip Karlín district. The knowledgeable owners know all the winemakers personally, and with their extensive expertise at the ready, you're bound to find the perfect glass or bottle in no time at all.

VNITROBLOCK Tusarova 791/31; vnitroblock.cz. To the northeast of the Old Town you'll find this factory hall-turned-coffee shop. A stylish combination of rough and refined, it's the perfect spot for a cup coffee.

Wine Not Masarykovo nábř. 8; wine-not.cz. This modern wine bar has an extensive collection of wines and provides excellent views of the bustling street and the Vltava River. *The* place to watch the sun set.

The Astronomical Clock

DANCE

Club TerMIX Třebízského 4a; club-termix.cz. Intimate, often crowded gay bar/club with cruising options. Open till 6am. Its sister club, *Club Termax*, is the largest LGBTQ+ club in the city, but only opens on Friday and Saturday till 7am.

Heaven Club Gorazdova 1995; heaven.cz. Heaven is more than just a club: it has a shop, bar, and dark rooms. A welcoming space, with DJs and drag events.

Nebe Cocktail & Music Bar Václavské nám. 56; nebepraha.cz/cz/vaclavske-namesti. Gigantic cocktail and music bar, providing great happy hour discounts. Reservations recommended in the weekend.

Radost FX Bělehradská 234/120; radostfx.cz. This vegetarian restaurant by day moonlights as a popular expat-friendly dance club, often playing house and techno music. Cover charge can be somewhat pricey.

SHOP

Kotva Department Store Náměstí Republiky 656/8; od-kotva.cz/en. After a long shopping session, take the elevator all the way up for expansive views of the city from this department store. It dates back to the 1970s, but has had a modern refit since then.

Shakespeare a Synové U Lužického semináře 10; shakes.cz. The façade may look a little kitschy, but this bookshop is a veritable treasure trove, carrying an extensive selection of literally thousands of new and second-hand English and foreign-language books.

U Elektry Flea Market U Elektry 7; blesitrhy.cz. At over 50,000 square metres, this is the largest flea market in the city. Trinkets, clothes, tasty food, and more are waiting to be discovered – if you're ready to hunt for them, that is! Take the free shuttle bus from the Hloubětín metro to get there.

Airship on the roof of DOX
Centre for Contemporary Art

The Dancing House

DO

Astronomical Clock Staroměstské náměstí 1. One of the most popular sights in Prague is the town hall's fifteenth-century Astronomical Clock, whose hourly mechanical dumbshow regularly attracts a large crowd of upward-gazing tourists. Little figures of the Apostles shuffle along, bowing to the audience, while perched on pinnacles below are the four threats to the city as perceived by the medieval mind. A cockerel pops out and flaps its wings to signal that the show's over, before the clock chimes and the crowds drift away.

Dancing House (Tančící Dům) Rašínovo nábřeží 80. Designed by Frank O. Gehry and Vlado Milunič, this building is known as the *Dancing House* (*Tančící dům*) or "Fred and Ginger building", after the shape of the building's two towers, which look vaguely like a couple ballroom dancing. The apartment block next door was built at the start of the twentieth century by Václav Havel's grandfather, and was where Havel and his first wife, Olga, lived in the top-floor flat until the early 1990s.

DOX Centre for Contemporary Art Poupětova 1; dox.cz. Modern art museum with thought-provoking temporary exhibitions, infrastructure, and more, all aimed at sparking conversations. Well worth the short taxi ride out of the Old Town.

Jazz Dock Janáčkovo nábř. 3249/2; jazzdock.cz/en. Swanky lounge bar primarily featuring local talent in the jazz scene. Located right on the river, it guarantees an atmospheric performance; the roof can be opened in good weather to let the sun shine in.

Kasárna Karlín Prvního pluku 20/2; kasarnakarlin. cz/en. Large multi-purpose venue just outside the city centre with bars, playgrounds, a volleyball court, and an outdoor cinema. The perfect place to chill with friends slightly off the beaten path.

MAT Karlovo nám. 285/19; mat.cz/kino/cz/restaurace-mat. For the discerning film connoisseur, this small café/cinema offers a unique collection of international and Czech films, shorts, and documentaries.

Střecha Lucerny Pasáž Lucerna 110 00; strechalucerny. cz/en. Concerts and exhibitions take place at this scenic rooftop spot, which you can access via a vintage elevator. Alternatively, just go for an unforgettable sunset. Entry costs 150CZK, and note there can be queues. Open spring and summer.

BERLIN
Winter

To say Berlin is gay friendly would be an understatement. Berlin is howlingly and proudly queer, and has been for centuries. LGBTQ+ tourists flock here for its anything-goes attitude – nudity and sexual experimentation isn't confined to backstreet bars or dingy dance basements. Berlin also caters well to anyone looking for a quieter but nonetheless fun and absorbing stay: there are cafés, bookshops, lecture halls and galleries a-plenty for those who don't feel like partying. Berlin's scene is famously respectful and inclusive. Anything goes, but everyone goes too.

The Pride flag in front of the Reichstag

DEM DEUTSCH

HISTORY

Berlin is a city that city resonates with modern European history, having played a dominant role in Imperial Germany, both during the Weimar Republic after 1914 and in the Nazis' Third Reich. It is also a city that has experienced a freeze/thaw oscillation when it comes to queer activity and gay rights; plenty of gay bars opened during Weimar Germany (170 operated during the 1920s), although homosexuality was still illegal. Even so, Berlin's queer scene wasn't confined to a just few bars and clubs; there were kiosks on the street that sold gay magazines and gay films played openly in cinemas. Magazines with titles like *The Third Sex* and *A Woman's Love* could be bought on the highstreet.

It was a remarkable culture for the 1920s, and arguably a culture that wouldn't be seen again until the 1970s after the Stonewall riots. Berlin's subculture flourished in the late 19th century thanks in part to a very tolerant policing policy, which meant that homosexuals could only be prosecuted if someone who witnesses to the act itself came forward – and because most 'acts' occurred in private and were consensual, they were rarely prosecuted: queer balls, clubs and cabarets blossomed. Dr Magnus Hirschfield was a German sexologist and physician who was exiled by the Nazis due to his work – but his legacy lived on in Berlin's Institute of Sexual Science, founded in 1897 to encourage legal reform of homosexuality.

Under the Nazi regime, being gay was considered a crime from 1935. It's estimated that around 50,000

VOLKE

homosexuals and LGBTQ+ people were sent to concentration camps, and perhaps around a fifth of those people died – archival work is ongoing.

Post-war, the city was partitioned by the victorious Allies and, as a result, was the front line of the Cold War. In 1961, its division into two hostile sectors was given a very visible expression by the construction of the notorious Berlin Wall. After the Wall fell in 1989, Berlin became the national capital once again in 1990. During this time, Berlin's queer subculture was flourishing on both sides of the Iron Curtain; East Germany decriminalised homosexuality ahead of the West, where there was the lingering effect of Nazism which lived on in cities like Frankfurt. In the first two decades of West Germany, more than 50,000 men were convicted under the law which criminalised homosexuality. Despite this, Berlin continued to operate as a bastion of gay culture: in 1985 at the height of the Aids Crisis, the Schwule Museum opened, celebrating homosexual culture and history, while in 2017, gay marriage was legalised.

As for the city itself, parliament now sits in the renovated Reichstag building, and the city's excellent museum collections have been reassembled. The physical revival of Berlin has put it at the forefront of contemporary architecture, and there is a plethora of dramatic new buildings around the city. The speed of change over the past few decades has transformed Berlin into an energetic and irreverent city that has become a magnet for artists and musicians. Culturally, it has some of the most important archeological collections in Europe, as well as an impressive range of galleries and museums, and an exuberant, cutting-edge nightlife.

layers and strip off when you arrive – even the strictest of door policies wouldn't expect you to freeze on the metro to and from the party!

Like in any big city, drugs form part of Berlin's club scene. If that's not your vibe, there's no pressure – there'll be plenty of people dancing the night away fuelled only with water. Do bear in mind, though, that Berlin's club scene is a lot less prescriptive than most: you're very likely to see speed, ketamine and MDMA passed around openly. However, drug-taking is generally seen less as a way to pump up individual egos and more as a way to best experience the music.

LISTINGS

STAY

Adlon Kempinski Unter den Linden 77; kempinski.com/en/hotel-adlon. Probably the most famous hotel in the city; Michael Jackson dangled his baby from one of the balconies here in 2002.

Axel Hotel Berlin Lietzenburger Str. 13 / 15; axelhotels.com/int/axel-hotel-berlin/hotel.html. Its tagline is 'we're hetero-friendly' – which they are. But this is a hotel aimed at queer people, located in the centre of Schöneberg – Berlin's pulsing gay district. Rooms are sleek, stylish, and there's a glitzy rooftop hot tub.

Circus Hotel Rosenthalerstr. 1; circus-berlin.de. An ecofriendly place just across the road from its sister hostel, *Circus Hotel* offers junior suites and apartments, decorated in striking colours with wooden floors and a mix of antique and modern furniture.

Hotel Zoo Kurfürstendamm 25; hotelzoo.de. This historic hotel's rooms are sumptuously appointed with high-quality wooden floors and furnishings. There's a restaurant and lounge, and two sixth-floor penthouse suites if you feel like splashing out.

My Gayhostel Nollendorfpl. 5; my-gayhostel.de/en. A hostel only for gay men, which offers dorms, single rooms and doubles. It's basic but centrally located, so you can stay gay on a budget.

Tom's Hotel Motzstr. 19. This friendly queer hangout has a great bar (*Tom's*), a vibrant café and is close to the gay scene of Nollendorfplatz. Rooms are artistically decorated and apartments feature a flat-screen TV.

Marlene Dietrich in the film *Blonde Venus*, circa 1932

EAT

Café BilderBuch Akazienstr. 28; cafe-bilderbuch. de. Lovely rambling café in the Viennese tradition. It doesn't look particularly special from outside, but the comfortable back parlour may well hold you captive for hours. Great breakfasts, delicious cakes, elegant coffees, and courtyard seating, too.

Cocolo Paul-Lincke-Ufer 39; instagram.com/ cocoloramen. Unarguably Berlin's best dedicated ramen spot. Enjoy slurpa-licious dishes (including sweet pork belly and kimchi ramen) at a shared table inside, or on the canal-facing terrace.

Katz Orange Bergstr. 22; katzorange.com. Tucked away in a restored, nineteenth-century brewery, the (slightly) glamorous "orange cat" offers a pleasant blend of casual and fine dining with an international menu. There's also a fantastic cocktail bar.

Witty's Wittenbergplatz 5; wittys-berlin.de. One of the city's first and finest organic sausage stands, *Witty's* has customers lining up for Currywurst and crispy fries.

SHOP

Bikini Berlin Budapester Str. 38–50; bikiniberlin.de. This trendy concept mall in a 1950s building place was, arguably, the place that put West Berlin back on the map. Spanning offices and a cinema, the lower three floors of the *Bikinihaus* offer chic retail and coffee stop options.

Prinz Eisenherz Bookstore Motstrasse 23; prinz-eisenher-buchkatalog.de. A Schöneberg bookstore celebrating queer literature since 1978, *Prinz Eisenherz Bookstore* is one of Europe's oldest surviving bookshops: it sells magazines and a wide range of books by international and German authors.

She Said Kottbusser Damm 79; shesaid.de. A bookshop packed with books from diverse, queer and trans writers. This is a seriously inclusive and celebratory bookstore which mainly sells books by authors who identify as women. *She Said* organises plenty of events both online and in real life with authors and literary figures.

The Schwules Museum

Rooms at the luxury hotel *Adlon Kempinski*

DRINK AND DANCE

://about blank Markgrafendamm 24c; aboutblank.de. Not all of Berlin's club scene is about dressing up and wearing black. If you just want to show up to a party wearing flipflops and tracksuit bottoms, this is a no-judgement venue with chill vibes: it's a left-wing bar with a lesbian-first ethos, but everyone is welcome.

Berghain Am Wriezener bhf; berghain.berlin/en. One of the world's most famous clubs, *Berghain* is a queer techno club (but welcomes clientele of all sexualities) and is probably Berlin's most famous. It's a judgement-free zone with an excellent sound system, housed within a former East German power plant. The doormen tend to prioritise people over the age of 30 and the queue can last for more than four hours. Once inside, people spend anything from 10–24 hours partying across the club's four levels.

Betty F*** Mulackstraße 13; instagram.com/bettyfvck. Small gay bar with DJ nights and friendly, well-stocked bar. Come here for great drinks and a night that descends into dancing, later on rather than techno heavy from the outset.

Clärchens Ballhaus Auguststr. 24; claerchensball. haus/en. At weekends, this authentic pre-war ballroom is taken over by one of the most diverse crowds in Berlin, drawn by the unique atmosphere of a live covers band and an unpretentious good time.

Möbel Olfe Reichenberger Straße 77; moebel-olfe.de. A bar on top of a Kottbusser Tor high-rise which has a regular Tuesday night gathering for queer women – very welcome in a city where it can sometimes feel like men have all the fun! Check website for male-friendly nights and kink events.

Mutschmanns Motzstraße 30; facebook.com/Mutschmann.info. Billed as Berlin's hottest club, this established venue is heavy on the cruising and high on the hedonism. Packed with attractive male locals, there's a naked-only party on Thursdays.

Schwuz Rollbergstraße 26; schwuz.de/en. Arguably Berlin's most inclusive club (and open since 1977!),

Schwuz is mixed, and welcomes a variety of ages, genders and kinks. Check the website for party nights, which range from fetish-driven darkroom affairs through to camp pop. Wheelchair users will be happy to know it ranks high for accessibility, with ramps and wide corridors.

Sudblock Admiralstrasse 1-2; suedblock.de. *Sudblock* is a woman-focused but definitely mixed club, located under the Kottbusser Tor roundabout in Kreuzberg. Go for drinks but stay for the club nights that play a mix of pop, rock and Latin music, depending on the theme. Happily, there's also better-than-your-usual club food fare – cheesy *flammekuchen* and spicy *currywurst* are on hand to see you through a long night of dancing.

Tom's Bar Motzstraße 19; tomsbar.de. *Tom's Bar* is one of Berlin's most popular cruising clubs: after midnight the darkroom tends to become more popular than the bar area. It used to exclusively be a leather bar, but it's much more casual now. Although not discriminatory, this is definitely a bar for gay men rather than lesbians and queer people of other genders.

DO

Babylon Rosa-Luxemburg-Straße 30; babylonberlin. eu. This striking yellow cinema opened in 1929 and remains one of the defining architectural landmarks of Rosa-Luxemburg-Platz. Today the cinema shows a mix of indie, trash, silents with live organ music and cult movies, as well as hosting concerts and over forty film festivals annually.

The Ballery Nollendorfstraße 11-12; theballery.com. A small art gallery that sits in the lively gay district of Schöneberg, *The Ballery* features art by queer people, about queer issues. Recent exhibitions include work about LGBTQ+ people living under oppressive and homophobic governments.

Der Boiler Mehringdamm 34; boiler-berlin.de. Described as the best gay sauna in the world, *Der Boiler* offers two Finnish saunas, a large jacuzzi and a steam sauna. It's also Berlin's only explicitly queer sauna, and men used to more sexually-oriented saunas may be surprised to hear that there are wellness and fitness programmes on offer (no, not euphemisms!).

The queue for Berghain is almost as legendary as the club itself

That said, there's still a significant cruising section with a sexy, industrial feel, so don't feel like you've come to the wrong place when you show up.

instinct.berlin Kurfurstenstrasse 31; instinct.berlin. A gallery and community space with a focus on queer masculinities, which acts as a safe space for people who identify as men.

Kraftwerk Berlin Köpenicker Str. 70; kraftwerkberlin. de/en. A cavernous events space in a former power station, *Kraftwerk* hosts all manner of performances, events and art installations. It's definitely worth checking the website to see what kind of avant-garde event is taking place during your visit, but you can be sure to expect cacophonous sound, incredible light installations, plenty of dry ice and lots of walking.

P6 Galerie Gossowstraße 6; galerie-p6-berlin.de. Founded in 2020 in a former ice cream parlour, *P6 Galerie* is an art gallery located in Schöneberg. There's a lovely garden and an array of striking contemporary art in temporary exhibitions on the walls.

The Schwules Museum Lützowstraße 73; schwulesmuseum.de. The Schwules Museum was founded in 1985 at the height of the Aids Crisis to celebrate Berlin's LGBTQ population and culture. From exhibitions about LGBTQ+ icons in East Germany to stacks of queer magazines from the city's underground presses, there are talks and rotating exhibitions to keep visitors and locals entertained.

Spinnboden Anklamer Str. 38; spinnboden.de. *Spinnboden* is a vital archive and library whose staff collect lesbian literature from all over the world. Readers wanting to dive deeper into the genre can borrow from their extensive archive.

Xposed film festival xposedfilmfestival.com. Berlin's annual *Xposed* festival is a celluoid extravaganza that celebrates some of the world's best LGBTQ+ shorts as well as full-length pieces. The festival takes across a number of the city's cinemas, including *Freiluftkino* open-air in Kreuzberg and *Kino Krokodil* in Prenzlauer-Berg.

Incredible costumes at Cologne Pride Parade

COLOGNE

Winter

The fresh scent of Eau de Cologne that wafts gently through the streets of the city, the spires of the cathedral that proudly welcome travellers from all over Europe, and the smiles of the locals make Cologne a pleasant surprise. While the city may not be the first queer destination to come to mind when thinking about Germany, the city plays host to a vibrant queer scene that doesn't stop at clubs but expands all over the city. Throw the naturally open and friendly attitude of Cologne's residents and an incredible calendar of events into the mix, and the result is the perfect destination for a queer vacation.

HISTORY

From a small village on the left bank of the Rhine, Cologne soon became an important Roman military base named Ara Ubiorum. Its current city-status and name find their roots in 50 AD thanks to Agrippina the Younger; the fourth wife and niece of Emperor Claudius was a native of this village and because of her power, the colony grew into a city with that bore the name Colonia Claudia Ara Agrippinensium (meaning "Claudius's Colony and Altar of Agrippina").

The fame of the city and its power continued to grow; within a few years, Cologne became the Roman provincial capital of Germania Inferior in 85 AD and in 260 AD, at the behest of Postumus, the city became the capital of the Gallic Empire.

After the conquest of the Franks in the fifth century, the city became one of the most important ecclesiastical and cultural centres in Europe. It became a royal residence towards the end of the Merovingian dynasty (during the second half of the eighth century) and at the beginning of the tenth century, Cologne became a city of the Holy Roman Empire and finally of Germany.

Thanks to its central location on the Rhine, Cologne emerged as the most important trading port in Europe in the late Middle Ages, and the city was catapulted to unprecedented levels of economic success. It was also during this era that the most iconic building of Cologne began construction; Cologne's gigantic Dom was started in 1248, and would not be completed until 1880; it was declared a UNESCO World Heritage Site in 1996. Today, this undisputed symbol of the city stands as a visual representaion of this Golden Age.

In 1475 Cologne formally became a Free Imperial City, a status it held until its annexation by France in 1796. The French occupation ended in 1814 when the region was conquered by Prussian and Russian troops making it a territory of Prussia.

The city underwent a radical change with the bombings of World War II; the city sustained damage to over ninety percent of its buildings. The reconstruction, entrusted to the architect and urban planner Rudolf Schwarz, was slow but effective.

Today, Cologne attracts thousands of tourists to its many museums, fairs and events including its annual pride event, the Christopher Street Day (CSD), which is among the largest pride festivals in Germany.

ICON

Though known internationally for her English-language songs, one of music's most famous modern LGBTQ+ icons is Kim Petras. Petras was born in Cologne in 1992 and is a well-known public figure, not only for her music but also for her activism and the media attention she garnered in Germany during her transition.

At the age of two, Petras's parents recognised that she suffered from gender dysphoria. Having supported their daughter early on, Petras was able to begin the transition at a young age. The age at which gender affirmation surgery is legal in Germany is 18, but thanks to Petras's tenacity and the support of her parents, it was possible to open a public discussion that led to the authorization of the operation at 16, two years before the legal limit.

A few years after becoming famous for her transition, Petras began her career in the music industry; she recorded her first English-language songs and performed mainly at the Cologne Pride festival. It was in 2017, however, that her first real international successes arrived thanks to the single "*I don't want it at all*" where Paris Hilton made a cameo in the music video. Since this song, Petras has collaborated with musicians such as Charli XCX on the song "*Unlock it*" and on "*How It's Done*" from the film *Charlie's Angels* (2019).

2022 represented a turning point for Petras; thanks to the song "*Unholy*", sung together with Sam Smith, she participated in the MTV Ema Awards, was nominated for best video clip, and became the first trans artist to ever arrive on the Billboard Hot 100 chart. From Cologne to the world stage, Kim Petras has officially become an LGBTQ+ icon in the history of world music.

A Cologne Christmas market

HIGHLIGHT

Winter in Cologne is taken very seriously. In this season, two much-loved events take place in the city: from the end of November to the 23rd of December, Cologne lights up with the many colourful lights of its famous Christmas markets, while in February, the city breaks out its feathers and sequins to welcome carnival lovers from all over the world.

The Roncalliplatz Market is one of the most famous and spectacular Christmas markets in the world: the massive Cathedral of Cologne is the setting for the hundreds of wooden houses that host artisans, food stalls and sellers of Christkindl Gluhwein, the famously hot and fragrant mulled wine from Cologne. The whole place rings with the sounds of carols and bells, and the square seems to glow yellow with warmth and cosiness despite the plummeting temperatures.

The oldest market, however, is that of Neumarkt and Alter Markt, in the historic centre of Cologne. Within the hundreds of sprawling stalls, you'll find handicrafts, decorative plates and the irresistible Kolner Spekulatius, the iconic spiced biscuits in the shape of the Cologne Cathedral.

Don't be frightened if you see strange little creatures at the Alter Markt Christmas market; these are the Heinzelmännchen, a kind of gnome- or elf-like creature from Cologne folklore to whom a beautiful fountain in the city centre is also dedicated. The tale goes that these small creatures would run around doing all the hard work of the citizens of Cologne during the night, so that the people could laze around during the day. Unfortunately, though, curiosity killed the cat and put an end to all the mischief. One day, a tailor's wife decided she wanted to see the Heinzelmännchen for herself so she scattered peas onto the floor of the workshop to make them slip and fall. The Heinzelmännchen were so angry at this trickery that they disappeared, never to be seen again. Since then, the people of Cologne have had to do all their work

A golden winged car on the roof of Cologne City Museum

Kim Petras at New York Fashion Week

themselves. The Heinzelmännchen are one of the main attractions of the Alter Markt Christmas market, together with the old carousel, the Ferris wheel and the large ice-skating rink.

On the south bank of the Rhine, close to the Chocolate Museum and the Ferris wheel (from which you'll get an unparalelled view of the city), you'll find the Harbour Christmas Market. Here, about seventy artisans set up an atmospheric maritime market. Of course, it gets its theme from its gorgeously picturesque location overlooking the Rhine and the watery theme is carried through via sea shanties and seafood dishes. You'll even find some stalls housed inside traditional wooden boats rather than huts.

Once the Christmas market season is over, Cologne becomes the perfect place to leave everyday clothes at home and opt instead for colourful costumes, extravagant make-up and flamboyant wigs. The Cologne Carnival (Koelner Carnival) officially starts on 11/11 at 11.11 am. with the greeting "*Kölle Alaaf!*" (Long

Live Cologne) and the presentation of the three main protagonists of the Carnival: Die Jungfrau (the virgin), Der Bauer (the farmer), Der Prinz (the prince). But it's not until February that the entire city goes really wild. In fact, it's during the six days before Ash Wednesday when you'll experience the real joy of Carnival, and can dance until the early hours of the morning in Cologne's many queer clubs and discos.

The most important days of the Cologne Carnival are Saturday, when the alternative Geisterzug Ghost Procession happens, and Monday, the day when Rosenmontagszug, the official parade and the largest carnival parade of floats in Germany, takes place. It's a must-see event, so be sure to get there early to claim a good spot.

If you are not in Cologne in the winter, the other main event is the Cologne Pride, one of the largest pride festivals in Germany, held between June and July and hosting countless political and cultural events, plus incredible parties.

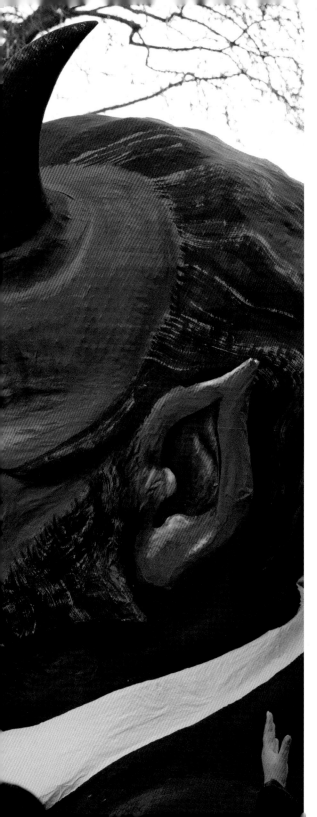

LISTINGS

STAY

Cologne offers varied accommodation options that won't break the bank. The city is relatively small which allows you to stay in more peripheral neighbourhoods, but still remain within easy reach of all the main places of interest on foot or using the widespread public transport system. Use the Queer City Pass (queercitypass.com/en/cologne-en) to travel on all metro (subway and tram) and suburban rail lines as well as buses, while benefitting from discounts from all Queer City Pass partners. It's always a good idea to book early if you intend to visit Cologne during the Christmas market season, Carnival or for Pride.

Hotel Flandrischer Hof Flandrische Str. 3-11; flandrischerhof.de. The location of this 3-star hotel is ideal for those who want to experience Cologne's Belgian Quarter to the fullest. The rooms are tastefully decorated, and it's pet-friendly.

Hostel Köln Marsilstein 29; hostel.ag/en. Stylish combination of budget hotel and hostel with a children's play area and an excellent central location. There are no dorms as such; rooms are only rented whole. Breakfast is included in the price.

Köln-Deutz City Hostel Siegesstr. 5; jugendherberge. de/jugendherbergen/koeln-deutz-450/portraet. Large and functional DJH hostel close to Deutz station, directly across the Rhine from the Altstadt. Facilities include a disco room.

Lindner Hotel City Plaza Magnusstraße 20; lindner. de/koeln-hotel-city-plaza/ankommen.html. A modern 4-star hotel with all the necessary creature comforts to guarantee a pleasant holiday. Each floor of the hotel is decorated with icons of the city: from the Eau de Cologne to the Cathedral, from the Three Kings to the famous Carnival. The breakfast is hearty and wholesome, and the staff very friendly.

Tante ALMA's Hotel Lasthaus am Ring Hohenzollernring 20; tante-alma-hotels.com/koeln. Eccentric and unique decorations for those who want to take a leap back into the twentith century, amidst coloured armchairs and wallpaper. The breakfast is plentiful and the rooms are very comfortable.

EAT

Bunte Burger Hospeltstraße 1; bunteburger.de. Organic restaurant famous for its excellent vegan burgers, vegan doner kebab and vegan *currywurst*. Be sure not to miss the brunch on Sundays with its hearty buffet of hot and cold dishes, soups and salads.

COCO Ramen WDR Arkaden, Breite Str. 26; cocoramen. de. This is *the* place to enjoy fresh, tasty Asian food in Cologne, serving up everything from curry to ramen and other traditional Japanese dishes.

Früh am Dom Am Hof 12–18; frueh-am-dom.de. Near the Dom and fronted by a marvellous fountain, this huge traditional Brauhaus has a long history and does really excellent, hearty German food.

Gaffel Am Dom Bahnhofsvorpl. 1; gaffelamdom.de. Just a few steps from the Cathedral, this brewery is has a typical tavern atmosphere. From local cuisine to seasonal highlights like mussels, chanterelles and asparagus, the food here is a real treat for the palate.

maiBeck Am Frankenturm 5; feinkost-maibeck.de. This top Michelin starred restaurant is known for its modern and sophisticated cuisine, made with regional and extremely high-quality produce.

Maison SEN Friesenplatz 7; maisonsen.de. Here you'll find regional cuisine of North Vietnam. Sweet-and-sour as well as spicy sauces and fresh fruits like mango, pineapple, lychee and coconut feature prominently on the menu, and there is a long roster of vegan options.

Mashery – Hummus Kitchen Roonstraße 36; mashery-hummus.de. Chickpeas, silky tahini, the freshest lemons and lots of love are the secret ingredients for the best hummus in Cologne. Dishes are prepared only with seasonal ingredients, mostly vegetarian or vegan.

Mühlenkölsch Heumarkt 6; muehlenkoelsch.de. Opened over 160 years ago, this beer tavern remains a genuine family brewery and it's the perfect place to try delicious local cuisine.

Peters Brauhaus Mühlengasse 1; peters-brauhaus. de. This popular beer tavern requires reservations if you want to eat, but it's worth visiting even if only to admire the grand Art Deco decor.

Vintage chocolate display inside the Chocolate Museum

A drag queen at the Cologne Pride Parade

DRINK

Baustelle 4U Vor Sankt Martin 12; baustelle4u.de. Very popular gay bar in the Old Town of Cologne. Famous for its themed events for fetish lovers, sneaker boys and bears.

BOlze.bar Friesenstraße 43; facebook.com/BOlze. bar. Despire the name, this is a cosy women-only bar with an industrial vibe; all women-identifying folk are welcome here – but be warned: if you identify as male, it's likely you will be turned away. The main event happens on Tuesdays evening, when they host the dating show "Princess Charming".

ExCorner Schaafenstraße 57-59; instagram.com/cornercologne. Super colourful and a bit kitschy, *ExCorner* is a real institution in Cologne. Be sure to come here for the famous happy hour (every day from 9 until 10pm you'll get two beers for the price of one), as well as to drink excellent cocktails and dance to good pop music. Especially popular on the weekend.

Exile Schaafenstraße 61a; exile-cologne.de. Situated in the heart of the LGBTQ+ district of Cologne, *Exile* is one of the most popular gay bars in the city. Drag shows as well as themed and games nights make this *the* place to dance and meet new friends.

Hennes Terrace Mauritiuswall 102; instagram.com/hennes_terrasse. A fabulous and friendly queer bar, especially very popular in spring when the weather is good. Known for its beautiful outside terrace and excellent cocktails that often come adorned with sweets, it's located near the Rudolfplatz and is a great place to stop by for a drink before going out dancing until the small wee hours.

Die Mumu Schaafenstraße 51; die-mumu.de. This queer bar has a slightly more lesbian-oriented clientele (though everyone is welcome!) and is very popular among young people. Come here for the delectable cocktails.

DANCE

The Altmarkt area is the main locus of nightlife for visitors; locals tend to prefer the western part of the city along the Ring, while students gather around Zülpicher Platz and Brüsseler Platz.

Backstage Diaries Ehrenfeldgürtel 127. A party that takes place on the second Saturday of the month and is perfect for indie and electronic music lovers.

GreenKomm Hohenzollernring 89-93; greenkomm.com. One of Cologne's most famous and longest-running afterparties. It has been held since 1993, usually once a month on the first Sunday, and attracts a mostly queer as well as queer-friendly clientele.

SEXY Bootshaus, Auenweg 173; sexyparty.cologne/events. The leading gay party in Germany hosts shows, performances and international guests.

SHOP

Belgian Quarter Around the Belgian Quarter you'll find countless young fashion designers' boutiques, vintage shops, handmade products and custom-tailored jewels.

Hohe Straße Clothes, shoes, souvenirs and electronic equipment are just some of the goodies you will find on this iconic street that runs from Wallrafplatz to Schildergasse. The cafés and restaurants on the Wallrafplatz are a great bet for a place to stop and rest with a beer after all that retail therapy.

Schildergasse Cologne's most popular shopping street, Schildergasse is the place to find major department stores such as Galeria Kaufhof and Peek & Cloppenburg shopping centre. The streets around Schildergasse also offer some serious shopping.

The Kölntriangle

Eau De Cologne for sale at the Farina Fragrance Museum

DO

Centrum Schwule Geschichte (CSG – Centre for Gay History) Gustav-Heinemann-Ufer 58; csgkoeln.org. Since 1984, the CSG has been carrying out the impressive work of collecting and cataloguing documents on the history of the German LGBTQ+ community. Their "Warme Meilen" city tour is a great way to get to know the untold story of the queer community in Germany.

The Chocolate Museum Am Schokoladenmuseum 1A; schokoladenmuseum.de. Cologne's most visited museum is throughly enjoyable for adults and children alike; in fact, it's perfect for chocolate-lovers of any age! The museum illustrates the history of chocolate from its origins to modern production methods. Best of all, though, you can taste a freshly made chocolate bar and a wafer covered with chocolate from the beautiful chocolate fountain overlooking the Rhine.

The Dom Domkloster 4; koelner-dom.de/en. Cologne's gigantic Dom is one of the largest Gothic buildings ever built. Climb the 509 steps to the top of the south tower for a breathtaking panorama over the city and the Rhine, and seek out the Domschatzkammer in the vaults, containing a stunning array of treasury items.

Eau de Cologne Farina Fragrance Museum, Obenmarspforten 21; farina.org/welcome. Step back into the early eighteenth century to when Italian chemist Giovanni-Maria Farina created the most popular fragrance in the world; he named it Eau de Cologne as a thank-you to his adopted city, and nowadays aftershave is also known the world over by the moniker "cologne". The amazing story is told in the exhibition at the Farina Fragrance Museum.

KölnTriangle Ottoplatz 1; koelntrianglepanorama.de/en. This massive glass tower was built in 2005 by the German architect Dörte Gatermann. At 100 metres tall, it boast the highest viewpoint in the city. In summer, the KoelnTriangle is open until 11pm, but the perfect time to enjoy the view is at sunset.

Street art Street art is ubiquitous in Cologne; just keep your eyes peeled and soon you will begin to see it everywhere. Try to spot the a winged car on the roof of a museum or the banana stencils, a new symbol of Cologne street art. Once evry two years, the city hosts the City Leaks Festival (cityleaks-festival.de/en), one of the most important festivals for street art, temporary installations and experiments in urban landscapes.

FESTLASTBILER.DK

COPENHAGEN
Winter

Velkommen til København! Copenhagen, Denmark's affluent and open-minded capital, is a cool, compact and caffeinated city nestled between the Baltic and North seas. Easily navigated on foot or by bicycle, Copenhagen has heaps to offer: from its now well-established 'New Nordic' cuisine to newer, more affordable pop-up eateries and restaurants employing the same principles. There are museums on every other corner, enough cafés and bakeries to give Paris a run for its euros and, during winter months, the city oozes *hygge*. Best of all, liberal Denmark consistently falls close to the very top of Rainbow Europe's Country Ranking for LGBTQ+ rights. *Lad os gå!* (Let's go!)

HISTORY

Copenhagen (*København*) is the capital of Denmark (*Danmark*), a northern European country which shares a land border with Germany to the south, counts Norway and Sweden as its closest neighbours (to the north and northeast respectively), and is made up of more than 400 islands – 70-something of which are inhabited. While the Danish section of the Jutland peninsula is larger in surface area, the island of Zealand, home to Copenhagen, is its most populous.

Positioned on the Øresund, a major waterway between the Baltic and North Sea, Copenhagen emerged as a fishing village and became a stop-off for passing trade, before growing to become a key naval port and commercial centre during the reign of Christian IV of Denmark (1588-1648). In fact, the Danish 'København' translates to 'merchant's harbour'. Though precise dates vary, Copenhagen was established as Denmark's capital city by the late fifteenth century.

As its cultural prominence grew during the 1700s–1800s, the city was repeatedly faced with wars, plagues and two notably devastating fires in which many of its earliest buildings were destroyed or

Rosenborg Castle and Christiansborg Palace spire

damaged – including the observatory at the top of the *Rundetårn* (Roundtower) which still stands proudly in the medieval maze of Indre By (literally 'Inner City').

By the nineteenth and twentieth centuries, Copenhagen was an established centre for culture, education and industry. Tivoli Gardens, the city's famous theme park created by Georg Carstensen, opened on 15th August 1843 counting the (LGBTQ+) author Hans Christian Anderson as one of its first guests. Come the 1970s, the squatter-built 'Freetown' of Christiania was founded during a period of unrest between citizens and police. Fifty years later, this bastion of freedom and self-governance still exists, attracting thousands of visitors every year. Make sure to leave cameras in pockets when visiting this spot so as not to perturb the locals, particularly on 'Pusher Street' where marijuana is sold openly.

On 1st October 1989 in a ceremony at Copenhagen's City Hall, gay rights activist Axel Axgil and his partner became the first LGBTQ+ couple ever to enter into a same-sex civil union. Denmark was the first modern nation in the world to legally recognise same-sex partnerships. Axel was also a founder of Denmark's first LGBTQ+ rights organisation, LGBT Danmark. In 2021, Copenhagen, along with its Swedish neighbour Malmö, hosted World Pride.

ICON

Here we turn to the beginning of the twentieth century and the celebrated Danish painter, Lili Elbe. Born in the winter of 1882, Elbe, a trans woman, was one of the first known people to undergo gender-affirmation surgery at an experimental clinic in Germany.

Before becoming Lili, she married fellow artist Gerda Gottlieb. The pair met while they were both students at the Royal Danish Academy of Fine Arts in Copenhagen. It was around this time that Elbe, then known under her birth name, rose to fame, becoming a highly respected landscape painter.

It's worthwhile noting that her partner Gerda, who depicted Elbe in many of her works, was an important painter in her own right – her boundary-pushing depictions of women in an Art Nouveau (and often provocative or sexualised) style were exhibited at Arken Museum of Modern Art in Ishøj from 2015–17.

In wider culture, Elbe is perhaps most famously known as the subject of Tom Hooper's 2015 film *The Danish Girl*, loosely based on Elbe's life. The film stars Alicia Vikander as Gerda and Eddie Redmayne as Lili; Redmayne said in the years following the film's release that he wouldn't take the role on if it were offered to him now, as he believes that Elbe should be portrayed by a trans actor.

The longstanding, annual MIX Copenhagen LGBTQ+ film festival has an award category named for Elbe and on 28th December 2022, she was featured in a Google Doodle by Dutch illustrator Hilde Sam Atalanta in celebration of her 140th birthday.

City Hall Square

HIGHLIGHT

Though most say Copenhagen comes to life in the summer months (and they're not wrong), May to August are also the city's busiest. This is when *københavners* take time to enjoy everything their waterfront city has to offer, while tourists flock to join them. Winter, on the other hand, is a more understated affair. Though temperatures drop and the days are shorter, there is magic to be found here during wintertime – just remember to wear an extra layer!

Even when it's cold outside, indoors Copenhagen thrums with *hygge*; think cosy pubs and steamy-windowed cafés, open fires, woolly jumpers and meals enjoyed with friends and family. Then of course there's *J-Dag*, Denmark's beery tradition which begins in November (at 8.59pm on the first Friday, to be precise) and runs throughout winter. This is the almost holy day when local brewery Tuborg release their Christmas brew and the streets of Copenhagen come to life with festive merriment, marking the beginning of the holiday season.

On top of this, Christmas markets abound, with the crowded but marvellous Tivoli Christmas Market and Freetown Christiania's crafty, alternative 'Jule Marked' being just two highlights. Equally, TorvehallerneKBH Market Hall throngs with locals filling up on fresh, local (though pricey) produce and carts pop up on bustling corners throughout Indre By selling *gløgg* (mulled wine with almonds, raisins and schnapps) and *rostade kastanjer* (roasted chestnuts). If snow falls, the central historic attractions of Rosenborg Castle and Christiansborg Palace both make for postcard perfect stop-offs.

One particular highlight of the winter months is Winter Pride. Yes, this city is so LGBTQ-friendly that they throw Pride *twice*! Taking place in February, Winter Pride acts as a veritable beacon of light during the city's darker months, as well as an opportunity for the queer community to come together and celebrate for a second time. The main event is housed at Huset-KBH (Rådhusstræde 13, 1466) close to the 'gay quarter', Studiestræde, a colourful shopping street that's not far from *Københavns Universitet*, Denmark's oldest university. The full Winter Pride programme of events is released in January.

LISTINGS

STAY

25Hours Hotel Copenhagen Pilestræde 65; 25hours-hotels.com/en/hotels/copenhagen. Centrally located and housed in a former porcelain factory and university building, *25Hours* revels in its *beau histoire* as a locus of art and knowledge. Vibrant, colourful and chic.

71 Nyhaven Nyhavn 71; 71nyhavnhotel.com. Two interconnected converted warehouses overlooking Inderhavnen and next door to the city's playhouse, *71 Nyhavn* is a charming place to stay. Although it is slightly on the small side, the hotel's magnificent location easily makes up for this slight shortfall. Superior rooms feature pretty French doors opening onto a balcony. Primarily a business hotel, there are some good deals to be had during summer.

Admiral Hotel Toldbodgade 24-28; admiralhotel.dk/en. A 200-year-old former warehouse, this waterfront hotel is both established and environmentally-conscious. Wooden-beamed and golden-hued, it sits opposite Copenhagen Opera House and within walking distance of the star-shaped Kastellet.

Next House Copenhagen Bernstorffsgade 27; nexthousecopenhagen.com. Close to Central Station, Tivoli and the trendy Meatpacking District in Vesterbro, dorms in this luxury hostel are basic but quiet and comfortable. Expect a youthful, beer pong-playing crowd on weekends.

Palace Hotel Rådhuspladsen 57; palacehotelcopenhagen.com. Wonderful Art Nouveau hotel from 1910 located next door to the Rådhus. A refurbishment has reinstated its original decor, featuring lovely details such as George Jensen silver door handles and abstract artwork; rooms have also been modernised with comfy beds and luxurious bathrooms. During its heyday many a Hollywood star stayed here, including the likes of Audrey Hepburn and Gregory Peck.

A colourful installation in the arty district of Christiania

EAT

Aamanns Øster Farimagsgade 10-12; aamanns.dk. This stylish ode to traditional Danish open sandwiches makes hands-down the city's best *smørrebrød*. Head chef Adam Aamanns ensures everything is free range and sourced from local Danish farmers. It's perfect for a visit with children, too, who love the bite-sized portions. You can either eat in or take away in smart little picnic-friendly boxes.

Conditori La Glace Skoubogade 3; laglace.dk. Traditional patisserie serving beautifully crafted cakes and pastries. Try the scrumptious HC Hat cake, made with chocolate, caramel mousse and lemon ganache.

DINA Vester Voldgade 19; dinabarkafe.dk. On the corner of Studiestræde and Vester Voldgade, *DINA* is all soft jazz, candle-lit tables and Parisian vibes. Serving quality coffee, sandwiches, salads and French–Danish mains as well as excellent cocktails.

DØP Købmagergade 52; døp.dk/en. Arguably the most upmarket of the umpteen hotdog carts that pepper the city (Copenhagen loves hotdogs), *DØP* uses only organic ingredients to create its mouthwatering 'dogs. Vegetarian options are also available.

Hija de Sanchez Kødbyen Slagterboderne 8; lovesanchez.com. Created by Rosio Sanchez, this is one of several branches of the award-winning taqueria, with a small but considered menu built on New Nordic principles: local, fresh, sustainable.

KanalCafeen Frederiksholms Kanal 18; kanalcafeen. dk. Founded in 1852, this cosy, historic lunchtime restaurant opposite Christiansborg serves outstanding, good-value *smørrebrød*. Inside, the decor is all heavy tablecloths and period oil paintings, while outside there's canal side seating in summer.

TorvehallerneKBH Frederiksborggade 21; torvehallernekbh.dk. Copenhagen's Market Hall, this is a must-visit for foodies seeking high quality local produce. Visit *Hallernes* for *smørrebrød*, *Rørt* for 'spread salads', and *Arla Unika* for cheese. Right by Nørreport Metro Station.

DRINK

1105 Kristen Bernikows Gade 4; 1105.dk. Cool, elegant, low-lit cocktail bar, where the mixologists wear crisp white lab coats. *1105* has made a name for itself with the creation of the Copenhagen cocktail, a delicious mix of *genever* (Dutch gin), cherry liqueur, lime juice and a host of secret ingredients.

Bibendum Nansensgade 45; bibendum.dk. Small, cosy basement wine bar with a huge selection of wine, all of which are sold by the glass as well as by the bottle. Also does good nibbles to soak up the alcohol, such as cheese and charcuterie platters and a delicious fish soup.

Bo-Bi Bar Klareboderne 4. Opened in 1917, *Bo-Bi Bar* sports Copenhagen's oldest bar counter and attracts a boho clientele of writers, students and intellectuals – great for peoplewatching. Serves cheap bottles of great Danish and Czech beers as well as local schnapps.

Cafe Intime Allegade 25; cafeintime.dk. Established in 1922, this Montmarte-inspired café-bar is worth visiting. Though the crowd is mixed, LGBTQ+ ephemera fills the walls. Pre-Christmas, expect live piano, hot *gløgg* and a warm welcome from locals. Note that smoking is still permitted indoors here. Cash only.

Centralhjørnet Kattesundet 18; centralhjornet.dk. Denmark's oldest gay bar according to local lore, cosy pub *Centralhjørnet* is a staple destination on the LGBTQ+ rounds. It's also the undisputed (unofficial) winner of the 'Most OTT Christmas Decorations in Copenhagen' award.

Curfew Stenosgade 1; curfew.dk. Lavish cocktail bar inspired by the speakeasy culture of the 1920s and 1930s, run by flamboyant Portuguese-born cocktail aficionado, Humberto Marques. Also serves tapas.

Kalaset Vendersgade 16 kalaset.dk. Quirky shabby-chic basement café which spills out onto the pavement during summer when it's an excellent spot to enjoy the sunshine while sipping a cool drink. During weekends a DJ gets the party going.

Mikkeller Viktoriagade 8, B-C; mikkeller.com/locations. The original *Mikkeller* bar, *Viktoriagade* opened in 2010 and the beer has been flowing ever

Orstedsparken

Bob Rockwell performs live jazz with his band at Jazzcup

since. Snug, unassuming and wonderfully *hygge*-worthy. On the same street as *Vela Gay Club*.

Nemoland Christiania; nemoland. dk. This lively café-bar with a large outdoor space is a popular place for visitors to sample purchases from 'Pusher Street' undisturbed. There are free gigs on a rickety stage outside on summer Sundays, featuring well-known Danish artists and lesser-known international acts.

Nørrebro Bryghus Ryesgade 3; noerrebrobryghus.dk. Microbrewery-cum-restaurant where you can try beer-glazed cauliflower and *panna cotta* served with beer syrup. Surprisingly, it all does seem to work, and the long wood-beamed tables are packed to capacity most nights. Hourlong brewery tours led by the chief brewer include four samples en route.

Oscar Bar Café Regnbuepladsen 9; oscarbarcafe. dk. *DINA*'s big brother is most popular with gay male clientele, though certainly not exclusively. Find coffee and *smørrebrød* during the day, upbeat bops, beers (and the odd bear) by night.

DANCE

Cosy Bar Studiestræde 24; denmarkcosybar.dk. *Cosy* (and it *is* cosy) is where the queers go to dance until dawn (6am, to be precise). Located on the particularly LGBTQ+-friendly Studiestræde and popular with a young, mixed crowd.

Culture Box Kronprinsessegade 54; culture-box.com. Spread over two floors, with a Berlin-style industrial decor, this popular bar-club keeps going until the wee hours of the morning. Revellers tend to get the party started first at *The White Box* cocktail bar next door.

Vega Enghavevej; vega.dk. A favourite amongst locals, this wood-panelled, mahogany-floored music venue hosts Danish and international acts alike. *Lille VEGA* is the more intimate of its two concert halls.

Vela Gay Club Viktoriagade 2-4; velagayclub.dk. Though open to all genders, shapes and sizes, *Vela* is generally where Copenhagen's queer women and non-binary folk flock. Serving beers, cocktails and folkloric foosball matches, *Vela* is more of a bar than a club.

SHOP

Designer Zoo Vesterbrogade 137; designerzoo.dk. Welcoming store run by eight designers selling own-made furniture, jewellery, knitwear, pottery and glass. A great place for that elusive Christmas gift.

Ecouture by Lund Læderstræde 5; ecouture. dk. You can now find the glamorous, bohemian women's clothing line with organic/socially responsible stance (hence the "eco" in the name) in a central location – although opening hours remain restricted.

Jazzcup Gothersgade 107; jazzklubben.dk. Excellent music store specialising in jazz, blues, soul and world music. It also has a small café and hosts regular, intimate live shows.

Paustian Kalkbrænderiløbskaj 2; paustian.dk. Superb designer furniture sold in a magnificent building designed by Jørn Utzon of Sydney Opera House fame. The vast range on offer includes own-brand furniture as well as iconic pieces such as Alvar Aalto sofas and Verner Panton chairs. There's also a stylish restaurant.

Royal Copenhagen Amagertorv 6; royalcopenhagen.com. Flagship store for the Royal Porcelain Factory's famous china, distinguished by its blue patterning. The beautiful gabled store building, from 1616, is one of the city's oldest, having survived countless city-centre fires. Pricetags are accordingly hefty.

Soul Books Læderstræde 13; soulbooks.dk. A warm nook of a bookshop in the heart of the city offering English and Danish-language books on mindfulness, spirituality, psychedelics, creativity, witchcraft and more. One for the soul seekers.

SummerBird Værnedamsvej 9; summerbird.dk. Dinky little chocolatier selling arguably the world's best chocolate. Try the otherworldly *flødeboller* (cream buns) – fluffy, chocolate-coated marshmallow treats.

Tranquebar Borgergade 14; tranquebar.net. A cosy, centrally-located book, music and gift shop specialising in travel, they also serve up a decent cup of coffee. What more could a sleepy visitor need? See their website for occasional events.

Post-it notes at the Happiness Museum where visitors answer the question: What makes you happy?

A panorama of the city at the Museum of Copenhagen

DO

Christiania Mælkevejen 69D; christiania.org. Copenhagen's alternative enclave, squatters declared *Christiania* a 'free city' in 1971. Stop in for the best falafel in town, their crafty Christmas 'Jule Marked', or visit the LGBTQ+ community hub and events space, *Bøssehuset*. Many stalls are cash only.

Danish Film Institute Gothersgade 55; dfi.dk/en. Much like London's BFI, the DFI celebrates Danish film and culture. Especially worth visiting during October's MIX Copenhagen — one of the longest running LGBTQ+ film festivals in the world.

The Happiness Museum Admiralgade 19; thehappinessmuseum.com. Visit the tiny but wonderful *Lykkemuseet* to find out why Nordic countries are some of the happiest in the world. An independent museum sure to put a smile on your face.

LGBT+ Library Vestergade 18E, 4th floor; lgbt.dk/en/lgbt-library. Less of a tourist attraction but worth highlighting, the LGBT+ Library is run by national organisation LGBT Danmark and serves as a resource for locals accessing queer literature, history, community and more.

Museum of Copenhagen Stormgade 18; cphmuseum.kk.dk. What it lacks in general pizazz, the Museum of Copenhagen makes up for in its 'Queer in Copenhagen' audio tour, a journey through 1000 years of the city's LGBTQ+ history.

Ørstedsparken Nørre Voldgade 1. With its hills and lake, this park is popular in winter for skating and downhill sledging. There are also two innovative playgrounds here, one with staff at hand to show you the ropes. Come nightfall it becomes a gay hangout.

Tivoli Gardens (Christmas Market) Vesterbrogade 3; tivoli.dk/en. You'll struggle to find a guidebook that doesn't list nineteenth-century amusement park Tivoli; what they sometimes neglect to mention is its Christmas Market. With *gløgg*, *rostade kastanjer* and 50+ stalls selling all manner of festive finery, it would be a shame to miss it if you're planning a winter trip.

Dublin Pride Parade

DUBLIN
Winter

Ireland's capital is fast-paced, lively and creative. Home to over a quarter of the country's population, the city's character is defined by its cosy pubs, fascinating historic buildings and progressive outlook. The city lights are up in winter and you can't help but be inspired as you wrap up warm to explore Dublin's markets, as well as its buzzing live music and vibrant food scene. Pulsating with history and charm, Dublin is shedding its more traditionally conservative past and embracing a new cosmopolitan outlook that welcomes diversity and multiculturalism.

HISTORY

Dublin sits on over a thousand years of history; the city's roots are in fourth century *Áth Cliath* (Hurdled Ford), seventh century monastic *Duiblinn* (Blackpool), ninth century Viking longphuirt and the resultant eleventh century Hiberno-Norse town. Its history is written in its buildings, from the Anglo-Norman walls of the old city; the derelict Georgian mansions of Henrietta Street; to the bullet holes riddling the General Post Office.

Dublin (and Ireland as a whole) is well-known for Guinness, which finds its origins here and is now sold in 150 countries around the world. If you're a fan of the stout (or indeed of Irish history of culture), head to the iconic Guinness Brewery to visit a key part of the city's history – it's located on the site where Arthur Guinness first set up shop in 1759. A shrewd businessman, he managed to haggle an impressive 9,000 year lease for just £45 a year. Whilst the factory located in the city no longer produces Guinness, it has instead become a museum for everything you could ever want to know about Dublin's iconic beverage and offers a very informative tour and, of course, pints of the good stuff. And as for the £45 lease – it's definitely worth noting that it's no longer in operation. Since the time of Arthur Guinness, the site has been bought out by the company and they now own it outright.

For bibliophiles, it's good to know that literature has always flourished in Dublin, the city has produced three Nobel Prize–winning writers – Yeats, Shaw and Beckett. James Joyce imagined and interpreted Dublin in his most famous work, *Ulysses*, and the city was also once home to Oscar Wilde; he was born here in 1854 to Irish parents and studied at Trinity College in the 1870s. When leaving Ireland, the author of *The Picture of Dorian Gray* was sentenced to two years in prison because of his sexuality; fast forward almost 150 years and Wilde's hometown is making history for all the right reasons as Ireland became the world's first country to hold a popular vote in favour of same-sex marriage. It was in May 2015 that the city's streets saw huge celebrations and the Dublin Castle lit up in the colours of the Pride flag as thousands celebrated the victory in its eighteenth century courtyard.

OF FINE SMOKING
OBACCO
Always in Stock

THE TEMPLE BAR

Traditional
Irish Music

The
TEMPLE BAR
Est. 1840
Traditional Food Fare
Meat Plate, Cheese Board
Fresh Oysters, Smoked Salmon
Charcuterie Meats, Olives
Toasted Sandwiches
Hot Roast Beef Rolls

ICON

Dubbed the 'accidental activist' and national treasure of Ireland, Panti Bliss is a world-famous drag queen who grew up in County Mayo but has called Dublin home since the mid-1980s. Otherwise known as Rory O'Neill, Panti Bliss was a prominent figure during Ireland's equal marriage campaign in 2015.

After starting drag, Panti quickly made a name for themself and by 1995 they were organising Dublin's best club nights, hosting the Alternative Miss Ireland competition and performing all over the world.

The 'accidental' activism started when Rory, Panti's male alter-ego, called out the homophobia they'd seen in national journalists on an episode of Irish talk show *The Saturday Night Show* on RTÉ, Ireland's national TV station; the incident came to be known as 'Pantigate' as several of the journalists named threatened RTÉ and O'Neill with legal action; the station issues a public apology and made large payouts to those

named. However, international support for O'Neill soon followed and Panti was invited to deliver a speech at the Abbey Theatre on the oppression they felt living as a queer person in Ireland. The speech quickly went viral and Panti was praised for their honest and eloquent words by the likes of Madonna, Graham Norton and Stephen Fry.

By the time Ireland's equal marriage campaign rolled round in 2015, Panti had become a figurehead for LGBTQ+ rights and was campaigning relentlessly for equal marriage in Dublin and across Ireland. In the same year, Panti featured as the subject of Conor Horgan's box office documentary hit, *The Queen of Ireland*. Taking five years to make, the film secured the highest ever grossing opening weekend of an Irish documentary in cinemas. The film follows Panti's life, from growing up in Mayo to their work and activism around the marriage equality campaign.

When you visit Dublin, make sure to visit Panti's very own *Pantibar* – a staple of Dublin's queer scene since 2007 that serves up drag shows and drinks in a relaxed atmosphere.

Rainbow outfits at Dublin Pride

HIGHLIGHT

Known as Dublin's 'cultural quarter', Temple Bar is an iconic neighbourhood that has transformed from a rundown, seedy neighbourhood into a bustling bohemian area full of the capital's favourite bars, theatres and cafés. It may be touristy, but a wander round the area's narrow, partly pedestrianised eighteenth-century cobbled lanes (featuring some original architecture) draws in the crowds for a reason.

The name Temple Bar is thought to have come from the Temple family, who built a house on the marshy lands way back in the early seventeenth century. However, other stories suggest that it may have been named after the area of London of the same name.

Today, it's hard to imagine Temple Bar as anything but a creative hub full of tourists and locals alike enjoying a drink on the busy streets; in the eighteenth century, however, it offered little more than brothels and rundown buildings. The area's decline continued until the 1990s, when the Dublin Council stepped in to revamp the neighbourhood by introducing business incentives, cheap rents and the idyllic cobbled streets that have come to personify the area.

Modern-day Temple Bar has everything you could want for a perfect day out in Ireland's capital. Whether you came to Ireland seeking to see live Irish folk music with a pint of Guinness, to wander round art galleries or to spend all night dancing in one of the street's queer-owned clubs – you'll find it all here, and there will be lots of other locals and tourists enjoying this spot along with you. If you find yourself wandering around during the afternoon, it's worth checking out cultural landmarks such as the Irish Film Institute, DESIGNyard and the National Photographic Archive. As the sun sets and the streets begin filling up with after-work revellers, grab a drink at *Street 66*; this intimate gay bar is packed with living room furniture, board games and regular drag performances.

Finally, to make sure that you enjoy the full experience and important history of the neighbourhood, make a beeline for Dublin's most famous pub, *The Temple Bar* itself. Established in 1840, it has stood tall during Temple Bar's decline and subsequent regeneration in the 1990s – as well as being home to Ireland's largest collection of rare whisky (450 types, to be precise).

A busker playing piano on Grafton Street

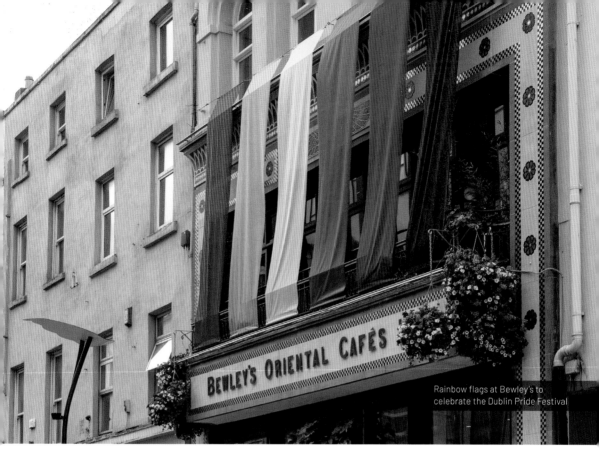

LISTINGS

STAY

Arlington Hotel O'Connell Bridge 23–25 Bachelors Walk; arlington.ie. Sensationally located 3-star hotel and pub on the north bank of the Liffey, in the absolute heart of the city, near O'Connell Bridge – handy for concert arenas, sightseeing, and theatres. Friendly staff and well-maintained rooms. The pub downstairs (facing the river) hosts Celtic Nights with live traditional Irish music and dancing.

Blooms Hotel 3–6 Anglesea Street, Temple Bar; blooms.ie. A convenient modern hotel in the Temple Bar area, *Blooms* is a decent choice for partygoers, but not for those planning a quiet night; *Club M* is just downstairs.

Central Hotel 1–5 Exchequer Street; centralhoteldublin. ie. A modest and comfortable hotel, furnished in Victorian style and well-located midway between Temple Bar and Grafton Street. The first-floor *Library Bar* attracts literary types.

Number 31 31 Leeson Close; number31.ie. This upscale B&B is a favourite with regular visitors to Dublin. It features spacious rooms, listed architecture, a sunken lounge with fireplace, and a fabulous Irish breakfast in the conservatory.

Wynn's Hotel 35–39 Lower Abbey Street; wynnshotel. ie. This old-fashioned city centre hotel has been a landmark since Victorian times and is just around the corner from the Abbey Theatre. This one is a favourite meeting spot for Dubliners, with a genuine local buzz, and a busy restaurant at lunch and in the early evening.

EAT

Aobaba 46A Capel St, North City; aobaba.com. Bringing Vietnamese street food to Dublin, *Aobaba* offers a wallet-friendly menu with scrumptious noodle soups and a huge range of bubble teas. Kumquat bubble tea, anyone?

Bambino 37 Stephen Street Lower; bmbno.ie. This places offers New York-style pizza slices that have garnered a lot of hype. Order a slice and sip on a beer to find out what everyone's been raving about.

Bewley's Grafton Street Café 78–79 Grafton Street; bewleys.com. No one should miss a trip to the original *Bewley's Oriental Café* with its Arts and Crafts stained-glass windows. Delicious fair trade coffee, teas, and a range of dishes are on offer for breakfast, lunch, and dinner. The location is perfect for a quick pit-stop while shopping and it's a popular meeting spot with locals and tourists alike. Visit the Bewley's Theatre (bewleyscafetheatre.com) for lunchtime and evening musical and theatrical performances.

Café en Seine 39–40 Dawson Street; cafeenseine. ie. Stunning Art Deco interior with three-storey atrium featuring intimate bars within bars. The casual, contemporary food – dry aged Irish beef, sustainable seafood, freshly baked bread – is on offer all day and well into the night. The menu is rich with something for every taste, all at prices your pocket will love. It's a lovely place to stay on for a drink afterwards too.

Daddy's Café 538 S Circular Rd, Rialto; daddys.ie. A lively café with bright tables and even brighter food. Come for the best Irish comfort food including tarts and sandwiches – all made with seasonal and local produce. Expect locally roasted coffee and homebakes. No booking; walk-ins only.

Saucy Cow 19 Crane Lane, Temple Bar; thesaucycow. com. A vegan fast food joint with all the fried chicken, sloppy kebabs and dirty fries you could dream of. Expect music, a good atmosphere and even some tote bags for sale should you want a souvenir.

Two Boys Brew 375 N Circular Rd, Phibsborough; twoboysbrew.ie. This is a thriving speciality coffee and food space located in the heart of Dublin 7. For groups of six or more, you can book ahead to guarantee your table at this popular brunch spot serving everything from your classic avocado toast to Asian-style fritters.

Gravity Bar

DRINK

All My Friends 61-63 Meath St, The Liberties; instagram.com/allmyfriendspub. An inclusive bar, venue and community space in the middle of Dublin's most famous market street. The perfect place for a weekly pub quiz or karaoke before a night out.

The Bailey Bar 1–4 Duke Street; baileybarcafe.com. A busy, trendy bar on the site of Leopold Bloom's house.

The Big Romance 98 Parnell St, Rotunda; thebigromance.ie. *The Big Romance* is an audiophile bar with a custom soundsystem, great music, craft beers and a friendly crowd. For jazz fans, make sure to head here on a Sunday.

Pantibar 7-8 Capel St, North City; pantibar.com. Owned by Dublin's national treasure, Panti Bliss, this bar is a great place for a relaxed drink and a drag show. Expect a variety of drinks, including prosecco on tap and Panti's Pale Ale.

DANCE

Centre Point Curved St, Temple Bar; centrepointclub. ie. This club is where all the biggest DJs play when passing through Dublin. From big names from Folamour to Chaos In The CBD, *Centre Point* is sure to provide you with a memorable night out.

The George 89 South Great George's Street; thegeorge. ie. Without a doubt, this is Dublin's most iconic gay bar and longstanding staple of the LGBTQ+ nightlife scene in Dublin, and is a favourite with locals and visitors alike. With drag shows, a huge dance floor and entertainment, it's the perfect place for a night out.

Yamamori Tengu 37 Strand Street Great, North City; yamamori.ie. This Japanese restaurant has a club in the basement where it hosts DJs from Dublin and across the world. Expect a bar stocked with both local and Japanese beverages, including the Nikka Sour. *Yamamori Tengu* is a guaranteed great night.

Temple Bar cocktails

Arlington Hotel on Bachelors Walk

SHOP

Grafton Street Dublin's main shopping street, a pedestrianised avenue jostling with shoppers and street entertainers. Located south of the river, this central thoroughfare is lined with stores including the famous *Brown Thomas* department store and high-end jeweller *Weir & Sons*. You'll also find the iconic *Bewley's* on this street, should you need a pick-me-up.

Gutter Bookshop Cow's Lane, Temple Bar; gutterbookshop.com. An independent bookshop in the Old City part of Temple Bar. Expect to find a range of quirky books you won't find in larger chain stores.

Hen's Teeth Blackpitts & Mill Street; hensteethstore. com. *Hen's Teeth* is a store, gallery and café that brings together great food, art, music and culture. It's great fun to lose yourself browsing the range of prints, clothing and homeware.

Moore Street Market Moore St, North City; visitdublin. com/moore-street-market. A lively open air street market with local food and vendors shouting in the recognisable Moore Street accent. Come here to buy fresh fruit, vegetables and flowers.

DO

Irish Film Institute 6 Eustace St, Temple Bar; ifi.ie. Come for the range of arthouse Irish cinema but stay for the bookstore, bar and restaurant. It offers an impressive range of craft beer.

Guinness Storehouse St. James's Gate; guinness-storehouse.com. The latest incarnation of the Guinness Brewery tour, and an ultra modern one at that. This selfguided tour begins on the ground level with ingredients, and ends in the very stylish *Gravity Bar* atop the brewery with a 360-degree view of Dublin.

Project Arts Centre 39 East Essex Street, Temple Bar; projectartscentre.ie. The centre of contemporary arts in Ireland, Project Arts Centre is a hub for artists and audiences. Their packed schedule offers 600 events a year including theatre and music; check out the schedule during your visit as there's sure to be something interesting on.

Tropical Popical Nail Bar 28 South William Street; tropicalpopical.com. Getting your nails done has never been so fun! *Tropical Popical* offers loud nail art with music to match, and pineapple margaritas in coconuts.

GLASGOW
Winter

Free from the shackles of its post-industrial malaise, the rejuvenated metropolis of Glasgow is perched on the banks of the river Clyde and throws up juxtaposition on every corner, from eighteenth-century mansions to innovative twenty-first century design. Roam its diverse neighbourhoods to take in elegant Merchant City (home to many LGBTQ+ venues), foodie Finnieston, East End markets and the super-hip southside. This is a city that's buzzing with pop-ups, world-class street art, live music, political resistance and all things creative. And as for that die-hard "Glesga" party spirit? It's indomitable – even in deepest winter.

HISTORY

Glasgow's earliest history is obscured in a swirl of myth. The city's name is said to derive from the Brythonic *Glas-cu*, which loosely translates as 'green hollow' – a name quite contrary to the sooty images of popular imagination.

William the Lionheart gave the town an official charter in 1175, after which it continued to grow in importance, peaking in the mid-fifteenth century when the university was founded. This led to city status in 1492, and Glasgow soon expanded into a major industrial port. The 1707 Act of Union between Scotland and England led to a boom in trade with the colonies until American independence.

Glasgow's population mushroomed in the nineteenth century, from 77,000 in 1801 to nearly 800,000 at the end of the century. By the turn of the twentieth century, its industries had been honed into one massive shipbuilding culture, but in the harsh economic climate of the 1930s, unemployment spiralled, and Glasgow could do little to counter its popular image as a city dominated by inebriate violence and (having absorbed vast numbers of Irish emigrants) sectarian tensions.

Shipbuilding died away almost completely in the 1960s and 1970s, leaving the city depressed and directionless. Then, in the 1980s, the self-promotion began, starting with the upbeat 'Glasgow's Miles Better' campaign and snowballing towards the year-long party as European City of Culture in 1990. Glasgow has since gone on to host a number of big events including the 2002 Champions' League Final and the 2014 Commonwealth Games. These various titles have helped to reinforce the impression that Glasgow has successfully broken the industrial shackles of the past and evolved into a city of stature and confidence.

It's been a fascinating journey towards equality in Glasgow. Despite male same-sex activity being legal in Scotland only since 1981 – fourteen years after it

was decriminalised in England and Wales – things were surprisingly lively back in the 1950s and 1960s. This was the era of discreet bars dotted across the city, while cruising area Glasgow Green was a well-documented meeting place for men. One notorious joint was the *Strand Bar* on Hope Street, where, according to the illuminating blog queerscotland.com, customers were assigned the name of the female film star that they most resembled upon entry.

By the 1970s and 1980s a gay scene proper had begun to emerge, with the opening of the still-standing *Waterloo Bar* and *Bennett's* (now *AXM*), the latter a wildly popular club which ran both gay-male and women-only nights. Another institution, *Delmonica's*, followed in 1991, and is also still open today.

These decades also saw the rise of political activism. In 1976 Glasgow Women's Centre became the first of its kind in Scotland, a resource soon home to pioneering lesbian and female-only groups. Meanwhile the Glasgow Gay Centre launched in 1977, the first openly queer community hub in the UK,

even though male same-sex activity was still illegal. Celebrity visitors included *Glad to Be Gay* singer-songwriter Tom Robinson and legendary raconteur Quentin Crisp. Another key landmark on the road to equality was the Glasgay Festival, created in 1993 as a response to the UK's discriminatory Section 28 laws. Running until 2014, it morphed into one of the UK's largest celebrations of LGBTQ+ culture, attracting headliners like Ian McKellen, Rhona Cameron and John Waters.

Fast forward to the present day and the age of both homosexual and heterosexual consent has been equal since 2001, while same-sex marriage was approved in 2014. The gender recognition reform (Scotland) bill passed at the end of 2022 before it was sadly blocked by the UK government at the start of 2023. Two unmissable events are October's Scottish Queer International Festival, and the largest LGBTQ+ event in Scotland, Pride Glasgow, which takes place in June with 50,000 people hitting the streets to be seen and heard – and, of course, to party.

The Clyde Arc (or Squinty Bridge) over the River Clyde

ICON

Sure, Glasgow is now a cutting-edge world city, but what was it like to be a queer kid growing up in the 1980s and early 90s? Glaswegian-born award-winning author Douglas Stuart offers unparalleled insights in his Booker Prize-winning debut *Shuggie Bain*. Set in the disadvantaged area of Sighthill, situated north of the Clyde, it's a stark but captivating portrait of a young gay child growing up with his alcoholic mother – yet it's strangely uplifting, too.

Written in English but with Scottish dialogue – whose idioms can take a little time to adjust to as a non-Scots reader – the lyricism of the prose and immersive nature of Stuart's writing provides a fascinating glimpse into the city's past. The book's mammoth success is all the more impressive when taking into account that it took ten years to write, while Stuart juggled writing with a successful career in fashion. The second Scottish writer to win the Booker Prize for a debut novel, *Shuggie Bain* has sold over 1.5

million copies, with a BBC adaptation in production.

Visiting fans can seek out a stunning mural on the wall of one of Glasgow's most famous music venues, the Barrowland Ballroom in the East End. Created in 2021 by the Cobolt Collective, which comprises Glasgow School of Art 2015 graduates Erin Bradley-Scott, Chelsea Frew and Kat Loudon, the towering work features a young Shuggie, accompanied by a quote from his mother Agnes: "You'll not remember the city, you were too wee, but there's dancing. All kinds of dancing."

In 2022 Stuart cemented his status as Glaswegian literary icon with a follow-up to his smash-hit. Entitled *Young Mungo*, the novel follows two teenage boys – one Protestant, one Catholic – as they embark on an affair in the early 1990s, the threat of violence never far away. Once again, Stuart's prose allows the reader to feel Glasgow in a uniquely powerful way: it's writing that transcends its humble roots.

HIGHLIGHT

Is there a more appealing wintry pursuit than hibernating in one of the UK's cosiest LGBTQ+ bookstores? If your answer is a firm no, head to Glasgow's southside and the must-visit neighbourhoods of Strathbungo (its exotic-sounding name has never quite been explained) and Govanhill, a grid of elegant Victorian streets packed with hip spots. Amongst the many independent cafés, stores, pubs and restaurants is *Category Is Books*, a local treasure which opened in 2018 as an essential resource for the area's ever-increasing queer community.

Situated just off the high street, bold handwritten slogans in the windows make its agenda unapologetically clear: 'Queer Books,' 'Trans Liberation Now', 'No Terfs' and 'Fight Racism. No, but really.' Inside, you'll find a space brimming with passion, knowledge and diversity: it's easy to spend an hour rifling through its new and second-hand stock, as well as varied magazines, graphic novels and zines. It's hard to leave without buying at least one badge.

Started by "wusband and wusband" Charlotte

(they/them) and Fionn ('Fin') Duffy-Scott (they/them), who have lived in Govanhill for a decade, the pair's dream was to create a space for the resident LGBTQ+ community to feel inspired. "We're an artist and designer respectively," says Charlotte, "who wanted to work together on something with a queer focus. We've both loved books all our lives, and at the time of setting up the shop were both discovering lots of queer history. A lot of this information was new to us, as we both grew up under Section 28 – so we created a space that could open up that world of queer books, histories, art, writing and activism to more people." For Charlotte and Fionn, their love of Glasgow doesn't start and finish in Govanhill. What's most beautiful about their city to them is "the solidarity, whether that be tenants' unions, or groups like Southside Strike Solidarity, the Kenmure Street Protests or the ongoing building work of community gardens. There's even a queer baseball team here."

Category Is Books also runs a helpful home delivery service and a lovely pay-it-forward system.

Wonderfully wacky costumes at Glasgow Pride

Kelvingrove Art Gallery and Museum

LISTINGS

STAY

ABode Glasgow 129 Bath St; abodeglasgow.co.uk. A classy hotel that delights on many levels, from the warm welcome and original cage lift. The rooms come in four categories ranging from 'Comfortable' to 'Fabulous'; the main difference between them is size and the odd extra (for example, Nespresso machines); nearly all feature tartan bedspreads, while a few retain the original stained glass windows.

The Brunswick 108 Brunswick Street; brunswickhotel. co.uk. Good-value boutique hotel, well-placed for Merchant City's LGBTQ+ venues on a street alive with the flutter of rainbow flags. Onsite café-bar, *The Amsterdam*, serves decent food and cocktails.

Grasshoppers 87 Union St; grasshoppersglasgow. com. A red-brick penthouse of 30 chic bedrooms right in the city centre, *Grasshoppers* occupies an unusual position, squatting on top of the main Central Station

– hence the name – with sweeping views over the undulating sea of roofs.

Kimpton Blythswood Square Hotel 11 Blythswood Square; kimptonblythswoodsquare.com. Luxury hotel boasting gorgeous Georgian architecture, with smartly renovated rooms and an on-site spa, plus a top-notch seafood restaurant, *iasg* (pronounced 'ee-usk') and posh cocktail bar.

The Revolver 62 Virginia Street; revolverhotel.co.uk. Geared towards the LGBTQ+ community, this design hotel in Merchant City above *Polo Lounge* club boasts a rooftop gym with sauna, as well as a democratic pricing structure to suit different budgets.

Z Hotel 36 North Frederick St; thezhotels.com. The handsome, sandstone facade of this former printworks conceals compact but fabulously sleek rooms. Each evening between 5 and 8pm there's a free wine and cheese buffet.

EAT

Gamba 225a West George St; gamba.co.uk. Continental contemporary sophistication prevails in this super basement restaurant where fish is king: once you've devoured the signature fish soup – a delicious mix with Portland crabmeat and prawn dumplings – perhaps try some seared king scallops with creamed celeriac and black pudding. A beautifully refined interior and outstanding service. Both the weekday two-course lunch menu and Saturday three-course menu are good value, and there's a pre-theatre deal too.

Laboratorio 93 West Nile St; twitter.com/LabEspr. The 'Lab' is a terrific little bolthole with cement board walls and recycled wood panelling, and super-friendly baristas who really know their beans; there's typically a single-origin espresso and a guest espresso on the go at any one time. You can perch inside, takeaway or grab one of the sought-after pavement tables.

Lobo 758 Pollokshaws Rd; loboglasgow.co.uk. Based in Strathbungo (extremely handy for *Category Is Books*) *Lobo* serves classy small plates with Middle Eastern and Mediterranean influences in a pared-back dining room.

Ox & Finch 920 Sauchiehall Street; oxandfinch.com. An acclaimed Finnieston hotspot serving sharing plates with interesting flavour combinations, from scallops with pearl barley and truffle to crab tartlet, apple and kohlrabi. Strong plant-based options, too.

The Spanish Butcher Merchant City, 80 Miller Street; spanishbutcher.com. This glamorous Merchant City dining room channels NYC with its sexy interiors and double-height ceiling, while the menu features tender Iberican pork, Galician prime rib and chargrilled octopus.

Trans-Europe Café 25 Parnie St; transeuropecafe. co.uk. Named after the Kraftwerk album, this fun, railway-style diner – with 80s-style bus seating – takes culinary inspiration from various European capitals, hence gourmet sandwiches like the Madrid (chorizo sausage, pesto and mozzarella) and the Monte Carlo (tuna melt with cheddar and mayonnaise).

Delicious cuisine at *Ox & Finch*

DRINK

Delmonica's 68 Virginia St; delmonicas.co.uk. Known locally as *Del's*, this fun gay bar with red-lit interior is located right in the heart of Glasgow's gay triangle in Merchant City. Themed nights range from Filth Friday to Drag-aoke.

Katie's Bar 17 John Street; katiesbar.co.uk. A petite basement bar serving up drag, poetry, burlesque, 'bender bingo', comedy karaoke and music acts. Soak it up with small plates, nachos and sharing platters.

Lunar 72 Nithsdale Road; instagram.com/lunar.cocktail. From the owners of the *Grunting Growler* taproom in the West End, queer-friendly *Lunar* dishes up imaginative libations in Strathbungo, as well as vegan and orange wines, plus a good alcohol-free selection.

The Riding Room 58 Virginia St; theridingroom.co.uk. There's a well-curated line-up of nightly burlesque and drag from LGBTQ+ performers (and "everything in between") at this vintage-style bar with its own bookable booths and classy cocktails.

Underground 6A John Street; facebook.com/ UndergroundGlasgo. It's a real hoot joining the rowdy bunch of up-for-it locals doing karaoke at this dimly lit subterranean queer dive bar. There's also drag queen bingo, quiz nights and more.

The Waterloo 306 Argyle St; waterlooglasgow.wixsite. com. Allegedly the oldest gay bar in Scotland (having been in operation for half a century), this essential stop on the LGBTQ+ trail focuses on retro nights and karaoke.

DANCE

AXM 90 Glassford St; facebook.com/axmclubglasgow. Scotland's largest LGBTQ+ nightclub with two floors, *AXM* plays host to some of the biggest Drag Race UK stars, including local superstar Lawrence Chaney.

Bonjour Glasgow 37-45 Saltmarket; instagram.com/ bonjourglasgow. A co-operative serving up one-off nights and events, as well as being community space for underrepresented groups in the LGBTQ+ community, such as people of colour, trans and non-binary folk, and queer women. This important cornerstone of the LGBTQ+ community has been facing funding issues of late, but is soldiering on with a packed calendar of events; check out their Instagram page for details and consider going along to lend your support.

Flying Duck 142 Renfield St; theflyingduck.org. Established in 2007, this stalwart of the underground music, vegan and drinking scene hosts everything from queer and non-binary artists to post-punk and grindcore.

Polo Lounge 84 Wilson St; pologlasgow.co.uk. Explore four different rooms at this popular haunt, with weekly queer student nights, 90s pop nights and 'Lipstick Sundays', in which local queens compete in lip-sync battles for prizes.

Sub Club 22 Jamaica St; subclub.co.uk. Underground club and purveyor of the finest techno and electro, regularly hosting DJs from Glasgow and beyond.

SWG3 100 Eastvale Place; swg3.tv. These repurposed warehouses and yards host everything from club nights to experimental arts performances. Adjoining studio *The Poetry Club* is the hangout for smaller gigs, film screenings and alternative clubs like queer night 'Hot Mess'.

SHOP

Barras 244 Gallowgate; barrasmarket.com. While Buchanan Street is the city's main shopping strip, don't miss this real East End institution. As atmospheric as a film set, it's open for bric-a-brac, vintage buys, sustainable fashion and streetfood at weekends.

The Lanes West End. Cobbled Cresswell Lane is home to indie vintage stores and art galleries (don't miss the eclectic boutiques on De Courcy's Arcade), while fairy-lit Ashton Lane houses a cinema, street art and abundant eating options.

Luke & Jack 45 Virginia St; lukeandjack.com. Feeling saucy? This adult entertainment store is an institution. Peruse the books, magazines, cards, underwear, fetishwear, jewellery, leatherwear, sex toys and more.

Timorous Beasties 384 Great Western Rd; timorousbeasties.com. Founded in 1990, this bohemian store is a must for anyone with a lust for interior design; here you'll find a plethora of surreal wall coverings, furnishings and fabrics.

A Victorian statue of an angel in the Glasgow Necropolis cemetery contemplating two modern high-rise tower blocks

The Kelvingrove Museum and Art Gallery

DO

CCA 350 Sauciehall Street; cca-glasgow.com. The cavernous Centre for Contemporary Arts contains a gallery, theatre, cinema and two café-bars, while the upstairs terrace hosts DJs in the evening. Don't miss the LGBTQ+ literature at the specialist bookshop in the foyer.

Glasgow Necropolis Castle St; glasgownecropolis. org. Every visit to Glasgow needs to be crowned with a gasp at the panoramic city view offered by the Victorian Necropolis, a sprawling hillside cemetery. The climb will shake off that hangover, too.

Glasgow Women's Library 23 Landressy St, Bridgeton; womenslibrary.org.uk. Open to the public since 1991, *Glasgow Women's Library* is the UK's sole accredited museum dedicated to women's history, lives and achievements, with a substantial lesbian and LGBTQ+ archive.

GOMA Royal Exchange Square; galleryofmodernart. blog. The most visited modern art gallery in Scotland,

this contemporary art powerhouse is housed in an iconic neoclassical building in Royal Exchange Square built in 1778. A real must.

Kelvingrove Gallery Argyle St; glasgowlife.org. uk/museums/venues/kelvingrove-art-gallery-and-museum. One of the country's most popular attractions with works by Rembrandt, Degas and Van Gogh, as well as key Scottish artists such as the Glasgow Boys. LGBTQ+ highlights include Peter Paul Rubens' *George Villiers, 1st Duke of Buckingham*, one of King James' male lovers, and Patricia Cronin's bronze sculpture *Memorial to a Marriage*.

River Clyde. The third-longest river in Scotland makes for a lovely stroll, and the Riverside Museum along Glasgow's redeveloped waterfront (100 Pointhouse Place; glasgowlife.org.uk) showcases the city's shipbuilding heritage. In summer you can take a cruise from the quay outside here on the world's last ocean-going paddle steamer to Dunoon and Rothesay, as well as other destinations around the Clyde Estuary.

The Spittelau incinerator in Vienna, built by the famous Austrian architect Friedensreich Hundertwasser

VIENNA
Winter

Famous for its sumptuous architecture, classical music and delicious cake, Vienna also boasts twinkling Christmas markets, historic cafés and quirky shops. The former home of Mozart, Beethoven, Freud, Klimt and Schiele, Vienna is far from old-fashioned, and is home to diverse communities and a thriving LGBTQ+ scene. The city's reputation for tolerance can be seen even at city street crossings, where traffic lights feature icons of both same-sex and straight couples crossing the road. One of Vienna's greatest attractions is the relaxed vibe you will encounter; it is a city that's perfect for culture lovers, foodies and café- and bar-hoppers alike.

Viennese drag artist Conchita Wurst

HISTORY

Vienna has existed as a settlement on the Danube for millennia, but it was in the eighteenth and nineteenth centuries that the city became a world-class centre of classical music, beautiful architecture and political power. Under the reign of the Habsburgs, the city became home to famous figures including the composers Ludwig van Beethoven and Wolfgang Amadeus Mozart. While art and culture flourished, restrictive laws criminalising same-sex relationships were introduced from the eighteenth century, with sodomy punishable by death.

By the early twentieth century, Vienna was the capital of the Austro-Hungarian Empire; the Empire totalled 15 nations and over 50 million inhabitants. The city became famous for its coffee house culture, which attracted intellectuals and other influential figures and big names from all over the world. At one point in 1913, Adolf Hitler, Leon Trotsky, Sigmund Freud and Joseph Stalin all lived within the same two square miles of the city.

World War I led to the collapse of the Habsburg monarchy and the Austro-Hungarian Empire. The interwar period saw the rise of antisemitism and fascism, as well as the beginnings of a lesbian and gay scene in Vienna. However, many members of the city's LGBTQ+ and Jewish communities were arrested, imprisoned and killed under the Nazi regime in World War II. A monument to Vienna's LGBTQ+ victims of this period is due to be unveiled in 2023 to accompany the existing monuments to Jewish victims of the regime.

Austria decriminalised homosexuality in 1971, and Vienna's first Pride event was held in 1996, coinciding with the end of another law which prohibited open displays of homosexuality. Another proud moment for the city was when Viennese drag artist Conchita Wurst won Eurovision in 2014.

History connected to the House of Habsburg can be seen everywhere in Vienna, from its spectacular palaces to the art and natural history collections in its museums and art gallery. Over centuries the Habsburgs became rulers of Bohemia, Hungary, Croatia, Spain and Portugal, making them one of the most important royal dynasties in Europe. What visitors to Vienna may not be aware of is that one of the last members of this royal family was an openly gay man.

Archduke Ludwig Viktor Joseph Anton of Austria was born in 1842. He was the youngest child of Archduke Franz Karl of Austria and his wife Princess Sophie of Bavaria, making him the younger brother of Emperor Franz Joseph I. Ludwig, known as "Luziwuzi" or "little Ludwig", was reportedly not particularly handsome; he possessed the notorious Habsburg jaw and was very short with a reputation for eccentricity. He spurned the offers of marriage made to him, including one offer that would have made him the next Emperor of Mexico

and Brazil, preferring the company of men. A news blackout regarding scandal surrounding the royal family meant that this fact was not widely reported in Vienna's press; however, when Ludwig tried to chat up the wrong officer at a cruising spot in Vienna's Central Bathhouse, he got into a fight, creating a scandal which proved to be the last straw for his brother, Emperor Franz Joseph. This ultimately led to Ludwig's banishment from court to his palace in Salzburg.

Ludwig's beautiful Viennese palace still stands in Schwarzenbergplatz. The Palais Erzherzog Ludwig Viktor was created by Heinrich Ferstel, the architect who designed Vienna's famous Votivkirche and Café Central. It is also possible to visit the baths where Ludwig's scandalous encounter unfolded, which still operates as a gay sauna today. Known today as *Kaiserbründl Herrensauna*, it is a gorgeous, lavishly decorated bathhouse where you can experience queer Vienna as it appeared to Habsburg royalty.

Kaiserbründl Herrensauna

HIGHLIGHTS

Most people who come to Vienna will pay a visit to at least one palace, the most spectacular of which are Schloss Schönbrunn and the Schloss Belvedere. Both palaces are surrounded by gardens which are free of charge to enter and give fabulous opportunities to take in views across the city.

To appreciate UNESCO World Heritage site Schönbrunn's privileging of sensuality over imperial pomp, be sure to visit the gardens before the palace itself. With the exception of the Kammergarten (Chamber Garden) and Kronprinzengarten (Crown Prince Garden) immediately left and right of the palace, the park has always been open to the public. The park, laid out in classical French manner, is dominated by the Gloriette, a magnificent colonnade perched on the crest of a hill. It is difficult to say

which view is prettier – the graceful silhouette of the Gloriette against a sunset viewed from the palace, or a bright morning view from the Gloriette over the whole of Vienna to the north and the Wienerwald away to the south. The woods and gardens stretch for miles, and contain a maze, an excellent zoo and an orangery, in addition to numerous statues, fountains and romantic vistas. There is also a greenhouse which is an almost identical copy of Kew Garden's temperate glass house in London. Those who are keen on Habsburg culture should also pay a visit to the interior of the palace itself, in which the opulence of the ballrooms is juxtaposed with the intimacy of the bedrooms.

Schloss Belvedere also offers formal French gardens, statues, and of course views. The palace houses the world's largest collection of Gustav Klimt

The elegant interior of *Café Central*

artworks, including Austria's most famous painting, *The Kiss*. As Klimt artworks are generally too fragile to be moved, many of his artworks can only be seen in Vienna.

Another highlight of Vienna is its unique coffee house culture, and a visit to a traditional coffee house is not to be missed; coffee houses in the city have such a strong cultural heritage that they were recognised by UNESCO in 2011. Featuring old-fashioned furnishings and elegantly dressed waiters, the traditional Viennese coffee house is supposed to feel like a living room (albeit a very fancy one), giving you the chance to sit for as long as you like, reading the newspaper while sipping a coffee. Most well-known is the grand *Café Central*, a former favourite hangout of Trotsky and Freud. Palatial *Café Savoy*, a particularly gay-friendly version of the traditional coffee house dating back to 1897, can be found near the city's famous Naschmarkt

food market in the "gay mile" district of Vienna – the square mile located between Naschmarkt, Mariahilferstraße and Kettenbrückengasse. Its mirrors are reported to rival those of Versailles Palace in size. Also worth a visit is the beautiful *Café Sperl*, hung with large mirrors and boasting a selection of English language newspapers. For a modern twist on the café theme, try the kitschy queer-friendly Vollpension café in Schleifmühlgasse; the cafés in this Viennese group are staffed by Viennese grandmas and grandpas to help them supplement their pensions and break down the barriers between generations. It's worth trying the cakes – they are made by the staff themselves following old family recipes, and will allow you a real taste of homemade Austrian cuisine. You can find another Vollpension café in the MUK (Musik und Kunst or Music and Art University), and there is also a kiosk on Schwedenplatz, near the Danube Canal.

LISTINGS

STAY

Bristol Kärntner Ring 1; bristolvienna.com. An Art Nouveau building dating from 1884 providing a bit more cosiness than many other five-star hotels. Its restaurant, the *Bristol Lounge*, is known for its light Viennese cuisine and distinguished wine list. There are non-smoking rooms and wheelchair facilities.

Do & Co Hotel Vienna Stephansplatz 12; docohotel. com. This überchic, gay-friendly design hotel may just occupy the best spot of any Vienna hotel, on the upper storeys of the Haas Haus and slap-bang in front of St. Stephens Cathedral. Bang & Olufsen-equipped rooms are complimented by one of the most popular bars (*The Onyx*) and restaurants in the city, which have amazing views and a choice of Asian or European cuisine.

Hollmann Beletage Köllnerhofgasse 6; crazyhollmann. com/en/beletage-vienna. It is hard to recommend this small (26 rooms) hotel enough. It's super-central, and

the rooms are contemporary and chic in their design and commendably well kept. The vibe is laid back and the reception even shuts down at night, leaving the guests to help themselves at the bar. Excellent value, and a hearty breakfast included in the price.

Hotel Altstadt Kirchengasse 41; altstadt.at/en. This boutique hotel is located in the hip Neubau district, within easy reach of Vienna's best bars, cafés and restaurants. Situated in a classic Viennese townhouse, the hotel features a collection of contemporary art and promises a calm refuge amid the nearby bars, restaurants and galleries.

Mooons Wiedner Gürtel 16; mooons.com. The characteristic façade of *Mooons* awakes curiosity but this great value hotel keeps its promise inside as well. Rooms have smart technology, and the large windows are a bonus. In addition to a quiet courtyard garden, a roof terrace offers panoramic views.

EAT

Beim Czaak Postgasse 15; czaak.com. A friendly Beisl with helpful staff tucked away behind the Old University, hence popular with students. The hearty menu includes superb *tafelspitz*, sinful desserts and an excellent selection of beers.

Bitzinger Sausage Stand Albertinaplatz 1; bitzinger-wien.at. Try munching on a *kaiserkrainer* (cheese-filled sausage) while sipping a glass of champagne at the Albertina Bitzinger stand near the Albertina art gallery. This is a popular pit stop following a night at the opera, so don't be surprised if you end up queuing alongside a couple in evening dress.

Demel Kohlmarkt 14; demel.com. One of the most famous places to sample *Sachertorte* and apple strudel is *demel*, a pastry bakery which has been in business since 1786. *Demel* now serves the Austrian fluffy cut up pancakes known as *kaiserschmarrn* to go. In winter this often leads to long queues forming of hungry pancake lovers outside, while chefs can be observed making huge quantities of *kaiserschmarrn* in the picture windows.

Esterhazy Keller Haarhof 1; esterhazykeller.at. A Stadtheurigen in a dark cellar; take the winding stairs down from the small doorway. Typical belt-stretching food and local wines. Atmospheric in a very Viennese sort of way.

Palmenhaus Burggarten 1; palmenhaus.at. A tropical greenhouse with a high arched ceiling, this is a lovely spot for a drink or a typically Austrian meal or snack in the First District. In summer, people throng the outside terrace overlooking Vienna's Burggarten park. The *Palmenhaus* is located next to Vienna's butterfly house, so you may be able to see butterflies fluttering about on the other side of the glass wall. In summer, people throng the outside terrace overlooking Vienna's Burggarten park. It is a little on the expensive side, but worth it for the location and surroundings. Handy for the nearby Albertina art gallery.

Restaurant Meissl & Schadn Wien Schubertring 10-12; meisslundschadn.at. It's all about the traditional Viennese *schnitzel* in this restaurant, where chefs can

Bitzinger Sausage Stand, the famous and award-winning food kiosk

be seen in the open kitchen breading and frying veal cuts in free range egg and artisanal breadcrumbs. Visitors can choose whether to have their *schnitzel* fried in butter or lard; the *tafelspitz* (boiled beef) also comes highly recommended.

Rudis Beisl Wiedner Hauptstraße 88; rudisbeisl.at. For a down-to-earth experience in a cosy Viennese Beisl (pub), head to *Rudis Beisl* for warming and comforting Austrian dishes such as *zwiebelrostbraten* (roast beef with onions), *backhendl* (deep fried chicken) or *eierknockerl* (egg dumplings). This is one of the most popular places to eat the traditional *martinsgans* (roast goose), in November in Vienna.

Villa Vida Café Türkis Rosa Lila Villa, Linke Wienzeile 102; villavida.at. This queer community café with bar and restaurant offers food, coffee and cocktails. It is located in the Türkis Rosa Lila Villa, a housing project, restaurant, events and counselling venue for LGBTQ+ people which emerged out of the squatters' movement. Founded by queer people, it has also been a centre for trans activism since the 1990s. The café also hosts regular karaoke, activism, queer meetups and drag brunches for Vienna's queer community. The "Queen's Brunch", featuring drag queen entertainment and breakfast food, is held on Saturdays.

DRINK

Café Alte Lampe Zentagasse 30; cafealtelampe.at. One of the oldest gay bars in Vienna, formerly known as Café Rüdiger, has moved from its former location in Rüdigergasse. Stylishly decorated with red furnishings, marble, gilt framed pictures and large mirrors, the café offers a welcoming vibe for Vienna's queer community. The café opens in the evening and offers an extensive drinks menu and some good snacks.

Flex Augartenbrücke 1; flex.at. A popular, down-to-earth club where you can listen to dance music or see live gigs; this club also attracts some of Vienna's best DJs. Situated on the graffiti art covered Danube Canal, it has a grungy, alternative vibe and is open until 6am. Live music offerings range from local newcomers to international acts.

Village Bar Stiegengasse 8; village-bar.at. This friendly and welcoming gay bar in the Margareten district is one of the most popular in Vienna. Located close to the Naschmarkt food market in Vienna's "gay mile", it features delicious cocktails and good music.

Why Not Tiefer Graben 22; why-not.at. The *Why Not* first opened as nightclub in the early 1950s and features three floors with three bar areas. It attracts a mostly mixed and LGBTQ+ crowd.

The Naschmarkt food market

SHOP

Innere Stadt The winding streets of Vienna's Inner City are a good place to start any shopping expedition. Although now increasingly dominated by international names, especially along Graben, Kohlmarkt and Kärntnerstrasse, there are still numerous interesting local places to ferret out. To the west, Mariahilferstrasse is the other main shopping area: a long series of shops that only peters out at the Westbahnof.

The Naschmarkt Wienzeile. Vienna's largest food market also borders the city's gay district and can be easily reached from either Karlsplatz or Kettenbrückengasse U-bahn stops. In total there are around 120 market stalls and restaurants offering everything from Israeli cuisine to Turkish, Chinese and fish options. On Saturdays there is a popular flea market where you can find antiques, works of art, household items, used books and records. The market is made up of a mix of 400 private individuals and professional dealers who sell a mixture of high-quality secondhand goods and unusual or kitschy junk items.

DO

Hundertwasser Haus Kegelgasse 36-38; hundertwasser-haus.info. A popular tourist attraction in Vienna is the social housing complex designed by the eccentric Austrian architect Friedensreich Hundertwasser, a pioneering environmentalist who notoriously disliked straight lines. The Hundertwasser Haus is a colourful building, covered in 200 trees on its balconies and roof terraces. Nearby is the Hundertwasser village, designed in a similar style with trees, wavy lines and colourful buildings. Also nearby is the Kunst Haus Wien where you can find about more about Hundertwasser's art, architecture and philosophy at the Museum Hundertwasser.

The Kunsthistorisches Museum Maria-Theresien-Platz; khm.at. Packed with paintings ranging from Breughel the Elder to Vermeer and Caravaggio, a dazzling array of treasures belonging to the Habsburgs, and Greek, Roman and Egyptian antiquities to boot, the Kunsthistoriches Museum should be the first port of call for culture lovers in Vienna. The museum also

A drag queen giving an art tour of the Kunsthistorisches Museum as part of EuroPride celebrations

Wiener Staatsoper

has a beautiful café, and hosts monthly '*Kunstschatzi*' ('art treasure') evenings, when it is possible to view paintings while enjoying cocktails and a DJ at the museum.

Leopold Museum Museumsplatz 1; mqw.at. The Austrian expressionist artist Egon Schiele has influenced, among others, British artist Tracy Emin. The world's largest collection of his work can be found at the Leopold Museum, along with works by his mentor Gustav Klimt and other Austrian artists such as Richard Gerstl and Oskar Kokoschka. Known for his naked portraits (considered so scandalous and gynaecological that posters advertising them were censored by London authorities in 2017), Schiele lived a short, but controversial life, dying of Spanish flu in 1918 at the age of 28.

Prater praterservice.at. This is Vienna's most extensive park, once reserved for the nobility but opened up to the public in 1766 by Emperor Joseph II. Its most prominent feature is the old-fashioned amusement park with the famous Riesenrad Ferris wheel (wienerriesenrad.com), which is usually open all day long and was immortalised in the film *The Third Man* (1949). Built in 1897, it is one of the oldest and largest Ferris wheels in the world, 65m (213ft) high, and provides sweeping views over the city.

Stephansdom Stephansplatz 3; stephanskirche.at. For more than eight centuries St Stephen's Cathedral has watched over Vienna. With its Romanesque western facade, Gothic tower and Baroque altars, the cathedral epitomises Vienna's genius for harmonious compromise, managing to meld the austerity, dignity and exuberance of three architectural styles.

Wiener Staatsoper Opernring 2; wiener-staatsoper. at. Vienna's world class state opera house opened in 1869, and it is worth a visit just to see its spectacular interior, even if not an actual opera. Tickets for the opera or ballet can run into hundreds of euros, but it is possible to buy *Stehplatz* (standing) tickets on the day of performances for under €20.

SMALL PRINT
INDEXES

CONTRIBUTORS

Josh Asmah (he/him; Amsterdam, Rotterdam and Prague) hails from the beautiful island of Bonaire, growing up between there, the U.S., and Ghana. He's been living in Amsterdam since 2015. He works in development finance and is a content writing/strategy freelancer, and loves travelling and eating out in his spare time. Find him on Instagram at @joshthenormal.

Safiya Bashir (she/her; Dublin) is a freelance writer with bylines in gal-dem, Shado Mag, Crack, Azeema and Bristol24/7. She particularly focuses on South Asian identity, music and their intersection. As well as writing, she works on @RepresentAsian_podcast – the podcast, radio show and club nights exploring South Asian representation in the UK music industry.

Daniele Catena (he/him) and **Luigi Cocciolo** (he/him; Cologne) are writers and LGBTQ travel bloggers based in Milan. They love discovering the World with a colourful approach through food and people. You can follow them @gaylyplanet and on their website, wearegaylyplanet.com.

Stephen Emms (he/him; Glasgow and Malta) was born in Margate and has written about travel for 15 years, his articles appearing in broadsheets and magazines including *The Guardian*, *Time Out*, *Conde Nast Traveller* and *Lonely Planet*. He especially loves the Kent Coast, pop-up beach saunas and negronis. Follow @stephenemms on Instagram.

Jesse Gillespie (they/them; Brighton) is a queer writer and artist based in Brighton. They focus on the representation of queer and neurodivergent characters through screenwriting. Subscribe to writingqueers.wordpress.com to be the first to read their latest work.

Emma Harrison (she/her; Madrid and Athens) is a travel and music writer based in Bournemouth. She loves gigs, sea swimming and exploring the street art, coffee shops and vintage stores whilst on a city break. You can follow her on both Instagram and Twitter @emmahwriter.

Lauren Hurrell (she/her; Reykjavik) moved from Bristol to London in 2014 and lives and works in Peckham. She specialises in queer culture and nightlife, the creative industries, lifestyle, entertainment and travel as both a freelance writer and full-time editor. She has travelled to four of the seven continents and hopes to see the other three as soon as she can afford it. Lauren has studied in London and North Carolina, always in literature, publishing or journalism, and aspires for the freedom to write from anywhere in the world.

Richard Matoušek (he/him; Lisbon and Puglia) is a journalist who covers Southern Europe and Brazil. A former resident of Puglia and Lisbon, both are close to his heart and he hopes you get a lot out of them. He loves receiving feedback on his tips, on Twitter @richmatousek or Instagram @richmatico.

Emma Midgley (she/her; Bologna and Vienna) is a writer and journalist based in Vienna. She loves everything Italian, hiking in the Austrian mountains and swimming in lidos. You can follow her at @emmamiggy or on her website at emmamidgley.com.

Danielle Mustarde (she/her; Brussels and Copenhagen) is a writer, mature (ish) philosophy student and curious soul who loves to travel – preferably by bicycle or train. Originally from County Durham in the northeast of England, she now lives in London with her girlfriend and cat-child. Follow her @wordsbydanielle.

Eleanor Ross (she/her; Berlin and Milan) is an editor, writer and sustainability strategist based in London. She loves hiking, being in, on, or around water, and spending time with her dog, Mabel. You can follow her at @eleanorross102 or get in touch via her website at eleanorross.net.

Max Siegel (they/he; Sitges and Stockholm) is a proud Trans man, content creator, speaker and writer living in Hastings. His goal is to prove that Trans joy exists, through sharing his life and travels with as many people as possible. You can find him on Instagram @theyrequeer.

Stephen Unwin (he/him; London, Manchester and Paris) is an award-winning editor and writer specialising in LGBTQ+ and luxury travel, celebrity interviews – Adele, Kim Kardashian, a Spice Girl or two – and vodka-martinis with, or without, a twist. You can see more of his work at stephenunwin.co.uk.

Annie Warren (she/her; editor) is an editor, writer, translator and occasional stand-up comedian based in Nottingham. She enjoys reading, wild swimming, and margaritas. You can follow her on social media @notanniewarren and on her website, annie-warren.com.

ACKNOWLEDGEMENTS

Josh Asmah would like to thank all the amazing people who've travelled with me, shown me some of the places included in this guide (and the many that didn't make the cut!), or simply come along to explore foodie spots across town. Thank you for helping me foster my love of travel, food and writing. You know who you are – look at us now!

Safiya Bashir would like to send a very special shout out to Fiona and Anna – my favourite Dublin duo and Bloemstraat misfits.

Stephen Emms would like to thank visitmalta.com, maltagayrights.org and especially Michael Owen, Vice President of Allied Rainbow Communities, which produces key listings resource gaymalta.com. He would also like to thank Charlotte and Fionn from Category is Books, the invaluable history resource queerscotland.com, and Rachel Fiddes and Paul Burt for their endless local knowledge as southside tour guides extraordinaire.

Jesse Gillespie would like to thank Annie Warren at *Rough Guides* for putting this compilation together, and Em Evans for being a constant inspiration to both their personal life and professional work.

Emma Harrison would like to thank the staff at *Rough Guides* (particularly Annie Warren) for your support, Katilena Alpe at DK Associates for your hospitality, Spyridon Kagkas at This is Athens for your tireless knowledge, The Greek Deputy Minister for Culture, Nikolas Yatromanolakis, for your insight and time and last, but not least Joe Flanagan for being the best plus one and for being my biggest support and champion.

Lauren Hurrell would like to send a special thank you to travel writers Carolyn Bain and Alexis Averbuck who were the first to tell me anything about Iceland in a travel book, and to Eileen Myles' travel essays in art, *The Importance of Being Iceland* and Marcel Krueger's *Iceland: A Literary Guide for Travellers*, for putting the heart behind the story and why I will keep going back to this beautifully moody home for the poets again and again.

Richard Matoušek would like to thank Scott Maxwell from The Big Gay Podcast from Puglia, Sergio Scardia at Italy Gay Travels, and Gilberto Genco at Masseria Wave, for their good chat and excellent work in raising awareness of the queer heel of Italy's boot.

Emma Midgley would like to thank Annie Warren at *Rough Guides* for her support, Andreas Brunner at QWien for the chat about Vienna's queer history and Patrick Molloy and Ian Hopper for their Bologna culture tips. Special thanks to Christian, Charlotte and Laurence Hill.

Danielle Mustarde would like to thank Annie Warren and Jo Davey for their guidance. Mara Ittel and Jessica Gysel from BAD Brussels and the wonderful British-Danish couple I spent an evening with at Cafe Intime, Copenhagen (celebrating 40 years together!). And Caro, most of all.

Eleanor Ross would like to thank Annie Warren for being a great and fast editor, and Hristina for demystifying Berghain.

Max Siegel would like to thank everyone at Visit Stockholm, with a special shout-out to Uwern and Christina from Stockholm LGBTQ, his fiancée Lori for helping him remember the names of restaurants (and being a great travel partner), and finally *Rough Guides* for ensuring that LGBTQ+ people have safe and enjoyable ways to see the world.

Annie Warren would like to thank all the contributors for their wonderful writing, the amazing production and pictures team at *Rough Guides* who have worked so hard to make this book fabulous, and Peter Bradley, who originally had the idea for this book and because of whom it exists.

PHOTO CREDITS

(**Key:** T-top; C-centre; B-bottom; L-left; R-right)

All images **Shutterstock** except:
Adam Mørk/Museum of Copenhagen 259
Adlon Kempinski 233
Annæmma Antonello/La Restuccia 126
Aromi Group 174
ATLI THOR/Matur & Drykkur 64
Bar Tomeu 77
Barceló Torre de Madrid 103
Cantina Bentivoglio Bologna 175
Design Hotels 184
Dosfotos/Shutterstock editorial 156/157
Eurostars Sitges 78
Fáilte Ireland 268/269
Fauzia B&B 197
Hoxton Brussels 182
Julia Claxton/Drakes Brighton 89
JustMe Milano/Vittorio La Fata 209
Kaiserbründl 287
Kent Wang/Flickr under CC BY-SA 2.0 license 183
La Restuccia 117, 127
Late Birds Lisbon 30
Lilith Coffee 136
Magnus Skoglof/B.A.R. 149
NAOMI VANCE/Ox & Finch 279
Schwules Museum 232
Small Luxury Hotels of the World 290
SuperStock 239
The Harbour Club/Tonio Lombardi 196
The Pavillon de la Reine Hotel 52
Wiener Staatsoper / Michael Pöhn 295

Cover The largest progressive pride flag in the world at Waterkant Amsterdam/Q-Park Europarking during Pride Amsterdam **Wut_Moppie/Shutterstock**

INDEX BY COUNTRY